Economic Growth & Stability

An Analysis of Economic Change and Policies

by Gottfried Haberler

Nash Publishing, Los Angeles

Library of Congress Catalog Card Number: 73-92965
International Standard Book Number: 0-8402-1337-9

Published simultaneously in the United States and Canada
by Nash Publishing Corporation, 9255 Sunset Boulevard,
Los Angeles, California 90069

Printed in the United States of America

First Printing

This volume is a publication of
The Principles of Freedom Committee

The great body of economic and political literature since World War II—both academic and popular—has presented a misleading picture of the performance of private enterprise and of the State in the economies of the free world. This literature exaggerates the defects of the one and the merits of the other. Freedom will remain in jeopardy unless the public gains a clearer picture of the workings of the free market and comes to realize that its greatest virtue is not its extraordinary capacity to produce widely diffused material benefits, important as this merit is, but its unique capacity to protect the great immaterial values of our Western Heritage.

As a means of increasing the flow of literature that would correct the picture and strengthen the foundations of freedom, a group calling itself the Principles of Freedom Committee was formed during the early 1960s to promote a series of books dealing with important economic and political issues of the day. To assist in the international publication and distribution of the books, the Committee recruited an advisory group of scholars from sixteen countries. *Economic Growth and Stability* is the eighth book in the Principles of Freedom Series.

The membership of the Committee has changed over the years through retirements and replacements by cooption. The original members were Professors Milton Friedman, F. A. Hayek, G. Warren Nutter, B. A. Rogge, and John V. Van Sickle,

Executive Secretary; Ruth Sheldon Knowles, Project Coordinator; and Byron K. Trippet, Committee Member Ex-Officio. Dr. Trippet retired in 1965 following his resignation as President of Wabash College. Professors Hayek and Nutter retired in 1968, and three new members were added: Gottfried Haberler, Galen L. Stone Professor of International Trade, Harvard University; F. A. Harper, President, Institute for Humane Studies; and Don Paarlberg, Hillenbrand Professor of Agricultural Economics, Purdue University. In 1970 Gottfried Dietze, Professor of Political Science at The Johns Hopkins University, joined the Committee, and Kenneth S. Templeton, Jr., assumed the duties of Executive Secretary from Dr. Van Sickle. In 1973 Professor Yale Brozen of The University of Chicago replaced Professor Friedman as a member of the Committee.

The original Committee requested modest nonrecurring grants from a number of corporations and foundations. These donors receive copies of all books as they appear, and their help in promoting the distribution of the books is welcomed. The Institute for Humane Studies handles the funds received from the project's supporters and issues annual reports. Decisions as to authors, subjects, and acceptability of manuscripts rest exclusively with the Committee.

Earlier volumes in the Principles of Freedom Series are:

Great Myths of Economics (1968) by Don Paarlberg

The Strange World of Ivan Ivanov (1969) by G. Warren Nutter

Freedom in Jeopardy: The Tyranny of Idealism (1969) by John V. Van Sickle

The Genius of the West (1971) by Louis Rougier

The Regulated Consumer (1971) by Mary Bennett Peterson

The Conquest of Poverty (1973) by Henry Hazlitt

Union Power and the Public Interest (1973) by Emerson P. Schmidt

Acknowledgments

I would like to thank several members of the staff of the American Enterprise Institute for their valuable assistance in the preparation of this volume. Lynn Gottesman patiently endured the typing of several versions of portions of the manuscript. Whenever necessary, she was cheerfully helped by Iris Lee McPherson. I am especially grateful to Anne Brunsdale, AEI's Director of Publications, for permitting two members of her highly competent staff, Betty Ashooh and Donna Spitler, to assist me. These ladies rendered invaluable service in getting the proofs ready.

Contents

Preface

The scope and aim of the book are explained in the first chapter. This preface contains, first, a brief sketch of the genesis of the work, a description of the arrangement of the material and some acknowledgments and, secondly, a short discussion of some of the policy problems dealt with in the book.

I started writing this book six or seven years ago but was interrupted several times by other work. The manuscript was completed in the spring of 1973 but numerous additions were made in the proofs. Parts of the material in the book have been published earlier in pamphlets and articles to which references are made in the notes at the conclusion of this book. The book summarizes and amplifies the results (but not all the theoretical underpinning) of my work in the area of business cycles, money and inflation, as well as international trade and development.

With a view to making the text understandable to intelligent citizens with no formal training in technical economics, more technical discussions, references to the literature, and criticisms of other views and polemics are relegated to notes which are assembled at the end of the book.

I owe a heavy debt of thanks to my old friend Professor John V. Van Sickle. Without his prodding the book would have been further delayed and might not have been finished. He has carefully read, checked and edited the whole manuscript and has made many important suggestions in regard to substance, style and presentation. In addition he has read the proofs and prepared the index.

I am also greatly indebted to the American Enterprise Institute and its President William J. Baroody. The Institute provided me most generously with a congenial surrounding, enough leisure and secretarial assistance to finish the work which took longer than had been anticipated when I retired from Harvard and moved to Washington in the summer of 1971.

* * *

During the postwar period and even while this book was being written, remarkable changes have occurred in the expert opinions of economists as well as in the attitudes of policy makers and the public at large concerning economic stability and growth, their causes and their interrelations with other policy objectives, and the relative desirability of different objectives. The changes in opinion were followed in due course by equally pronounced changes and reversals in economic policies. These developments are discussed at some length in the following chapters. But a few may be mentioned here, especially some very recent changes that have occurred since the final version of the book was finished early in 1973. (On recent changes see also the postscript to chapter 5 on the 1973 inflation and the discussion of the 1973 price freeze in chapter 6, which were added in the proofs.)

During and for some time after World War II, economic thinking was dominated by the traumatic experience of the Great Depression of the 1930s. Under the influence of the

"Keynesian revolution" most economists saw in deflation, mass unemployment and secular stagnation the great dangers looming in the postwar period.

Actually during the years since the war there has been no deflation in any country, either in the sense of falling prices, declining aggregate expenditures (money national income) or shrinking money supply. There have been several recessions characterized by mild unemployment and slack—mild in comparison not only with the Great Depression of the 1930s but also with many earlier crises—but no real depressions. Furthermore, rates of growth have been on a high level by historical standards.

Thus, the postwar record of performance of the economy has been excellent. But we had to pay a price—the creeping inflation which recently has gone into high gear. The current rate of inflation—three months ending October 1973—as measured by the annual rise in consumer prices is close to 11.4 percent in the United States, 12 percent in Great Britain, 8.9 percent in Italy, 5.5 percent in Germany and 10 percent in Switzerland, just to mention a few highly developed industrial countries. The alarming rise in prices has renewed the fear in some quarters that, contrary to what the great majority of economists had come to believe, serious depressions may not be entirely a thing of the past.

The business cycle—alternating periods of expansion and contraction of economic activity—which on several occasions in the past had been declared dead prematurely, was again in the eclipse after the war. But it was soon discovered that the cycle is still alive, although in a much attenuated form, playing around a rising trend of prices, with the price level at best remaining stable in recessions rather than declining as had been the rule before World War II.

In the postwar period, as a consequence of Keynesian thinking, the role of money and monetary policy was discounted by many economists and had to be rediscovered. Fiscal policy was increasingly relied upon to steer the economy on a full employment course. In the 1960s American policy makers thought they had mastered the art of "fine tuning" the economy; by changing taxes and central government expenditures, they believed they could iron out even mild fluctuations in economic activity and achieve continuous full employment. Actually, fiscal policy proved to be a clumsy instrument. By and large, government finance has been a destabilizing factor in the economy, partly but by no means entirely, because of the expenditure explosions caused by the wars in Korea and Vietnam. What the "fine tuners" accomplished was to lay the foundations for the new wave of inflation which has engulfed the United States and the rest of the world. An unexpected and ominous development, unsettling especially for those brought up in the Keynesian tradition, has been the spectacle of "stagflation"–that is, the simultaneous appearance of inflation, unemployment and stagnation.

The distinction between "demand inflation" and "cost or wage push inflation" has been a recurrent theme in the postwar period. It is extensively discussed in Chapter 6. At this point I wish to add a few comments on the surge of inflation in 1973 which finally got under way after the text was completed.

There is general agreement that last year's inflation is a case of demand inflation. Skyrocketing food and raw material prices in world markets have nothing to do with wage pressures. Labor unions like everybody else were taken by surprise and their reaction to the spurt in the cost of living has been astoundingly slow.

Two comments seem to be in order. First, the unexpected mild reaction of organized labor unfortunately does not provide any basis for optimism concerning the future. Earnings of workers rose by about 7 percent per annum during the first half of 1973 and are showing a strong tendency to go to higher levels. This rate of increase is not excessive under the current rate of inflation, but it is entirely incompatible with long-run price stability. It will be very hard to reduce the rise of money wages to the 3 to 4 percent level which is probably the maximum reconcilable with full employment at tolerably stable prices. The chances are that we shall continue to be faced with an awkward choice between excessive inflation and excessive unemployment, or a combination of both. In other words the problem of wage push has been temporarily covered up by inflation but is no nearer a solution. An analysis of these tricky concepts "demand pull" and "cost push" and what to do about the latter will be found in Chapters 6 and 7.

The second remark concerns the policy reactions to last year's inflation in the United States and many other countries. The United States repeated what it tried in 1971—a price freeze (but not a wage freeze) for sixty days to be followed by detailed controls.

The justification for the U.S. freeze in 1971 had been that "excess demand had been eliminated" from the system and that the continued rise in prices was due to "cost pressures" and "inflationary psychology." That kind of inflation, it was said, could be cured only by means of incomes policies and controls. It was not easy to make sense of the assertion that "excess demand had been eliminated" because neither the quantity of money (M) nor total expenditure (MV) had stopped rising. But whatever the meaning of excess demand, there is agreement that in 1973 wage pressures were not the moving force.

The U.S. 1973 price freeze immediately ran into most serious troubles; it produced shortages and waste, forced the shutdown of numerous plants and had to be hurriedly dismantled ahead of schedule as an unmitigated blunder. The real reason why the price stop in 1971 did not have the same immediate impact as in 1973 was that it came at a time when the rate of inflation was declining anyway—it had started to taper off a year earlier—and there was still much unemployment and slack in the economy. In sharp contrast 1973 was a period of accelerating inflation, practically full employment, widespread labor and material shortages and hardly any idle capacity anywhere. These are conditions singularly unpropitious for a price freeze, especially when farm prices cannot be controlled and wages are exempt from the freeze. True, the effect of rising wages would be gradual. But such a lopsided program could not inspire confidence or douse inflationary expectations.

In fairness to the administration it must be said that it acted under terrific pressures from the Congress and public opinion. The Democratic caucus in the Senate voted unanimously for "a ninety-day freeze on prices, profits, rents, wages and salaries, and consumer interest rates." Many even wanted a rollback of prices. (The same senators voted cheerfully for a large increase in the minimum wage which, in effect, is a vote for more inflation and larger unemployment. The effects of minimum wages on inflation and employment are discussed in Chapter 6.) The administration, weakened by the Watergate affair, was unable to ignore these irrational and hysterical demands which had strong support in public opinion and the news media. One almost gets the impression that the administration deliberately tried to demonstrate the absurdity of general price control. In that, it may have succeeded to some extent. The majority of the senators who had demanded a general price freeze voted a few weeks later, when beef became scarce, to abolish the freeze on beef prices. Moreover there is evidence that the debacle of the American price freeze in 1973 had a restraining effect on some other countries not to make the same mistake. (The 1971 price freeze probably had the opposite effect because it was sold as a great success which, in reality, it was not.)

The disillusionment with controls is a very healthy development. But there is danger that it may go too far in one respect: the tragedy was that price controls were applied indiscriminately to a largely competitive economy. The debacle of this policy should not be allowed to compromise monopoly control. And labor unions are the most powerful monopolists. The basic differences between controlling competitive and monopoly prices are repeatedly stressed in the following text.

Many American policy makers are acutely aware that the central problem of price stabilization remains how to prevent labor unions from pushing up wages much faster than the slow rise in labor productivity permits. General price controls and freezes are regarded by these experts as indispensable, though costly, concessions to organized labor. This seems to be the only rational explanation of recent policy moves. Unfortunately the success of this strategy is quite uncertain. It is a great pity that the bearing of union wage pressure on inflation is still a highly controversial issue among economists. (For details see Chapters 6 and 7.)

The international character of the recent wave of inflation has been more generally and more quickly recognized than that of earlier ones. Monetary authorities in practically all countries have seized the opportunity to plead innocence and to blame inflation on other countries and on anonymous world markets as if the inflation bacillus had been flown in from outer space. It is true, small and medium-size countries cannot escape the worldwide inflationary trend unless they are ready to float their currencies; and even floating does not assure immediate success. Indeed, it cannot, unless monetary growth is curbed, and this often meets with stiff resistance. Imported inflation, too, cannot proceed unless it gets a helping hand from a permissive monetary policy. But in very large countries such as the United States the scope for blaming others is very limited. In the United States inflation is made at home. The excessive monetary expansion in 1972 combined with a large government deficit surely was the major cause for the American inflation in 1973, although it has been sharply aggravated by the devaluation of the dollar and the enormous rise in raw material prices on international markets.

To some extent these price rises can be traced back to repercussions of earlier deficits in the American balance of payments and the rise in international liquidity caused by the dollar flood. The question of "imported" and "exported" inflation is a very complicated one and cannot be taken up in this book. (It is discussed in my paper "International Aspects of U.S. Inflation" in *A New Look at Inflation*, American Enterprise Institute, Washington, D.C., 1973.)

Along with stability and inflation, economic growth is still of overriding importance for economic policy, notwithstanding the antigrowth movement that has sprung up in recent years. The case for growth and the modern disenchantment with growth are discussed in Chapter 2 and the relation between stability and growth and possible conflicts between the two objectives in Chapter 5.

Chapter 8 is devoted to a discussion of some international aspects of economic growth and stability. Section A, "International Trade and Economic Growth," deals with the contribution international trade has made and is still making to long-run growth of national income and economic welfare of nations. In this connection the ancient problem of free trade and protection is taken up with special reference to the case of the "less-developed countries" in our times.

Section B, "International Aspects of Economic Stability and Stabilization Policies," deals with international monetary arrangements in historical perspective. The analysis starts with the gold standard and leads up to recent developments. Arguments for and against fixed and flexible exchange rates are presented and evaluated. It is hoped that this analysis will be useful in forming a judgment about contemporary problems.

In this area the great event of 1973 was the final breakdown of the Bretton Woods system of semifixed exchange rates, the so-called system of the "adjustable peg." It has been replaced, for the time being, by a floating currency system. In the International Monetary Fund a Committee of Twenties, consisting of the ministers of finance of the major countries and their deputies, is hard at work on proposals for a new international monetary system which is expected to be put into effect in two or three years. The contours of the reform have not yet been divulged, and the details are still to be worked out. But it has been indicated that the new system will again be one of fixed or rather semifixed, "stable but adjustable" exchange rates (as the disingenuous phrase goes), not one of generally floating rates, although temporary floats "in particular situations" are not excluded.

A detailed discussion and evaluation of the chances of the reform presently contemplated goes beyond the scope of the present study. I venture, however, the following remarks. The chances of survival of a system of semifixed exchanges in the present inflationary environment are just about nil. The ministers of finance would be well advised, before they try to replace the present system of floating by one of fixed or pseudo-fixed rates, to go back to base and do their homework, that is to say, to curb inflation. The reasons for this advice are the following: fixed or semifixed exchange rates require mutual adjustment in many areas, such as monetary, fiscal and wage policies. Expressed differently, fixed parities require mutually consistent rates of inflation. (Note: not equal rates but consistent rates, a little more inflation for some countries, a little less for others according to circumstances. Some of the circumstances are identified in the previously mentioned paper "International Aspects of U.S. Inflation.") It is conceivable, although by no means easy or certain, that the major countries could achieve such a mutually consistent pattern, if rates of inflation in the world are very low. For in that case no country would find itself saddled with a very high rate of inflation. But it is practically inconceivable that there can be found such a mutually consistent and acceptable pattern, except among certain groups of countries, if inflation rates cluster around an 8 percent price rise or more per annum as they do at this time.

G.H.

Washington, D.C.
September 1973

NOTE ON THE OIL CRISIS

After this book was set in type, the energy crisis hit the world economy with full fury. The enormous rise of the price of crude oil imposed by the cartel of the producing countries is a crushing blow for many less developed countries. Moreover it will give a most dangerous impetus to producers in other areas to try to corner the market and will provoke protectionist reactions in many countries.

For the United States the burden of the higher price of oil imports is a most unwelcome additional expense but not an unbearable burden, although one has to add the temporary dislocations caused by the shifts in demand, for example, in the automobile industry. But large changes and shifts in demand, for example, in the automobile industry. But large changes and shifts in demand occur every year in our economy. In the short run the price hike of imported oil increases the magnitude of the problems of stability and adjustment to changes in demand, but it does not add an unmanageable new dimension. The rate of growth will be lower for a little while, but will return to its' normal level so that the former volume of GNP will be restored in a matter of a few years at the latest.

What may in the end cause more damage to the economy than the Arabs and is really depressing are the irrational reactions in the news media and in Congress (with a few notable exceptions), and the ready echo they find in public opinion.

A rational way to deal with the crisis would be to let the price of oil and oil products rise sharply to provide a strong incentive to consumers in households and businesses to economize in the use of oil, and to producers to expand domestic production and develop substitutes for oil. If, at first, prices overshoot the mark, as may well be the case, they will soon come down. This price behavior would greatly discourage hoarding. This basic policy could be supplemented by measures to provide relief in hardship cases and to tax away some of the extra profits but avoid blunting incentives for steeped-up production and exploration.

What we do instead is grudgingly let prices go up slowly while hinting at the same time that prices will go higher in the future, thus providing the strongest possible inducement to hoard and to withhold supplies from the market ; we substitute crude government allocations, which inevitably lag behind changes in the underlying situation and have to be changed continuously, for the delicate market mechanism which was quite effective in dealing with these problems; we continue exceedingly complex price controls (distinguishing between imported oil, "old" domestic oil, "new" domestic oil, etc.,); we create queues at the gas stations and force consumers to waste time, effort, and gas to fill their tanks. This policy breeds black and gray markets and corruption; it requires the creation of a sprawling new bureaucracy and diverts thousands of Internal Revenue agents from their work to the checking of prices at thousands of gas stations. An immense number of man-hours, of highly skilled, highly priced managers and executives, and legal and engineering experts are diverted from productive work to the sterile task of analyzing, anticipating, evading and circumventing government controls. These inconveniences and wastes further stimulate the hysterical clamor for tighter price controls and rationing.

Far too many people, innocent of the way in which the price mechanism can handle crisis of this sort, blame the whole trouble on the greed of big business and demand tight controls, punitive taxes, and even nationalization of the oil industry. Congress, too, and the news media with few notable exceptions, are mainly concerned with the side issue of high profits of the industry in some years—forgetting low profits in other years—instead of concentrating on the central task of providing incentives for stepped-up production and economies in consumption. Thus an embattled administration finds it necessary to make concession after concession to the advocates of controls and rationing.

If, in fact, the oil companies enjoy excessive tax privileges (for example excessive depletion allowances on foreign and domestic production), Congress should change the tax laws. But this must not interfere with the much more important job of stimulating production of oil, natural gas, and other fuels. The greatest folly would be to "roll back" the price of domestic oil, as is now demanded by influential senators. That would check production, encourage consumption, and exacerbate "scarcity," in other words increase the existing imbalance of demand and supply which breeds black markets and corruption.

Many countries have handled the oil crisis much more effectively than the United States. For example, West Germany has neither price controls nor rationing. Therefore it has no "scarcity," that is no imbalance of demand and supply. Prices of oil and gas have, of course, gone up sharply and are much higher than in the United States (as they always were). High prices have attracted additional supplies from abroad, have induced consumers to economize and industrial users to substitute coal for oil wherever possible, even in the short run. Scare buying and hoarding, which occurred when the oil war started and the introduction of controls was debated, has stopped and the ban on Sunday driving was lifted. Switzerland and many other countries had the same experience as Germany. There are, of course, counterexamples of countries, such as Italy, which imposed controls and created chaos. The Netherlands, Sweden and a few other countries panicked and introduced coupon rationing for gasoline. But they gave it up a few weeks later when they discovered that high prices did the rationing much more effectively and cheaply by increasing supply and reducing demand. This almost certainly would be the outcome in the United States, if rationing were introduced; but it probably would take longer and the damage would be greater for the paradoxical reason that the United States, unlike the countries mentioned, is blessed with large domestic supplies of oil that can be squeezed. Foolish government policies often turn a blessing into an evil.

The discussions in chapter 7 of price and wage controls and price freezes, especially the analysis of the debacle of the price freeze of 1973, provide the economic logic behind what has been said in this postscript.

The fantastic rise of crude oil prices—they quadrupled in the course of a few months—poses grave problems for the international monetary system. For the industrial countries alone, the extra cost of imported oil will be in the order of $50 billion in 1974. For the non-oil producing, less developed countries, the extra cost is estimated at $10 billion-$20 billion a year. This is equivalent to unilateral payments of $60 billion-$70 billion— ransoms, reparations, or whatever you wish to call it—to the oil producers from the rest of the Western world. How are these enormous sums to be transferred?

A part of the extra money will be spent by the oil producing countries on additional imports. A sizeable part will, no doubt, be used for development projects in the producing countries, "greening of the Arabian deserts," involving large imports of machinery, equipment, know-how from the industrial world. Some money may be used to give aid to less developed countries. But a large part, probably the bulk of the additional receipts, will be invested abroad, and a very large part of this in dollars. For the industrial world as a whole it means that the additional money they have to pay for oil will come back from the oil countries, either in the form of additional exports or as investment ("capital imports"). If the oil countries leave part of their foreign investments in liquid form—fail to spend them— monetary policy in the industrial countries can offset the deflationary effect.

The conclusion is, that as far as the industrial world *as a whole* is concerned, there will be no serious transfer difficulty. (This does, of course, not mean, that the the higher price paid for oil is no burden. Somebody has to tighten his belt. But for the industrial countries the burden is not unbearable.)

The reader may ask what will happen to exchange rates? Still treating the industrial world as a single unit, the answer is that it would make no sense to say that the currencies of the industrial countries should be devalued vis-à-vis that of the oil producers. The dollar need not bow to the Saudi riyal or the Kuwaiti dinar. The reason is that the oil countries—or at least the most important ones—are wide-open economies which spend an unusually large fraction of their incomes on imports and that the oil revenue accrues to the governments. The governments will spend the money on public projects or invest it abroad and need no exchange incentive to do so. (This is not to conclude that some oil countries with a broader domestic production base, such as Venezuela, may not find it expedient to appreciate their currency.)

When we cease to regard the oil importing countries as a

single unit and consider the differential impact of the oil price rise on different countries, the transfer problem becomes much more complicated. For example there is no doubt that many less developed countries will be hard hit because they are poor *and* because they will get little or none of the oil countries' foreign investments. Also, it is generally assumed that Europe and Japan will be harder hit than the United States. This is the main reason that, late in 1973 and early 1974, the dollar rose sharply vis-à-vis the European currencies and the Japanese yen.

The differential impact of the oil squeeze on different countries raises extremely complex problems. Here only a few of the main issues can be taken up. The analytical background will be found in chapter 8, especially in the last section on flexible exchange rates. (The problem is discussed in somewhat greater detail in my *Two Essays on the Future of the International Monetary Order* with a postscript on the impact of the energy crisis (Washington, D.C. 1974 American Enterprise Institute).

Since there is no reason to doubt that the international position of the United States will be less affected by the oil crisis than that of Europe and Japan, the appreciation of the dollar is a rational reaction of the market. But nobody is in a position to predict, even approximately, the comparative impact of the squeeze on different countries and the realignment of exchange rates that will be required. The everpresent uncertainties are especially great in the present unprecendented situation. The oil war impinged on an already highly fluid and disturbed world economy, plagued as it is by rates of inflation in all industrial countries unheard of in peacetime.

These high rates of inflation, because they significantly differ from country to country, make fixed or semi-fixed exchange rates impossible, even without the additional complications introduced by the oil crisis.

The inescapable conclusion is that there is no alternative but to continue the existing system of widespread floating. The oil crisis did at least one good thing to the international monetary system: It has forced the men in charge of the system to recognize, at long last, the necessity for exchange rate flexibility. For example, the managing director of the International Monetary Fund, Mr. H. Johannes Witteveen, declared that "in the present situation a large measure of floating is unavoidable and indeed desirable." And on January 19, 1974, France abandoned a long-standing position in favor of gold and fixed exchange rates which was firmly held by the ruling Gaullist regime and let the French franc float in the market. The float is supposed to last for six months; so was the detachment of sterling from gold in 1931.

Floating exchange rates are necessary—a necessary evil if you like—in the modern world, especially in an inflation-torn world economy, but they are not a panacea. They cannot reduce the basic burden of the higher oil price or obviate a certain amount of reshuffling of production resources inside each national economy and in international trade. They can only facilitate the necessary adjustments. The system of floating rates will be put to a severe test by the turmoil produced by the oil crisis. It is imperative that its limitations be understood fully. What they can do and what they cannot do is discussed in the last pages of this book.

Economic Growth & Stability

Chapter 1

Introduction

The principal purpose of the present study is to identify the public policies and the instruments primarily in the monetary and financial areas that are best suited to realize two economic objectives peoples almost everywhere regard as highly desirable —economic stability and growth. Since objectives determine the choice of instruments, a few comments on these two objectives are in order before going on to the question of the instruments best suited to their attainment.

OBJECTIVES

Obviously, economic stability and growth, while very important, are not the most basic. For most people, certainly for those in the West, there is a more basic objective: freedom, real personal freedom.

3

Personal Freedom

To be free a person must have a large array of choices: as to the work he wants to do, where he wants to do it, whether he wants to work for himself or for another. The individual must have control of his person and of the fruits of his labor. The preservation of these liberties implies respect for private property and the existence of free competitive markets where rewards (economists call them prices) are determined by market forces, that is, by the interplay of demand and supply. Price fixing, that is, determination of prices by government decree at other levels than those determined by market forces almost always leads to infringements on the freedoms just mentioned. (The only exception is governmental price fixing in case of a monopoly situation such as in the public utility area.) Especially fixing prices *below* the competitive level, which is so often done in the vain attempt to check inflation, implies formal or informal[1] consumer rationing and allocation of resources and thus violates freedom of consumer choice and free enterprise.

The above is a value judgment.[2] For those who accept it, as does the writer, it follows that the search for the best tools for realizing the economic objectives of stability and growth must be restricted to those who respect the rights of the individual and are consistent with the *modus operandi* of the free enterprise system. The instruments available will obviously be fewer for a government operating under these restraints than for one that can treat its people as pawns for its purposes.

Growth

While growth is not as overriding an objective in the mature industrial countries as it is in the less-developed countries and in the Communist world, it is nonetheless a basic goal everywhere. And I say this despite the recent clamor in this country for a

4

zero rate of growth. (The recent disenchantment with growth will be taken up in the following chapter.) The modern opposition to growth appears to be due to some extent to a misunderstanding of what economists mean by the term "growth" and of their ways of measuring it. Gross national product (GNP), now in universal use as a measure of changes over time in the economic conditions of a country and as a means of comparing international rates of growth, smacks of crass materialism. Its use may well have contributed to the violent denunciations of growth presently heard in this country and elsewhere. The term needs defining as does the companion term "stability."

These definitions appear in the next two chapters. They will, I believe, not only support my contention that growth is a basic goal of policy in all countries, but that it is a proper goal of policy.

Stability

The ideal goal should be to maximize the rate of growth with full employment and price stability maintained continuously. This, of course, may not always be possible, either because of ideally unnecessary but practically unavoidable mistakes, or because of the intrinsic impossibility of fully realizing all three of the objectives at the same time. It will be argued later that pressing for continuous full employment or even for an unduly high level of employment will not only conflict with price stability but also with the growth objective. Suffice it to say at this point that when conflicts among the basic objectives appear, policy makers, including the citizen-voters who think about these things, must make a choice: in economic parlance, there must be a "preference scale" or "trade-off function." Those who make or influence policies must have some idea how much stability of prices or employment they are willing to sacrifice for how much growth. If the choice is not made consciously and explicitly, it is implied by policy action—or inaction.

There may exist other policy objectives that, in the opinion of some people, should take precedence over growth and stability. Let me briefly mention one of them—greater equality of income distribution in some sense, including the fight against poverty.

Since it has become apparent that the growth records of Communist countries are not as good as was thought; that they cannot compare with those of many Western countries—for example West Germany, Italy (until a couple of years ago) or Japan—left-wing radicals have tended to scoff at growth and to stress equalization of income distributions as the prime goal of economic policy.

Obviously, much can be done in capitalist countries by tax policy, social welfare measures, and public expenditures on health and education to help the lower classes and to reduce poverty. But there clearly exist limits beyond which greater equality (however defined) can be obtained only by increasingly sacrificing overall growth. I shall not further discuss that problem. Winston Churchill once put it in a nutshell when he said: "Capitalism suffers from the vice that wealth is distributed unequally. Communism has the supreme virtue that misery is shared by all!"[3]

INSTRUMENTS

I turn now to the question of the instruments best suited to promote stability and growth available to the countries with a free enterprise economy. As mentioned earlier, the present book is primarily concerned with measures of a monetary and fiscal nature, "macroeconomic" policies as they are called. But first a few words on the basic problem of conserving competition, the indispensable foundation of the free enterprise system.

Antimonopoly Measures

The most powerful instrument at the disposal of governments is the power to prevent monopoly. Monopoly is the enemy of the free competitive enterprise system. The monopolist keeps the price above the competitive level, that is, above costs, defined in such a way as to allow for "normal" profits, the reward for riskbearing, and an adequate compensation for the labor of the manager or owner (wages of management). The difference between price and average cost in that comprehensive sense constitutes the monopoly profit.

The best way to eliminate monopoly profit and to bring prices down is to eliminate barriers to competition. In most cases this can be achieved by denying special privileges (licenses and other government-enforced or tolerated restrictions), and by the removal of import restrictions (import duties, prohibitions, quotas, import licenses, etc.). Few monopolies could survive without government protection of one sort or another. In these few cases primarily in the area of public utilities (transportation, communication, and the like) a good case can be made for some price fixing or control.

There is a basic difference between regulating monopoly prices and fixing competitive prices below the market level. If a monopoly price is fixed below the price the monopolist otherwise would charge (but not below the competitive level) the monopolist-producer will expand production, since the competitive price covers "normal" profits. No rationing is required, unless the mistake is made of fixing the price too low, that is, below the competitive level in which case the "monopolist" would curtail production and the consumer would suffer.

Actually real monopolies are rare. They are most likely to exist in the area of public utilities (telephone, telegraph, railroads, electricity, etc.). It would be irrational and inexpedient to have two telephone companies in one city or two subways on the same street. There is thus justification for public regulation aimed at imposing the rates that would be charged if there were competition. In fact, public utilities are frequently overregulated and the degree of competition which exists even in this field (between railroad, airlines, buses, and between electricity, oil, gas, etc.) is often grossly underestimated. Thus, when railroads are increasingly subjected to competition by new modes of transportation, old regulations, although they have lost their justification, are apt to persist. But bad practices do not alter the fact that some "natural" monopolies do exist, and that regulating monopoly prices, if not overdone, does not have the same deleterious effects as fixing prices in areas in which competition is reasonably effective.

So far we have discussed business monopolies. Far more powerful in the United States and Great Britain, as well as in a number of other countries of the West, are labor union monopolies. They are monopolists in the sense that they exert tight control over the labor supply and thus destroy competition, push up wages and make them almost entirely rigid downward. But their mode of operation is different from that of industrial monopolies. The existence of powerful labor unions is a headache for the policy maker and the theoretical economist. They strongly influence the effectiveness of the other instruments to be discussed presently.

Much is made nowadays of "oligopolies," "monopolistic competition" and other deviations from perfect competition. It is common practice in pure economic theory to define competition in the very strict sense of a situation where the individual producer has absolutely no influence on prices or, in economic parlance, where he is a "price-taker" who is confronted with a "horizontal demand curve." The wheat or cotton farmer is in that position. In these cases, we speak of "perfect, atomistic" competition. But already the village grocer and gas station operator have a tiny bit of "monopoly power"; they can raise

8

their price slightly without losing all their customers as they would if competition were of the perfect-atomistic type. The fact that some monopoly power is almost ubiquitous in manufacturing does not justify a policy of price fixing or price "guidance" over a very wide range. This kind of reasoning has become the wedge for the introduction of far-reaching policies of wage and price regulations under the name of "guideposts for noninflationary wage and price behavior" or "incomes policy."

This is a very important matter which will be taken up later (see page 177ff.), but here is not the place to pursue it further. Suffice it to say at this point that the conditions for effective and workable competition are much less stringent than abstract theory would make us believe. The so-called "monopolistic competition" comes in most cases much closer to perfect competition than to monopoly. In other words, modern economies, especially the American economy, blessed as it is with a huge internal free trade area, are much more competitive than the perfectionist definition of competition in pure theory and fanatical "trustbusters" would make us believe. (See Chapter 5.)

Summarizing, let me say once more, freedom of consumer choice, freedom of choosing one's residence and occupation, and free enterprise are values and policy objectives more important than those of growth and stability. Their preservation requires free markets and absence of price controls. Fortunately, these freedoms, far from being in conflict with the goals of growth and stability, are conducive to bringing about rapid growth and stability. These freedoms, thus, are means and ends at the same time.

Macroeconomic Policies

As mentioned, this book will focus attention primarily on overall monetary and fiscal policies, what economists now often call "macroeconomic policies" or "demand management." These policies are called macroeconomic policies (and the underlying theories macroeconomics) because they deal with broad aggregates such as the quantity of money, national income, total expenditure (often called "effective demand"), average price (price level), average wage (wage level), and government expenditures and revenues. The opposite of macroeconomic policies are microeconomic policies. This latter term comprises a large number of policies dealing with individual sectors of the economies or industries, with individual prices and wages. Antimonopoly measures and antipollution policies are examples of microeconomic policies. The distinction is important although, as is usual in economics, the dividing line between the two categories is not always sharply drawn.

To promote stability and growth the liberal economist—liberal in the original sense of *laissez-faire,* not in the modern perverted sense—prefers macroeconomic instruments, monetary and fiscal policies. Fortunately, as we shall see, these are quite effective, so that meddling with individual industries and firms (micromeasures) can be largely avoided—antimonopoly, antipollution and similar measures apart.

Monetary Policy

Monetary policy deals essentially with the issue (creation) of money and the regulation of its quantity by the "monetary authorities," that is, the Central Banks in most countries and the Federal Reserve System in the United States. Money stock or supply is usually defined as currency (bank notes and coins) in circulation plus demand deposits ("checking deposits") in commercial banks.[4] "Deposit money" is an integral part of money; in fact, in the United States where the great bulk of payments are made by check, demand deposits are the much larger part of the total money supply. It follows that "banking policy" and "credit policy," which regulate the volume of deposits, are integral parts of monetary policy.

The most important concrete instruments of policy at the

disposal of the monetary authorities are discount policy (rates and conditions at which private business, especially banks, can borrow from the Central Bank); "open market operations" (purchases and sales of government securities in the market by the Central Banks); and the setting of reserve requirements for commercial banks (the regulations concerning cash reserves commercial banks must hold against deposits). Numerous other more detailed regulations, "selective monetary measures," into which monetary policy often tends to proliferate, will be mentioned later. For the most part we shall deal with "general" monetary policy wielded by the three instruments mentioned.

Fiscal Policy

By fiscal policy we mean the policy that attempts to influence aggregate demand and total spending in the economy by manipulating overall government expenditures and receipts. Thus an excess of government expenditures over receipts—that is, a budget deficit, brought about either by an increase in expenditures or a decrease in receipts (tax cut)—adds to aggregate demand and stimulates the economy. An excess of receipts over expenditures or budget surplus, brought about by a tax increase or a cut in expenditures, tends to reduce total demand and to counteract inflationary pressure, and to "cool off" or depress the economy.

By its nature, fiscal policy must be to a considerable extent selective. Changes in expenditures cannot well be spread evenly over the whole range of government activity, and changes in tax rates are rarely across the board. Nonetheless, it will be useful to distinguish between general fiscal policy and selective fiscal policy. Selective fiscal policy attempts to influence particular sectors of the economy, for example, business investment or construction of houses; general fiscal policy aims at a general strengthening or weakening of overall effective demand and expenditure.

11

Monetary and fiscal policies are usually regarded as alternative methods of stimulating or slowing down the economy, counteracting inflationary or deflationary pressures as the case may be. But we shall see that the effectiveness of fiscal policy depends crucially on certain monetary conditions. If a deficit is financed in a "noninflationary" manner by borrowing from the public rather than from the banks, funds for private investment will be restricted and interest rates driven up. A reduction of private expenditures will partly or wholly cancel the stimulating effect of a governmental deficit.[5] Similarly, a government surplus must be withheld from the capital market (must be "sterilized") if the budget surplus is to have its dampening (antiinflationary) effect. These monetary preconditions for effective fiscal policy, which are very important and subtle, are often ignored, slurred over or implicitly abstracted from, in the predominantly Keynesian literature. We shall come back to these problems later.

Furthermore, monetary and fiscal policies have different side effects, for example, on growth and on the international balance of payments. Hence the two types of policy are far from being entirely interchangeable, and their "mix" or "blend" often becomes an important issue. When we refer to both and stress their basic similarity rather than differential side effects, we shall speak of "financial policies."

Apart from overall financial policies, modern governments often try to promote stability and growth by influencing individual sectors of the economy, by tampering with symptoms in many different ways. Control of individual prices (usually by fixing a maximum price below the free market price), and rationing (which effective price controls entail) are the most important forms of symptomatic measures. In the United States and elsewhere, these "direct controls," the opposite of "indirect controls" through overall financial policies, were extensively used during World War II and the immediate postwar period. They proved increasingly ineffective and distasteful and were thoroughly discredited when later in the 1940s, in country after country, the free competitive price mechanism was restored and financial policies, especially monetary policy, took over from direct control. A landmark in this process of liberalization was the monetary reform and abolition of the tight net of controls, at one stroke, in West Germany in 1948 under the leadership of Ludwig Erhard. This reform ushered in a period of spectacular expansion of the German economy which has continued uninterruptedly to this day. Many other countries followed the German example with similar favorable results.

In recent years a hybrid form of price control has become popular which, in the United States, was first called "guideposts for noninflationary wage and price behavior" and later became known as "incomes policy" first in Europe, later also in the United States. It is a sort of across-the-board price and wage guidance aimed at approximating the state of affairs that would obtain in a smooth-working, competitive economy. Actually the system, if kept over extended periods, either becomes ineffective and, if not abandoned, degenerates into comprehensive price and wage fixing. Thus, in the United States and elsewhere the discredited system of detailed price and wage control was again introduced in October 1971 as Phase 2 of the so-called "New Economic Policy" which had been inaugurated with a general price and wage freeze for ninety days on August 15, 1971. We shall ignore these aberrations for the time being, but discuss them in some detail later (see Chapter 7).

INTERNATIONAL ASPECTS

Following the usual procedure we shall discuss the problem of economic growth and stability and of stabilization and growth-promoting policies first under the assumption of a closed economy; in other words we first disregard, except for occasional hints, international complications and disturbances. This does not mean, however, that international aspects are insignificant. On the contrary they are of the utmost importance. As will be shown in the last chapter, in most countries modern economic growth and development would have been, and now is, nearly impossible if these countries were forced to live in isolation from the rest of the world. And economic stability is profoundly affected by influences from abroad. Especially price stability and inflation are for all countries—except the biggest ones, the United States and USSR—largely determined from the outside. Thus the postwar inflation is essentially an international phenomenon and so were periods of inflation and deflation under the rule of the gold standard. If some countries inflate more than others, they are forced to devalue their currency either openly or disguised in the form of numerous controls. It is impossible for any one country, under a regime of fixed exchange rates and freely convertible currency, to stay out of an inflationary trend in the rest of the world. Whether and to what extent it is possible for any country to maintain price stability and to ward off other threats to economic stability (for example, to full employment, in an inflationary or deflationary world by periodically changing or by floating its exchange rate) will be discussed in the last chapter.

Chapter 2

Growth and Growth Policy

INTRODUCTION

We live in the age of growth and development. Economists, policy makers and the public at large have become growth-conscious. While thirty years ago, in the heyday of the "Keynesian Revolution," employment and economic stability largely monopolized the attention, emphasis has shifted to the problem of long-run economic growth. Growth has become the overriding objective of economic policy in the "developed" industrial countries of the West, as well as in the "less-developed" world and in the Communist countries of the East. The rate of growth has also become an election issue in all democratic countries. Success or failure of democratic governments is often judged by the speed of the economic growth they are supposed to have secured or failed to secure by their economic policies. Many gullible individuals have been dazzled by fantastic claims of speedy growth in Communist countries.

15

In view of the recent antigrowth agitation in the United States and Western Europe, many readers will question the above assertion. I would ask them to suspend judgment. I shall discuss the antigrowth movement presently, arguing that although pollution and overpopulation are of course serious problems, it rests on misunderstanding of what economists mean by growth and is marred by other fatal defects.

In the present essay, our principal concern is with this question: How and to what extent can growth be influenced by monetary and fiscal policies in a modern and predominantly free enterprise economy with a fairly large public sector and a government budget accounting for 25 to 35 percent of the gross national product (GNP)? I make this latter assumption not because a large public sector represents an ideal state of affairs guaranteeing a maximum rate of growth—far from it—but because it is the economic environment in which we live. It gives fiscal policy the great weight it now has, making it, for better or worse, a powerful instrument for influencing growth and stability. To illustrate the great change that has taken place, consider this: If in 1931 or 1932, before the bottom of the Great Depression had been reached, the individual income tax had been cut 50 percent as an antidepression measure, it would not have arrested the downward movement of the economy because at that time the yield of the income tax was but a minute fraction of aggregate expenditures. Today, such a step could turn a deep depression into a runaway inflation[1] —so much larger is the relative size of the public sector and so much greater the weight of the income tax in total expenditures.

MEANING AND MEASUREMENT OF GROWTH

Economic growth or development[2] is now usually defined or measured by the increase in aggregate GNP or, better, GNP per capita or, still better, by the average increase in output per

16

worker employed or man-hour worked; in other words, the increase in average productivity of labor. In the short run, there is little difference between aggregate GNP and per capita GNP, although they diverge in the long run. Both reflect, in addition to long-run trend in output, short-run (business cycle) changes in the rate of employment. Care must therefore be taken when measuring long-run growth to choose periods that begin and end with the same cycle phase, for example, peak years of the cycle when the economy presumably operates at or near full employment.[3] In other words, long-run growth must not be confused with short-run (business cycle) recovery as would happen if we measured the average annual increase in GNP over a period beginning with a depression year and ending with a boom year, or vice versa.

The third measure, output per man-hour input (what is usually called productivity of labor), to some extent abstracts from cyclical changes in employment (because only labor that is actually used is counted and not unemployed labor) and is therefore a better measure of long-run trends over short periods.[4] In addition, this measure gives a better impression of long-run growth because it allows for the shortening of the workweek. When a country gets richer and incomes rise, people "consume" some of their higher incomes in the form of leisure; they work shorter hours, take longer vacations and retire earlier. Hence, output per man-hour worked will rise faster than total output or per capita output. The former faster-rising figure evidently gives a better impression of increasing economic welfare than the latter slower-rising measure which disregards increased leisure time.[5]

These relationships must also be kept in mind when making international comparisons especially between highly developed and backward countries. Both for contemporary comparisons between countries and for comparisons of rates of growth over time, output per man-hour is for most purposes the more appropriate measure. The interpretation of growth figures raises especially intricate economic and statistical problems when comparisons are made between countries in different stages of economic development—mature industrial countries and less-developed countries. In the latter, statistics are generally poor and GNP figures are apt to give excessive weight to industrial production, neglecting unduly the contribution of agriculture, especially subsistence farming. Comparisons of growth rates in capitalist and Communist countries are notoriously tricky.

As far as the less-developed countries are concerned, Peter Bauer, S. Herbert Frankel and others have extensively and convincingly dealt with these issues. Abram Bergson, Warren Nutter and others have done the same for comparisons between the United States and Russia. Suffice it to say here that GNP has to be defined comprehensively. It is, of course, not identical with industrial production and certain "imponderables" should be taken into consideration, such as freedom and range of consumer choice, quality of products, leisure, working conditions, quality of public services, and so forth.

DETERMINANTS OF GROWTH

While formal theories of growth, extensive measurement of growth rates and preoccupation with economic growth in popular discussions are a fairly recent development, going back not more than thirty or forty years, economists have always been concerned with growth, though using other words and terminologies. Adam Smith's great book would not have been falsely labeled had he titled it *The Economic Growth and Development of Nations* instead of *Inquiry into the Nature and Causes of the Wealth of Nations.*[5a]

It is often asserted, especially by Keynesians and modern interventionist-protectionist writers on economic development, that while the old classical writers had a theory of development and growth, "neoclassical" economists of all descriptions—members of the "Cambridge," "Lausanne" and "Austrian" schools—were and are not interested in the dynamic problems of growth and development; that they were entirely concerned with "static efficiency," "static allocation of resources," with value and price formation, with monopoly and competition—in brief with microeconomic problems, as the modern phrase goes, and had nothing to contribute to the explanation of growth and development. Modern neoclassical economics is dismissed as inapplicable or irrelevant for the economic problems of the less-developed countries—"developing" countries, as they are officially called (an inappropriate term because it suggests that the advanced countries are not growing or not interested in growth).[6]

This type of criticism is really quite superficial. Since the days of early classical writers, economics has grown in width and depth and has become much more complicated. Like scholars in other fields, economists specialize nowadays to a much greater extent than in the old days and only a few dare to cover the whole field. Thus some neoclassical writers did not write explicitly on growth, but others had a good deal to say. Let me only mention the names of Eugen v. Boehm-Bawerk, J. B. Clark, Alfred Marshall, and Joseph A. Schumpeter.

The charge of neglecting dynamic problems of growth and development can be leveled, however, against the Keynesian system. Keynes' *General Theory of Employment, Interest and Money* is entirely static. True, investment, an intrinsically dynamic phenomenon and important determinant of growth, plays a key role; but in the formal theory (apart from numerous asides, digressions, *obiter dicta)* the dynamic, output-raising effects of investment are consciously and explicitly ruled out. Only the short-run multiplier employment effects of investment are considered.

It is true that later writers have dynamized the static Keynesian system and constructed long-run growth theories in Keynesian foundations. But it is precisely the rigid Keynesian foundations which make these latter constructs, such as the so-called Harrod-Domar models of economic growth, wholly unsatisfactory and unrealistic. The objectionable assumptions are, concretely, that there is a constant (or only exogenously changing) capital-output or capital-labor ratio and that the proportions of incomes people save do not adjust to changing circumstances.[7] These assumptions imply that only changes in income and employment can equilibrate savings and investment; that capital and labor cannot be substituted for one another in response to changes in prices, wages and interest rates. It is one thing to say that in the short run, in the business cycle context, there are limitations on the speed at which such adjustment can take place and that this often leads to temporary disequilibrium, unemployment, recessions or depressions; it is an entirely different thing, and it is wholly unrealistic, to deny the existence of any tendency for such adjustments and substitutions in the long run.[8]

These "Keynesian"[9] theories make - aggregate effective demand or expenditures the fundamental determinant not only of short-run fluctuations but also of the long-term rate of growth. It can be argued that an adequate rise in aggregate monetary demand is a *necessary* condition for continuous real growth and that it is possible to interrupt growth by deflation, a contraction of aggregate monetary demand, and to slow it down by continuous deflation. But surely aggregate demand, an essentially monetary phenomenon, is not *sufficient* to assure rapid growth unless certain "real" conditions are fulfilled.

Although the present volume is, to repeat, not a monograph on economic growth, let me briefly review the "real" factors that would seem to have a strong bearing on the rate of growth. Everybody agrees that saving and investment is one of them. The more current consumption people are willing and able to forego (save) and to put to productive use (invest), the greater can be the future stream of output available for consumption or for further investment. There are many questions of detail, for example, where to draw the line between consumption and investment. They are often difficult in the public sector. What goes as "government investment" should often be classified as consumption if not as waste—"honorary investment," as Professor Sir Dennis Robertson once called it.[10] But also in the private sector the border line between consumption and investment is sometimes not easy to discern or is nonexistent. [11] Modern theorists are concerned with such cases when they speak of investment in "human capital," such as expenditures on education and self-betterment.

Another aspect which will not be discussed at this point is the possibility of occasional short-run hitches in the process by which savings are converted into investment. The capital market which performs the function of translating savings into investments is not perfect. This is connected with the phenomenon of cyclical depressions and recessions which will be discussed more fully in Chapters 4 and 5.

Nobody argues any more, as many Keynesians did during the Great Depression of the 1930s, that there are literally no investment opportunities left (except those created by population growth and new inventions) and that, since savings habits do not easily change, we are faced with a permanent excess of savings over investment and thus condemned to secular unemployment and stagnation from which only government expenditures and deficits can rescue us. This theory of "secular stagnation," which grew on Keynesian soil and became very popular in the 1930s, is wrong in its factual assertion that there are no investment opportunites left and in the conclusion that such a situation, if it existed, would necessarily cause permanent stagnation in the sense of chronic unemployment.[12] (This latter point will be taken up in connection with the problem of stability).

Today, most economists are again agreed (as they were before Keynes) that there exist practically unlimited opportunities for investment, that is, possibilities of increasing future production by plowing back current output even if we make the unrealistic and almost undefinable assumption that technological knowledge stops increasing here and now. There is, of course, even greater agreement that inventions, innovations, and increases in technological know-how are equally or probably more important for the speed of economic growth than the mere accumulation of capital. In fact, the two, capital formation and technological improvement, are very closely interrelated. Clear thinking requires conceptual separation, although even that is difficult. But however we draw the line, the two factors are clearly complementary in the sense that, on the one hand, most improvements and innovations, though certainly not all, [13] require additional capital investment and, on the other hand, new investment often yields unexpected new vistas on how to do things better than before.

The growth of technological knowledge and the speed at which improved methods of production and new products are invented and introduced involve enormously complicated social processes which far transcend the realm of economics and the competence of economists. They have their deepest roots in religious and philosophical attitudes and beliefs, and are conditioned by social developments.

Let me single out some of the specific economic aspects. Economists distinguish between inventions and innovations. Invention is the discovery of new products or methods in the scholar's study and in the laboratory; innovation, on the other hand, is the actual introduction of new methods of producing existing types of products or of producing and marketing entirely new or improved products. Economists are more concerned with the innovator than with the inventor. The dynamic producer who introduces new methods or products, the innovator, is called the entrepreneur. The entrepreneurial, innovational function is thus distinguished from the function of the production manager as well as that of the inventor.

As usual in economic matters, it is not easy to draw the line sharply between the "dynamic" entrepreneur and the "static" production manager. In a sense, innovational activity takes place throughout the industrial system, from the top-flight executive down to the lowly foreman. Each may be moved, in his own sphere, to innovate, to break out of established routine, to do things better or more cheaply and with less effort than they were done before, especially when confronted with unforeseen difficulties. But conceptually it is necessary to make the distinction, and it has been possible to identify important innovations that shape major advances in the economy. The interpretation of historical economic development in terms of innovational activities of individual entrepreneurs has been very fruitful; the "entrepreneurial approach" to economic history has yielded many useful insights.

The entrepreneur has been the driving force in Western economies and entrepreneurial activity is bound up with technological progress and growth. There has been much speculation as to why some countries and periods have generated more entrepreneurial activity and growth and others less. Some writers attribute the comparative backwardness of certain areas to the dearth of entrepreneurial talents. Actually, it would seem that institutional differences, social structures, government policies and monetary arrangements are primarily responsible for stimulating or retarding the flowering of entrepreneurial activity, the flow of innovations, and thus the speed of technological progress and growth. Otherwise, how could we explain the way in which emigrants from areas allegedly undersupplied with entrepreneurial talent—Eastern European and Middle Eastern Asian countries, etc.[14] —when coming to a favorable milieu, for example the United States, suddenly develop surprising entrepreneurial activities. There evidently was no, or little, scope and opportunity for entrepreneurial activities in their native lands.

Concretely, a milieu favoring successful operation of free entrepreneurs would have approximately the following characteristics: an open, competitive society; in other words, absence of any caste system, of rigid social taboos, and of formal or *de facto* restrictions on the setting up or expanding of businesses based on racial, social or religious grounds; wholehearted acceptance of the profit and loss system as a spur to disciplined risk-taking, which excludes confiscatory taxes with very high marginal rates; liberal policies concerning the immigration of foreigners;[15] the setting up of business by foreign corporations, and the free importation of foreign capital. "Direct investment," as distinguished from "portfolio investment," is especially important because capital imports for direct investment carry with them technological know-how and entrepreneurship. Monetary stability which excludes excessive inflation and deflation favors entrepreneurial activity. *Repressed* inflation, which entails price fixing, rationing, allocation of resources and exchange control, is poison for free enterprise and stifles innovational activity. *Open* inflation, if applied intermittently in moderate doses, may even stimulate entrepreneurial activity and growth.

Experience has repeatedly shown that even a country poorly endowed with natural resources can expect lively entrepreneurial activity, rapid and steady growth and consequently a high and rising standard of living and well-being if the enumerated conditions are approximately fulfilled. Switzerland, Hong Kong and Singapore are striking examples.

Experience has also shown that relatively affluent countries abundantly endowed with first-rate natural and human resources can sink into stagnation when the above-mentioned conditions to growth are absent. A glaring example is Argentina. Colin Clark years ago in his famous book *Conditions of Economic Progress*[16] predicted that Argentina would in the not distant future enjoy a standard of living close to that of Canada or the United States. Thanks to the policies of Colonel Perón (who recently returned to the presidency as General Perón) which discouraged agriculture, fostered overrapid industrialization and coddled labor unions, economic growth was stifled, and although Argentina has no business being underdeveloped it is still classified as a semideveloped country. Other examples of interrupted growth and stagnation are the late Salvador Allende's Chile and Fidel Castro's Cuba. Such regression is invariably due to bad government policies.

In the postwar period the political and economic climate in many less-developed countries has been very unfavorable for foreign capital; private foreign capital, direct investment and

24

entrepreneurship find a chilly reception or are not admitted at all. The emergence of strong Communist parties, frequent revolutions, outright expropriation of foreign enterprises even by non-Communist governments are clearly not conducive to attracting foreign capital and enterprise.

But apart from adverse political factors, there are certain features of modern economic policies, prevalent in different degrees in many less-developed countries, that have slowed economic growth and restricted the supply of capital from foreign and domestic sources. The two closely interrelated conditions I have in mind are excessive government interventions in the economic process and inflation. The first manifests itself in many different ways—nationalization of whole industries; hypertrophic growth of red tape and bureaucracy; excessive protection of domestic industries from foreign competition; a maze of import and payments restrictions, quotas, exchange control (all that is nowadays euphemistically called a "policy of import substitution"); overelaborate measures of social welfare introduced at an early stage of economic development; heavy arbitrary taxation, and so forth. Most developed countries have, of course, been moving in that same direction, but they can better afford such interventions because they are rich and their administrative capabilities are much greater than those of the less-developed countries.

Views differ about the comparative and absolute efficiency of public administration and enterprises. I personally am convinced that public enterprise is practically always less efficient and more wasteful than private enterprise. But there can be no doubt, in my opinion, that a tolerable degree of honesty in government and efficiency in public administration can be reached only at a comparatively late stage of economic development. This is especially true under democracy.

Many less-developed countries overload their governments and public administrations with tasks for which they are not ready—tasks which the now developed countries did not dream of undertaking in the corresponding stage of their development.

The hypertrophy of government activities in the public sector impedes the working of the private sector, impairs the efficiency of public administration in the legitimate areas that are important for economic growth (health, education, general administration of law and order, etc.), causes inflation and thus retards growth. The impact of inflation on growth will be taken up later. At this point, I confine myself to saying that huge deficits in government budgets are the main sources of inflation in less-developed countries and that they are in most cases due to the heavy burden placed on government budgets by grossly inefficient and overstaffed public enterprises and nationalized industries.

Fortunately a growing number of less-developed countries follow a policy of enlightened liberalism, give freedom to private enterprise, native and foreign, pursue liberal trade policies, welcome foreign capital and direct investment and avoid excessive regimentation of the economy. Shining examples are Taiwan, Mexico, Brazil, Greece and Malaysia, in addition to Hong Kong and Singapore which were mentioned earlier. The countries with liberal economic policies—liberal in the original sense of relative laissez-faire—have consistently outproduced and outperformed the interventionist and protectionist countries.[17]

WHY GROWTH POLICY?

Government policies can and do promote—or retard—economic growth in many different ways. For example, policies aimed at maintaining or restoring the basic conditions for lively entrepreneurial activity would go a long way to promote economic growth. In fact, a very effective, and from the economic and administrative point of view, comparatively simple (though politically by no means easy) way to increase the rate of growth would be to remove the man-made obstacles to growth by radically changing the policies that we just described. This was, in fact, achieved by Brazil after the overthrow of the Communist Goulart regime in 1964. The success of the new policy was spectacular. There are many other ways in which government can accelerate growth. Let me only mention the vast area of education, training and retraining of workers, designed to promote the mobility and versatility of the labor force.

A thorough discussion of these policies is not the subject of the present volume. Our main concern is with the impact of fiscal and monetary policies on stability and growth. But there is an important preliminary question which needs to be raised at this point: Why should government be concerned with growth? Why not let the rate of growth be determined by the decisions of individuals and by the forces of the market? We do not, as a rule, interfere with consumer choice. Should the principle of noninterference not apply to individuals' choices between consumption and saving, choices which determine the level of investment and thus help to determine the rate of growth? Individuals' decisions concerning consumption and saving are not the only ones that affect growth. Decisions concerning education and resources devoted to scientific research and development are equally important. Concerning all of these, the same question can be asked—why not leave them to individual households and firms? Why make them a business of the government? In short, why growth policy at all?

Before trying to answer these questions, we must *first* distinguish between growth and recovery and between growth policy and recovery policy. Starting from a situation with widespread unemployment—depression, recession, stagnation—output and GNP can rise rapidly. This we call recovery. When full employment is reached, output per head can still grow, but it requires growth of productivity, capacity, technological progress, saving and investing. Monetary or fiscal measures designed to bring about recovery and to speed the return to full employment, or to prevent lapses from full employment, belong to stabilization policy and are not growth policy proper, although they may have some impact on long-run growth. Thus, to prevent or terminate long periods of massive unemployment—deep depression or stagnation—surely is also conducive to long-run growth. The precise relation between stability and growth and possible conflicts between the two objectives will be discussed in greater detail in Chapter 5. At any rate, this is not the type of growth policy, if we call it such, to which the doubts mentioned above apply—why growth policy at all; why not leave the outcome to market forces and to the decisions of the individuals?

There is a *second* category of measures and policies affecting growth to which these doubts do not apply, namely, all those microeconomic measures and policies that influence growth indirectly by eliminating wastes and inefficiencies, thus directly bringing about a *once-for-all* increase in output and income. Examples are the elimination of barriers to competition; abolition of government controls and restrictions; reduction of import tariffs and other impediments to trade which permit more extensive international division of labor and a more efficient use of domestic resources. Such measures and policies can only bring about a once-for-all increase in output; they are thus not growth policies in the strict sense.[18] But any once-for-all increase in GNP brings with it a potential, and in all probability some actual, increase in growth for the indefinite future, because out of a larger income (GNP) some part presumably will be saved and invested.[19]

I now come to the *third* group of policies aimed at increasing the rate of growth—growth policies proper. These are policies and measures that stimulate saving and investment at the expense of current consumption. A straightforward example is a compulsory saving scheme. Current consumption can be reduced by appropriate taxes and the proceeds channeled through the capital market into private (or public) investment, resulting in larger output in the future. Investment in this connection should be defined broadly enough to include "investment in human beings," for example, in education through lengthening of compulsory school attendance and stimulating young people to go to high schools and colleges.

(Needless to add that we are here interested only in the growth potentialities of such policies. The actual effectiveness of concrete measures of this sort will not be discussed.)

It is with respect to measures of this type that the questions posed above can be legitimately asked: Why should the government try to influence growth? Why should growth not be left to be determined by the decisions of individuals and forces of the market?

For reasons set out in greater detail in the appendix to the present chapter (Appendix A), I believe that a good case can be made for a growth policy along the lines sketched above, even if one accepts (as the present writer does) the principle that the government should not try to substitute its own preferences for those of individuals. It does not mean government should replace the capital market and price mechanism by central planning. In our individualistic economy the capital market and the price mechanism, in particular pricing of capital (i.e., the interest rate), perform the indispensible function of allocating the supply of capital (saving) among the practically unlimited opportunities to invest.[20] In a free society growth policy, if it is to be efficient, must work with and through the market by channeling savings extracted by suitable taxes through the capital market into private or public investments.

But even so, growth policy does constitute a deviation from the principle of laissez-faire. Nonetheless, as is shown in Appendix A, this can be justified on two grounds: *first,* the pragmatic one that a conscious policy of stimulating growth may do no more than offset the adverse effects on growth of many other public activities; *second,* the fact that the laissez-faire principle loses its clear meaning and makes it impossible for government to remain entirely neutral (i.e., not to intervene in any way with individual decisions) when saving and investment decisions involve future generations.

It is hardly necessary to add that recognizing the validity of the case for growth policy does not imply accepting and condoning everything that modern governments do in the name of growth. (See Appendix A for details.)

DISENCHANTMENT WITH GROWTH

During the last few years professional and popular attitudes toward economic growth have undergone sharp changes. Until very recently it was primarily conservative economists who questioned the wisdom of elevating economic growth to the rank of an overriding policy objective and spoke sarcastically of "growthmanship" and "growthmania." Now the extreme left has become disenchanted with growth, and many regard the pursuit of economic growth as an expression of crass materialism.

The reasons for and the roots of the rejection are, of course, not the same on the right and on the left. To a considerable extent the modern hostility to growth stems from semantic differences about definitions and meanings of the word "growth" and from misgivings, often justified, about the actual execution of growth policy. For example, when conservatives criticize excessive preoccupation with growth they have in mind that actual growth policies are too often concerned with industrial production only and neglect agriculture, services, environment, etc., or that in practice the provisions for the future in the name of growth go so far beyond the wishes of individuals as to slow growth by reducing incentives and efforts or by inducing a rate of inflation that makes sustained growth impossible.

These are, of course, real dangers. To warn about them is justified, but does not really imply rejection of the growth objective if the term is properly understood and the policy is properly carried out—admittedly big ifs! Only if growth is defined in terms of a comprehensive GNP which includes agriculture, services and an adequate allowance for "deterioration of the environment" (more on this later) can a deliberate growth policy be justified. Furthermore, it cannot be justified if it has to be financed by rapid inflation since the resulting growth invariably proves unsustainable (see Appendix A for further explanation).

For the radical left disenchantment with growth is largely the consequence of their belated realization that many capitalist countries, especially Japan and West Germany, but also Brazil, South Africa and others, have scored extremely well on the growth scale. Not only are the Communist countries no longer so successful with respect to growth as they appeared to be in the past, but closer contacts have revealed their general backwardness, the shabbiness of many of their products (except military hardware), the general drabness of the life of the masses. Having lost the race for faster growth the easiest way to save face is to change the rules of the game and to say that growth is bad or not really important.

For faithful Marxists there remains the embarrassing fact that the Russians and their satellites seem still addicted to the cult of growth. That makes it difficult to reserve the opprobrium of "crass materialism" for the capitalist world. Some candid Marxists,[21] perhaps in moments of despair, solve that problem radically by declaring that Russia and Eastern Europe are not really socialist countries in the true Marxist sense anymore. Maoist-China, they allege, is the only major country that is really moving in the direction of true socialism. Since we are not very well informed about what is going on in China, it is still safe to bestow liberal praise on that regime.

The recent backlash against growth is, however, not all semantics and ideology. Growth, if conventionally defined in terms of GNP, is not costless. Important substantive problems are involved: the deterioration of the environment, pollution of air and water, overcrowding and "uglification" of the cities, despoiling of the landscape by unsightly litter (beer bottles, garbage dumps), traffic congestion, and so forth. All of these are the concomitants of population growth and rising affluence. Most of them are economic in nature and, at least in principle, are amenable to approximate quantitative evaluation. But not all. Damage to the beauty of the landscape, disturbance of the "peace of nature," destruction of wildlife,[22] psychological or sociological effects on the human race through the gradual disappearance of the frontier of undisturbed nature and wilderness—these

31

and other real or alleged dangers of advancing civilization clearly involve "philosophical" questions of *Weltanschauung* and value judgments and go beyond the competence and expertise of the economist; these noneconomic issues will not be further discussed in the present essay.

But to return to the deterioration of the physical environment—"pollution" in the broad sense—caused by population growth and growing affluence (growth of national income per head): this is by no means an unfamiliar problem for the economist. The dangers of unlimited population growth (overpopulation) have been recognized by economists even before Thomas Robert Malthus (1766-1834) spread the alarm around the world—prematurely and exaggeratedly as far as the Western world is concerned if we keep in mind that long-term growth is measured by growth of GNP per capita, not global GNP. Per capita GNP makes allowance for the adverse impact of population growth, provided it is not defined too narrowly.

The problem of "pollution" (in the broad sense) has been extensively discussed by economic theorists. Pollution and damage to the environment is a case of what economists have been calling "external economies" since the days of Alfred Marshall (1842-1924). External economies, "externalities" as they are now often called, are more or less pervasive effects on other industries or on the economy as a whole, emanating from the expansion of individual firms or industries, or of industry (including agriculture and mining) as a whole. These "external" influences can be either positive and favorable, in which case they are called external "economies"; or they can be negative and damaging—then they are called external "diseconomies." External economies, positive or negative, are contrasted to "internal" economies. The latter are the well-known advantages (or disadvantages from a certain point on) of large-scale production. Internal economies are taken into consideration by private cost accounting and are passed on through the market to the buyers of the product. Therefore, they do not give rise to a discrepancy between private profitability and social productivity. External economies, also called nonmarket influences, are not taken into consideration by the private cost accounting of the firms involved; they thus give rise to a discrepancy between private profitability and social productivity. [23] The negative external economies have attracted most attention. [24] Pollution of the air by smoke and of the water by waste disposal have been the standard examples. A firm which pollutes the water or the air does not consider the damage done to others. Therefore, its "social product" (its net contribution to national income which makes allowance for the damage done to others) is smaller than the private income which it generates. In extreme cases its net contribution could conceivably be negative. [25]

To sum up what is new in the contemporary concern about pollution and deterioration of the environment is not the substance but the strong emphasis. The fear about deterioration of the environment, although justified in principle, has in many cases gone to absurd lengths, mainly among scientists and ecologists. An extreme although no longer rare example is the following:

> The ecologist must convince the population that the only solution to the problem of growth is not to grow. This applies to population [growth] and, unless the population is declining, to its standard of living. It should be clear by now that standard of living is probably beginning to have an inverse relationship to the quality of life. An increase in the gross national product must be construed, from the ecological point of view, as disastrous. (The case of underdeveloped countries, of course, is different.)[26]

In 1972, with tremendous fanfare of publicity, a book appeared entitled *The Limits to Growth: A Report of the Club of Rome's Project on the Predicament of Mankind.* [27] The Club of Rome consists mostly of scientists and engineers who believe that "the momentum of present growth" will "overshoot the carrying capacity of this planet" with "chilling" implications for ourselves and our children—not in the distant future but in the next 50 or 100 years. Not only will growth gradually come to a halt, but by "overshooting"—or running head-on against a wall—there will be catastrophic decline.

The authors of *The Limits to Growth* have discovered, as T. R. Malthus did about 200 years ago (without the help of computers), that exponential population growth in the face of an absolute limit of arable land must eventually lead to disaster. To Malthus' growth of population the new prophets of doom have added the exponential growth of industrial production and of garbage (pollution), and to the land-restraint they have added the limitation of supply of many raw materials and "the quantitative restraints of the world environment." They are convinced that realization of the imminent danger ahead will initiate "new forms of thinking that will lead to a fundamental revision of human behavior and . . . of the entire fabric of present-day society." "Entirely new approaches are required to redirect [world] society towards goals of equilibrium rather than growth." They "have no doubt that . . . concerted international measures and joint long-term planning will be necessary on a scale and scope without precedent." But "the brake imposed on world demographic and economic growth must not lead to a freezing of the *status quo* of [unequal] economic development." Therefore it "will be demanded from the economically developed countries, for a first step . . . to encourage a deceleration in the growth of their material output while, at the same time, assisting the developing nations in their efforts to advance their economies more rapidly."[28]

In other words the Club of Rome demands that the inequality between rich and poor nations be reduced from both ends, by slashing the rate of growth of the rich and by massive transfers from the rich to the poor to raise the standard of living of the less-developed countries.

It would not be necessary to report at length on *The Limits to Growth* if it were not for the fact that it has made a great impression among scientists, policy makers and the general public. (Details can be found in Professor Beckerman's paper cited below.)

How immediate is the danger of world disaster if growth of population and GNP are not brought to an early stop? Is there more to this dire prediction than to that of Malthus 200 years ago? What is the reaction of economists, especially experts on growth, to *The Limits to Growth?* The criticisms can only be described as devastating. Simon Kuznets called the conclusions "simplistic." Robert M. Solow, economist at M.I.T., said politely that the model "had too slender a data base for the sort of predictions made." Henry Wallich declared it "a piece of irresponsible nonsense." [29] The most detailed and withering criticism came from Professor Wilfred Beckerman.[30] He demonstrates in detail that the whole approach is flawed by a failure to understand that mathematical models without adequate empirical data cannot tell us anything about the real world. And the statistical data fed into the computer are sketchy, arbitrary, unreliable—in short, totally inadequate—too "slender," in Solow's words, to support the prediction of doom.[31]

Nobody, of course, denies that population pressure and pollution are pressing problems in many countries. The dangers are real. But recognition of this fact does not require dethronement of economic growth as a major policy objective. To halt or slow down growth may even increase pollution by denying us the resources needed for developing pollution-reducing methods of production.

What is needed is first to take specific measures to cut down pollution and to reduce the birthrate where it is too high, and second to define and measure growth properly.

As for concrete measures, much is being done in many countries. Here is not the place to go into details. Let me only say this: There exist in every country innumerable antipollution regulations, and countless proposals have been made and are under consideration for the alteration and strengthening of existing regulations and the introduction of new ones. Examples are building codes, forest regulations to prevent deforestation, smoke and noise control, prevention of waste disposal into streams, lakes and the sea, and so forth. Much has been achieved already, often at moderate cost (see Beckerman's paper for examples). And much more can and should be done with the help of the price mechanism, by "internalizing externalities" through taxes, thereby providing an inducement for private enterprise to search for nonpolluting products and methods of production.[32]

Very often the government itself is the worst polluter. The dangerous and damaging side effects of the High Aswan Dam on the Upper Nile[33] were completely ignored by the Egyptian and Russian planners of that great enterprise. Or on a larger scale, in many less-developed countries the policy of the forced industrialization at breakneck speed, brought about by drastic import restrictions—"import substitution" as it is euphemistically called—has paid scant attention to the pollution of air and water and has created monumental urban slums. What is objectionable is not industrialization as such, but the excessive rapidity with which it is carried out, the neglect of agriculture and disregard for external diseconomies.[34] Further discussion of that problem will be found in Chapter 8, Section A.

As far as the meaning and measurement of growth is concerned it should be recalled that the relevant definition is output (GNP) per head and not aggregate output. It follows that stimulating growth does not necessarily imply that population growth should be welcomed. On the contrary most experts believe that in many densely populated countries population growth is a drag on economic growth, especially if it is defined so as to make allowance for pollution (in the broad sense).[35]

Correctly computed growth figures should allow for the deterioration of the environment. In other words a deduction should be made from conventional output figures measuring the cost of preventing the pollution caused by increase in output.

The problem is analogous to that of allowing for the depletion of capital resources. As far as ordinary capital equipment (buildings, machinery, inventories) is concerned, it is, of course, routine in private cost accounting to make a capital depletion allowance. Correspondingly in the computation of net national income a deduction is made from gross output to cover the cost of keeping the capital stock intact (replacement cost). A similar depletion allowance should be made and is usually made for the reduction of the stock of exhaustible natural resources (coal, ore, oil deposits and the like). It is only one further step in the same direction to conceive of the environment as an exhaustible resource and to make allowance for its depletion (deterioration). All this amounts to defining "real" growth as the rate of growth of national income net of depletion of capital resources (both natural and man-made) and making allowance for the deterioration of the environment, measured by the cost of preventing further pollution.

The precise statistical evaluation of these corrections of the GNP figures is an extremely difficult job. But it should be possible to arrive at a rough estimate of the order of magnitude of the changes of the GNP figure that are necessary. Economists have been aware of the problem, and promising studies are underway to further clarify the issue conceptually and to determine the magnitude of the necessary correction. Fully reliable concrete estimates are not yet available, but preliminary guesses indicate that no radical changes in growth figures will be involved; after the deterioration allowance has been made the growth rate will be somewhat lower but will, by no means, be negative.[36]

Chapter 3

Economic Stability

TYPES OF INSTABILITY

Economic stability like economic growth is a complex matter. The meanings in which stability can be said to be an objective of financial policies must be carefully defined.

Every business firm is conscious of the importance of stabilizing its activities as far as possible. This is part of its endeavor to minimize cost of production and to maximize profits over the long run, because steady employment of the labor force and continuous utilization of plant and equipment minimizes cost of production and maximizes profits. Internal arrangements such as multiple shifts, holding of inventories, maintaining standby equipment, go some way to guard against costly interruption of production and to guarantee continuous activity, that is to say, to maintain stability. Diversification through mergers and acquisitions are other measures directed at the objective of internally compensating divergent fluctuations in different divisions and thus maintaining stable levels of overall activity.

Despite all efforts, complete stability is rarely attained. Individual firms have their ups and downs, they wax and wane, and occasionally disappear. The same is true of individual industries. Output and employment change; occasional lapses from full employment are unavoidable. There is always some "frictional" unemployment—workers on the way from one job to another. When a man loses his job, he seldom finds an immediate opening suitable to his training and skills and in an acceptable locality. "Frictional" unemployment is often assumed to amount to 3 or 4 percent of the labor force; actually, it must be expected to change according to circumstances.[1]

There is, furthermore, what is called "structural" unemployment. It occurs when a larger sector or locality of the economy is affected by a specific disturbance while other sectors or localities enjoy brisk demand and seek to attract labor. "Structural" unemployment and excess capacity shade off on the one hand into "frictional" unemployment and, on the other hand, into general unemployment and excess capacity ("cyclical" unemployment), to which we come in a moment. (Different types of unemployment will be discussed in greater detail in Chapter 5.)

In a dynamic, growing economy, where new methods of production and new products are continuously introduced by innovating entrepreneurs, "frictional" and "structural" types of instability and unemployment cannot be removed by monetary and fiscal policy. They are the price a people pay for progress. They could be eliminated only by preventing progress and growth itself. Financial policies, on the other hand, can mitigate or possibly eliminate what we call the business cycle in the broad sense, especially the downswing or contraction phase of the cycle, cyclical depressions or recessions and the associated general (cyclical) unemployment.

THE BUSINESS CYCLE

The business cycle is a complex phenomenon. It has a "real" side or aspect and a "monetary" or "price" side or aspect. Conceptually, we must distinguish between "real" stability and instability on the one hand, and, on the other, "monetary" and "price level" stability and instability. By "real instability" we mean fluctuations in output and employment; and by monetary or price instability, we mean fluctuations or excessive increases and decreases in the value of money (price level) and the stock of money. In the business cycle, real and monetary fluctuations are inextricably intertwined, but their amplitude can be of an entirely different order of magnitude. There are no physical limits to monetary and price level changes, while fluctuations in real output (GNP in "constant prices") are rigidly bounded by the full employment ceiling on the upside [2] and very rarely (never in the ordinary business cycle) fall below 75 percent of the peak values.

I now indicate the basic characteristics of what one may call the "classical" business cycle. [3] Later we discuss the question whether the cycle still exists; this is being seriously doubted in some quarters.

As the word "cycle" suggests, the business cycle has basically two phases—expansion or upswing and contraction or down-swing. The expansion phase is separated from the next contraction by an upper turning point or "peak" and the contraction phase from the succeeding expansion by a lower turning point or "trough." The peaks and troughs are almost always well marked and there is little controversy about their precise location. The National Bureau of Economic Research has established a "cyclical calendar" for the United States and other major countries which fixes the historical turning points on a monthly scale. These dates are generally accepted as accurate. [4]

41

Other words frequently used instead of *expansion* and *contraction* are *prosperity*—depression, stagnation or recession ("pause," "period of hesitancy," "mini-recession")—and *boom*—slump. Formerly, economists tried to distinguish more than two phases. For example, some writers divided the upswing in a recovery and prosperity phase and the downswing in a depression and recession phase. But in the end it turned out that it was not possible to give precise criteria of these subdivisions which would fit all cases. Therefore today most economists accept the two-phase scheme, while realizing that the length and intensity of the two phases vary from cycle to cycle. There are long and short upswings, and the expansion can be rapid or slow. Similarly, the downswing can be short or long and the decline precipitous or gradual; in other words, there are deep depressions, shallow recessions and "pauses" or "mini-recessions" which are too mild to be entered into the cyclical calendar as a recession.[5] The length of the whole cycle, measured from peak to peak or from trough to trough, varies from one to ten or twelve years.

In the nineteenth century and up to the Great Depression of the 1930s the turning points from cyclical expansions to cyclical depressions were usually marked by "financial crises"—sharp slumps on the stock exchanges, numerous bankruptcies, runs on the banks for cash and similar phenomena. It was these spectacular financial crises which first caught the attention of the economists. "Theories of crises" were the forerunners of the theories of the business cycle. It was only late in the nineteenth century that it became generally recognized that financial crises were not an invariable feature of every cycle. Not all upper turning points have been marked by financial crises, and some crises have occurred at other points of the cycle. For example, the breakdown of the American banking system in 1933, the last financial crisis of the nineteenth century type in the United States, occurred near the lower turning point of the business cycle. Since then full-blown financial crises have been absent.[6]

GENERAL CHARACTERISTICS
OF THE BUSINESS CYCLE

While cycles vary greatly in length and intensity and while some have special features such as financial crises not shared by others, there are certain general characteristics which apply to all; these general features establish the business cycle as a distinct class of phenomenon different from other types of economic movements. Business cycle expansions and contractions are very pervasive, affecting almost all branches and aspects of the economy; during the upswing GNP and its principal subdivisions, especially industrial production as a whole (although not necessarily every single industry), rise; during the downswing they decline. In very mild cycles it may be only the rate of growth that declines in the contraction phase without an absolute decline of GNP.[7] Employment and unemployment move with output—unemployment, of course, in an inverted fashion, falling during the upswing and increasing during the downswing. Aggregate effective demand (money national income, aggregate expenditures, money times velocity of circulation of money, MV for short) fluctuates parallel with real output and employment.

A further general characteristic is that investment fluctuates more violently than consumption and, related thereto, the cyclical amplitude of production of durable goods and producer goods is greater than that of nondurables and consumer goods. For the United States it has been definitely established that agricultural *production* has no cyclical pattern. On the other hand, prices of agricultural products and consequently farm income did fluctuate sharply in a cyclical fashion, before comprehensive price support policies for agricultural products were introduced in the 1930s. The same is largely true of other countries, both developed and underdeveloped.

Especially important and very suggestive is the fact that in

43

the short run, that is to say in the business cycle, money flows (aggregate expenditures, money national income) and real flows (real income, aggregate output and employment) run parallel.[8] This means that the cycle has a monetary aspect or element. It does *not* by itself prove, however, that the cycle is always caused by monetary factors. While the cycle has a monetary element it is not a "purely monetary phenomenon" as some earlier writers have maintained. But it is not too much to say that every business cycle upswing has an inflationary touch, either the quantity of money (M) or the velocity of circulation of money (V) or both increase, and every downswing has a deflationary element, either M or V or both decrease.

We may go one step further and say that the *proximate* cause of the *real* cycle, i.e., the cycle of output and employment, is fluctuations in aggregate monetary expenditures ("effective demand"). This statement does not rule out the possibility that the mechanism which brings about the alternation of expansion and contraction of the "money flows" ("aggregate effective demand") may be or usually is nonmonetary in nature. For example, it may consist of an interaction of "multiplier" and "accelerator" as described by innumerable "Keynesian" cycle theorists, or it may be produced by the innovational behavior of free entrepreneurs as described vividly by J. A. Schumpeter (see note 4). But money plays at least a *permissive* role, even in these "nonmonetary" theories, in the sense that either the quantity of money (M) or its velocity (V) must adjust to the real forces, or else the cycle, as we know it, could not develop. Moreover, there can be no doubt that money very often plays an *active* role in the cycle in the sense that monetary policies initiate and intensify, or retard and interrupt, the process of expansion or contraction.

It is generally agreed that the business cycle is the result of an "endogenous" process, i.e., that there exists an internal mechanism which produces cyclical fluctuations. Few, however, would deny that the actual movement of the economy is often profoundly influenced by disturbances from the "outside," including government policy. The endogenous mechanism is rarely allowed to operate for a long time undisturbed without more or less powerful exogenous impulses of one kind or the other. Thus, the business cycle must be regarded as an amalgam of endogenous and exogenous forces.[9]

Exogenous shocks of a stimulating (inflationary) or depressing (deflationary) nature can arise in many different ways. They can come from abroad. Expansion and contraction, inflation and deflation are transmitted from country to country through ups and downs in exports and imports of goods, services and capital via the balance of payments. Naturally, the smaller and the more open vis-à-vis the rest of the world a national economy, the more important is the international impact. In small countries international developments often completely dominate the domestic cycle.[10]

So long as agriculture was a large sector of the U.S. economy, harvest changes due to weather conditions constituted powerful external shocks. They became especially strong when, as sometimes happened, a good crop in the United States coincided with poor ones abroad, thus giving a strong boost to exports and leading to an inflow of funds. Today, agriculture is a negligible factor for the cyclical ups and downs in the United States and most other industrial countries.

Today the most important source of exogenous expansionary (inflationary) and depressing (deflationary) shocks is government finance. Governments everywhere have become cycle conscious. They try to conduct their financial affairs in such a way as to smooth out and counteract cyclical or other fluctuations of the economy. These countercyclical policies in general and antidepression measures in particular are, of course, one of the main subjects for discussion in the present volume and will be taken up presently. But despite the efforts directed at stabilization, government finance often operates in a destabilizing manner, accentuating inflationary booms or occasionally interrupting healthy expansions. Such destabilizing conduct of government finance is usually the consequence of massive expenditure variations forced by war and defense needs and other emergencies. But it also results from mistakes made in stabilization policies and from sheer negligence and lack of coordination of the far-flung government programs and activities. In many less-developed countries endemic inflation due primarily, even in peacetime, to huge government deficits[11] is an exogenous force which often swamps the endogenous cycle altogether.

DOES THE BUSINESS CYCLE STILL EXIST?

Some economists assert that all this concern about business cycles is obsolete. There is no more business cycle. In the second half of the twentieth century, the only threat to stability is inflation and occasional periods of stagnation caused by misguided and inept attempts to stop inflation.

Certainly there has been a lot of inflation in the last thirty years. Many less-developed countries, with few notable exceptions, live under almost continuous strong inflation. And even in the industrial countries the inflationary trend since the Great Depression is unmistakable. But let us not exaggerate and oversimplify. That there is an inflationary trend does not necessarily mean that prices rise continuously at the same rate without interruption. What it means is that the shape of the price curve over a long period has changed. Up to the 1930s the price curve had the shape of a wave[12]; since then it looks like an ascending staircase. Periods of rising prices no longer alternate with periods of falling prices, as was the case until the 1930s. Periods of acute inflation and rapidly rising prices are followed by periods of slowly rising prices or, at best, by short periods of uneasy price stability. The United States enjoyed such a plateau of fairly stable prices from 1958 to 1965. During these six or seven years, wholesale prices remained practically stable while consumer prices rose by something like 1.2 or 1.3 percent per annum, which is tolerable in view of the inaccuracies of the statistics and their failure to take sufficient account of quality improvements and new products. Since 1965, wholesale prices have gone up again at something like 4 percent and consumer prices by 2.5 to 3 percent per annum. In 1968 inflation accelerated to almost 5 percent per annum, in 1969 to 6 percent, and in 1973 to 7 or 8 percent.

Recent price rises in periods of cyclical expansion can still be regarded as moderate by comparison with price rises in earlier upswings in the United States or with contemporary inflation in other industrial countries. In fact, the purchasing power of the dollar has been better preserved over the medium and long run than that of other important currencies, the Swiss franc and German mark included. Nonetheless, an inflationary trend does exist in the above-defined sense of intermittent price rises uninterrupted by offsetting price declines. Its implications and possible consequences will be explored later.

Here I only wish to point out that the existence of an inflationary trend does not make the business cycle obsolete. Attempts at stopping inflation practically always lead to temporarily higher unemployment and slower growth. True, the business cycle has been much milder in the postwar period than in earlier periods of comparable length whether measured in "real" (output or employment) terms or in prices (price-level changes) or monetary terms (money GNP or monetary aggregates)—money supply in any of its meanings. But in the basic sense of alternating periods of expansion and contraction of overall employment, unemployment and real output—contraction in output at least relatively to a rising trend in production—the cycle is still here. The only difference from the earlier pattern is that the real cycle has been much milder and the price cycle has been playing around a more steeply rising long-run price trend.

In Western Europe and Japan the cyclical pattern has been somewhat blurred and the determination of the dates of cyclical turning points complicated by the rapid growth these countries have enjoyed during the postwar period.[13] Suppose the population (or labor force or labor-force participation) grows rapidly, there is rapid technological progress, a high level of investment, and that entrepreneurial activity is accorded substantial freedom from government interference and is not hampered by restrictions imposed by labor unions. Under these conditions output and employment will exhibit a steep upward trend, and cyclical recessions will assume the form of a retardation of growth (decline in the annual rate of growth) rather than an absolute drop in output and employment—"growth cycle" we call this phenomena.

In every other respect, however, such a cycle in the growth rate will be essentially the same as a cycle in absolute output. For example, there will be *absolute* changes in the volume of unemployment.[14] In a recession, unemployment will rise in absolute terms (number of unemployed) and as a percentage of the labor force while employment may go on rising because of the growth in the labor force.[15]

That the business cycle is still with us does not contradict the fact that, because it is so much milder, the cycle is quantitatively, or even qualitatively much less of a problem than it used to be. But subjectively and hence politically, it may be more of a problem for the policy maker, because we are much more sensitive even to small changes in employment than thirty years ago.

The endogenous causal mechanism that produces cyclical fluctuations appears to operate much as it did earlier in the century, but in a very different environment. And this constitutes a change of very great importance. Governments everywhere know that they have the power to influence economic activities and are much more ready than formerly to make full and continuous use of this power. They frequently fail to accomplish the ends sought. To what extent they can possibly succeed will be discussed in the following chapters, but at any rate purely endogenous cycles no longer have any chance to run their course undisturbed.

Chapter 4

Policies for Stabilization

BUSINESS CYCLE POLICY

Business cycle policy in general and antidepression policies in particular, as well as the views of economists, statesmen, politicians and of the public at large concerning such policies, have undergone profound changes during the last forty years. This was the period of the "Keynesian Revolution," and the emergence of the so-called "New Economics." Many will say that the change in outlook was more or less the handiwork of Keynes and his disciples. While it is true that the change we are going to describe has gone in what broadly may be called the Keynesian direction, it is a mistake as I shall argue later, to give all the credit—or all the blame—to Keynes and the Keynesians. But first let me describe the change in policies and doctrines that has taken place.

Formerly, it was widely held that little could be done about depressions once a downward movement had actually started or after a boom had really gotten underway. The alleged reason was that in every business cycle upswing or at least in its later stages[1] "real maladjustments," disproportionalities in the structure of production, not matched by similar shifts in effective demand, developed. The gradual elimination or absorption of these real maladjustments was the essence and function of the depression. Since the distortions caused by the boom were "real" (not purely financial or monetary), their correction required some reshuffling of productive resources including some relocation of the labor force. These changes inevitably took much time and were bound to be painful. It followed that the only effective antidepression policy should aim at preventing, controlling or moderating the boom. Once an unhealthy inflationary boom had been allowed to develop and to cause a distortion in the structure of production, the ensuing depression became unavoidable; it could perhaps be somewhat alleviated, but any attempt to prevent it or suppress it altogether by monetary or fiscal measures would perpetuate and magnify the real maladjustments and thus lead to a more severe depression at a later date.

This view was never fully accepted either in theory[2] or in practice, but it was widely held and has strongly influenced policy. "The [Federal Reserve] System was operating [in the 1920s and 1930s] in a climate of opinion that in the main regarded recessions and depressions as curative episodes, necessary in order to purge the body economic of the aftereffects of its earlier excesses."[3]

Gradually, however, even those who did regard depressions as the unavoidable consequence of the real maladjustments that develop during the upswing of the cycle have come to realize that depressions "feed on themselves," creating "vicious, self-reinforcing spirals of deflation" and excessive, self-contagious "waves of pessimism" that will usually drive the contraction beyond, sometimes far beyond, what may be necessary to correct real distortions created by the boom. Albert Hahn and Wilhelm Roepke called this further contraction "the secondary deflation." From there it was only a small step to realizing that this (avoidable) "secondary deflation" may be, and in most depressions certainly is, quantitatively much more important than what the theory in question calls the "primary" or "essential" (and unavoidable) deflation needed to eliminate or absorb the real maladjustments left behind by the preceding boom.[4]

Since the Great Depression of the 1930s, emphasis has definitely shifted from preventing depressions by somehow manipulating and moderating the upswing to counteracting depressions once they have gotten underway. This does not mean that no attempt whatsoever should be made to influence the upswing. It means that the emphasis is on cures rather than on prevention; there is more agreement on methods of cure than of prevention. However, most experts would agree, at least in principle, that inflationary excesses, which sooner or later threaten most, though not all business cycle upswings, should be restrained. Naturally, opinions diverge on when and where the inflationary danger becomes acute. Some are willing to tolerate fairly high degrees of inflation in order to forestall a decline in output and employment. Others, especially in countries such as Germany that have experienced catastrophic inflations, are frightened by quite moderate price rises, either because they are afraid of insidious long-run consequences of inflation or because they assume the existence of a strong correlation between the degree of inflation accompanying the upswing and the severity of the following recession or depression. The latter fear does not seem to be well founded. There is no evidence of a close correlation between the degree of inflation in the upswing and the severity of the following depression.

Periods of rapid and prolonged inflation have not as a rule been followed by correspondingly severe and protracted depressions,[5] and some very severe depressions have followed periods of only mildly inflationary upswings. Thus the Great Depression of the 1930s followed a period of exceptionally stable prices from 1922-1929. In fact, the unusual stability of the general price level during the prosperous 1920s lulled many economists into a sense of false security. There was much talk of a New Era; many economists were confident that the business cycle had been definitely conquered by skillful monetary management which, for the first time, had succeeded in keeping prices stable during a long upswing. It is true that others were apprehensive and pointed to speculative price rises in certain areas, such as real estate and the stock exchange, which occurred while the overall price level remained stable. There were, furthermore, many *ex post* rationalizations. But it is safe to say that nobody foresaw the catastrophic severity of the depression, at least no one who based his foreknowledge on rational grounds. (There are, of course, always irrational prophets around who predict the doom of the world in and out of season).

After the depression had struck, Marxian economists took the economic catastrophe simply as a confirmation of Marx's theory that depressions would become more and more severe until the capitalist system would come crashing down in a final bang. (By now, this view has lost conviction, even among the faithful). Others who lacked the prophet's guidance through the maze of history had a harder time explaining the slump. Some spoke vaguely of big real maladjustments in the structure of production that had somehow accumulated during the 1930s. Meantime, the Keynesians fashioned their theory of secular stagnation.[6] These explanations carry little weight today.

In general, we can say that the severity of depressions depends much more on institutional weaknesses in the financial structure and on policy mistakes made during the depression rather than on "real maladjustments" and inflationary excesses that may have characterized the preceding prosperity period. This is especially true of severe depressions.

It is now possible to say with confidence that the extraordinary severity and excessive length[7] of the Great Depression of the 1930s was due primarily to the wholesale destruction of

52

money, and that this in turn was largely due to certain institutional weaknesses in the financial structure in the United States and elsewhere and to incredibly poor policies on the national and international level. Let me mention some of these: the collapse of the American banking system, the bankruptcy of thousands of banks and the overly timid monetary and fiscal policies which failed to stop the raging deflation—these factors explain the "darkest hues" (Schumpeter) of the depression in the United States from 1929 to 1933. The depression could not have become nearly so severe as it was if there had existed then, as there exists now, effective insurance of deposits in commercial banks or if the United States, instead of the archaic unit banking system, had had an efficient branch banking system.[8] For if either one of these two reforms had been carried out in time, the destruction of money could not have been as massive as it actually was. Moreover, even with the financial structure as weak as it was, a more energetic monetary policy (for example, much larger open market operations than were actually carried out) could have prevented or at least greatly alleviated the deflation which actually occurred.

Early New Deal measures must be held responsible for the fact that the recovery was very slow and incomplete, that in 1937-38 another very severe slump was superimposed on a still severely depressed situation and that at the outbreak of the second World War in 1939 unemployment was still over 17 percent of the labor force. The mistake was not, however, that excessively "Keynesian" policies were adopted but rather that the New Deal rushed through a number of poorly conceived reforms which fostered monopolies of business (NRA) and labor (Wagner Act), thus raising costs and frightening investors, instead of concentrating, at first at least, all energies on expansionary measures to bring about quick recovery. Keynes, among others, had in fact advised Roosevelt that the reforms should be postponed until recovery had made good progress.

Policy mistakes of a similar kind and magnitude were made in several other countries, for example, in pre-Nazi Germany and

France. France, under the premiership of Léon Blum, had its own New Deal similar to the American version; the consequences were disastrous from the economic and political point of view—slow growth and stagnation until the outbreak of the second World War.[9]

Several countries, following the advice of local economists and well before the appearance of the *General Theory,* did manage to extricate themselves from the maelstrom of the Great Depression by the adoption of expansionary monetary and fiscal policies which can be described as "Keynesian," although they owed nothing to the "Keynesian Revolution." Examples are Australia, the Scandinavian countries and Nazi Germany.[10] In all these countries, including pre-Nazi and Nazi Germany, high quality scientific rationalizations of expansionary policies had appeared long before 1937. These are some of the reasons for my statement that the impact of Keynes on economic policy has been greatly exaggerated.[11]

International economic and monetary policies were just as badly managed as domestic policies in major countries. The slow-motion, beggar-my-neighbor devaluation of all currencies of the world at intervals of a few years—sterling in 1931, the dollar in 1933-1934, the so-called "gold bloc currencies" in 1936, and so on—inflicted successively on different groups of countries protracted periods of overvalued currencies, causing balance-of-payments deficits and losses, further trade restrictions and more depression. Although each of these devaluations in isolation can be defended as unavoidable and even conducive to relieving deflationary pressure in the depreciating country, the time pattern and impact of these devaluations on other countries stamped the whole approach as a sadistic policy, calculated to maximize pain and destruction. It was like cutting the tail of a dog piece by piece instead of all at once. The proper way would have been to increase, perhaps to double, the price of gold. In the end, the real value of gold did rise sharply. Commodity prices in terms of gold fell precipitously as a consequence of the successive currency devaluations, on the one hand, and of deflation (i.e., decline of prices in terms of the various national currencies) on the other hand.[12] But because of the piecemeal way in which it was done, the volume and value of world trade contracted tremendously in the process. The dollar value of world exports in 1932 was a third of what it had been in 1929! Deflation and depression in country after country was greatly intensified.

ANTIDEPRESSION POLICIES

The cataclysmic depression of the 1930s decisively influenced economic thinking and economic policy and also had a profound impact on world history. Soviet Russia and the Communist movement around the world were immensely strengthened by the economic disaster that engulfed the Western world. Hitler would hardly have come to power without the deep depression in Germany or he may not have remained in power; at any rate he would have found the going much harder if the depressed state of the German economy had not presented him with the golden opportunity of being able to give the German people guns and butter at the same time. It was tragic that the greatest Western democracy, owing to misguided policies of the New Deal, missed the opportunity to match the economic success of the Nazi dictatorship.[13] If that had not been the case and if the economic and political strength of France, the Western country with the largest army at the time, had not been sapped by the French version of the New Deal, it is not unreasonable to speculate that the onslaught of Nazism could have been repulsed without frightful bloodletting and destruction. This would have deprived Stalin of his victory and might well have changed the course of history.

It is extremely important to realize that the Great Depression was not just an ordinary business cycle downswing. There is no reason to believe that it would have been exceptionally severe had it not been for the easily avoidable or curable institutional weaknesses and policy mistakes, of commission and omission, perpetrated after the onset of the depression. Yes, easily avoidable or curable! We are justified in saying that now, in the light of what happened and what we have learned during the last twenty-five years, although it evidently was not "easy" at the time of the tragic events.

What then have we learned and how much agreement is there now on how to fight depressions and prevent them from getting really bad? There exists, I believe, fairly general agreement among scholars as well as policy makers on some basic principles—an agreement that was lacking forty years ago and should not be allowed to be obscured by controversies about the instruments to be used for basic policy objectives and by differences in judgments on concrete situations and numerous finer points of stabilization policy.

Let me first set out what I consider as generally accepted principles and then go into controversial issues.

THE BROAD CONSENSUS

There is now general agreement, I believe, that it is always possible by a combination of easy money and expansionary fiscal policy to prevent a recession from becoming a serious and long drawn-out depression and to cure a deep depression after it has developed. It is also generally realized that the task of anti-depression policy is greatly facilitated by the existence of "automatic stabilizers." Even if no conscious effort were made to manipulate government expenditures and revenues in an anticyclical manner, when economic activity declines, the government budget will be automatically pushed in the direction of a larger deficit (or smaller surplus) because tax revenues will decline and certain government expenditures, such as unemployment relief and welfare payments, will automatically increase. The government budget functions like an automatic balancing wheel, becoming expansionary in a recession and antiexpansionary when the economy expands.

The mechanism works automatically, but the decision has to be made to let it work. This means that deficits and surpluses must be accepted and handled in such a manner as not to induce offsetting reactions on the part of the private sector of the economy. The monetary implications of effective fiscal policy will be taken up in greater detail later.

It stand to reason that the tremendous growth of the public sector has greatly increased the scope and the weight of automatic stabilizers. The size of the balancing wheel is much greater now than it was forty years ago in absolute terms and in proportion to the economy. Whatever that may imply for long-run growth and efficiency, it certainly is a potent stabilizing factor.

"Discretionary" fiscal policy (as distinguished from the "automatic" stabilizers) was, under the influence of Keynesian thinking, for a long time taken as practically synonymous with government deficits brought about by *ad hoc* increases in government expenditures—"public works." Only later was it realized that deficits can be created just as well by reducing tax rates.[14] It was only in the 1960s that the so-called "New Economics" discovered the idea of using tax cuts rather than expenditure increases to stimulate the economy. By overdoing it, piling large expenditure increases (for war and so-called Great Society purposes) upon tax cuts and thereby creating huge budget deficits and inflation, there is danger that the sound idea of tax cuts be compromised in the eyes of the general public and of legislators. It can be argued that dollar for dollar an increase in expenditures is more effective ("has a larger multiplier attached to it") than a tax remission, because expenditure increases can be directed at specific branches of the economy where unemployment is concentrated and because taxpayers may save more, i.e., not increase their consumption expenditures by the full amount of the tax remission[15] and may not immediately invest their savings. These qualifications do not seriously detract from the effectiveness of tax cuts as a general stimulus to the economy. One could allow for a smaller multiplier by increasing the size of the tax reduction.[16]

How far overall financial policies can and should be pushed in the pursuit of eradicating recessions and depressions is still a matter of controversy. To these questions we shall turn presently. But there is general agreement, in which the present writer fully concurs, that overall financial policies can prevent mild recessions from snowballing into severe depressions and drastically mitigate severe depressions if and when they have been allowed to develop. It is probably no exaggeration to say that severe depressions are a thing of the past. Modern governments have the power, the knowledge and the will to prevent them. The danger is that they will do too much rather than too little, that they will press closer to literally and continuously full employment than is compatible with long-run, noninflationary growth. Although it may sound ˙paradoxical it is, fortunately, true that it is easier to deal with severe depressions than with mild recessions. The more virulent the disease, the easier the cure.

To be a little more precise, by severe depressions I mean depressions more severe than the recessions we had in the postwar years when industrial production fell on the average by about 9 percent and unemployment rose on the average by about 3 percentage points, but very substantially milder than the depressions of 1920-1921 or 1937-1938 when industrial production fell by over 30 percent and unemployment rose from 4 percent and 11 percent to 20 percent respectively. To prevent catastrophies like the acute contraction of 1929-1933 when industrial production fell by more than 50 percent, or the prolonged depression of the whole decade of the 1930s, avoidance of the policy mistakes mentioned earlier and the crudest kind of expansionary monetary and fiscal policies would have sufficed.

All this is now generally admitted. Even many Marxists have all but given up Marx's famous theory that depressions under capitalism will inevitable become so severe and socially intolerable as to bring the whole capitalist system crashing down. Many former Marxists have accepted the Keynesian theory that depressions can be prevented by appropriate financial policies. What they say now, many of them probably without real conviction, is that the "capitalistic ruling class" will prevent the adoption of the financial policies that could forestall severe depressions. Since profits suffer more than any other type of income in a recession, this argument is singularly unconvincing. At any rate it is a far cry from the original Marxist position. Marx surely did not want to say that capitalism would go on forever were it not for the stupidity of "the ruling capitalist classes" to obstruct the adoption of financial policies that would prevent profits from tumbling in severe depressions!

CONTROVERSIAL ISSUES

There remain a number of important controversial issues, some due to differences about fundamental policy objectives, others to differences of a more technical-economic nature.

Liberals (the word used in the original sense to identify those who wish to maximize the scope of individual action and minimize government intervention) want to rely as much as possible on automatic stabilizers described earlier and to use as sparingly as possible discretionary policies either of a fiscal or monetary nature. If discretionary policies have to be used, the liberal economist has a strong preference for overall monetary as against selective measures; he prefers broadly based tax remission rather than selective tax changes and ad hoc expenditure variations, because the latter extend the public sector and have to be, in the nature of the case, more or less selective. (Changes in government expenditures can hardly be "across the board.")

Given these preferences, two major questions remain on which even liberal economists are not agreed. The *first* is this: Is it possible to rely *entirely* on automatic stabilizers? Or formulated differently, if we relied on automatic stabilizers, would cyclical movements become so mild and recessions so short that it would be impossible to reduce them still further by discretionary measures? Would attempts at finer stabilization, "fine tuning" as it is called, if at all feasible, lead to intolerable inflation? How close can one get to continuous full employment? This leads to the broader issue whether at some point the pursuit of the stabilization objective does not come into serious conflict with the growth objective.

The *second* controversial question is whether monetary policy can or cannot do the whole job. I have already indicated that fiscal policy, if it is to be effective, presupposes certain monetary conditions. A government deficit must be financed to some extent in an "inflationary" way by borrowing from the banking system which creates deposit money rather than by borrowing current savings from the public without an increase in the quantity of money. Otherwise it would drive up interest rates and thus could reduce—"crowd out" is the expression now often used—private investment so much that there would be no *net* increase in aggregate effective demand.[17] Some writers then go so far as to regard fiscal policy as a superfluous adjunct of monetary policy, a ritual as it were for which the best that can be said is, given certain prejudices and superstitions, it may be a necessary act of window dressing to make the only really important monetary measures palatable.

These two controversial issues, fine tuning and fiscal vs. monetary policy, are taken up separately in two following sections, although they are closely interrelated.

FINE TUNING

Professor Milton Friedman, more than anyone else, has demonstrated that *discretionary* monetary and fiscal policy measures, aimed at offsetting cyclical fluctuations in the economy, may easily turn out to have destabilizing effects. He goes so far as to say that "most" monetary and fiscal policy measures "deliberately taken to promote stabilization have had the effect of destabilizing the economy."[18] His reasoning points to real difficulties which even those who do not accept the somewhat extreme statement just quoted should recognize as important.

The trouble is not that discretionary monetary or fiscal expansionary measures, once they have been taken, fail to raise aggregate demand and to stimulate the economy.[19] Rather, it lies in proper timing of stabilizing measures and stems from the lags and delays to which both monetary and fiscal discretionary measures are unavoidably subjected. There is, *first, the diagnostic lag;* it takes time to diagnose a cyclical upturn or downturn. Correct diagnosing is by no means easy. Little ripples and changes in statistical series may or may not mark cyclical turns, the beginning of an expansion or contraction. Prompt economic reporting and diagnosing has been enormously improved during the last twenty years, due mainly to the patient work of the National Bureau of Economic Research (NBER). But prompt diagnosing is far from perfect and has unavoidably an element of forecasting. The two, diagnosing and forecasting, shade off into one another and cannot be sharply separated. Diagnosing an observed small change in economic activity as the beginning of a cyclical expansion or contraction rather than a fortuitous and purely transitory ripple implies a forecast of what will happen in the future. There is agreement that forecasting economic movements even for short periods is still a highly fallible and hazardous enterprise.[20]

There is, *second,* what may be called the *administrative lag.*

The diagnosis must be translated into concrete measures. This is easier in the area of monetary policy than in fiscal policy because monetary authorities can act more promptly and reverse their actions more easily. In the fiscal field, legislation and parliamentary decisions are usually necessary and it takes time, often much time, for changes in expenditures to be executed. Quick reversal of fiscal measures, either on the expenditure or revenue side, is often impossible, prohibitively wasteful or ineffective.

Thirdly, there is what may be called the *operational lag.* The effects of expansionary or antiexpansionary measures are seldom immediate. This is especially true of monetary measures; changes in the quantity of money and/or in interest rates usually require six to nine months to exert their effect on aggregate demand. Furthermore, the effectiveness of expansionary measures may be helped or hindered, speeded or retarded, by psychological reactions and anticipatory action on the part of private business. The last word on these problems has not yet been spoken, and much painstaking research must still be done. But that discretionary policy changes almost always involve considerable delays cannot be doubted.

If the combined lag of expansionary measures is long compared with the length of the recession, such measures instead of counteracting the recession will intensify the subsequent expansion. What is true of expansionary measures holds also for antiexpansionary measures. If their effects are delayed, they will intensify the following recession instead of counteracting the preceding inflation.

Postwar recessions have been on the average ten months long, and the combined lags of expansionary measures may well be in that order of magnitude. Thus the danger pointed out by Friedman, that discretionary stabilization policies may be in fact destabilizing, is a very real one. It would not be difficult to find instances where that has actually happened,[21] although Friedman's conjecture that this is true in *most* cases still remains to be carefully checked and tested.

Clearly there are limits to the stabilization that can be accomplished by overall financial policies. Yet to repeat what was said earlier, it is easier to deal with severe and long depressions than with mild and short recessions. It is probably not possible to "tune the economy much finer" than it was tuned in the postwar period without producing a much stronger inflationary trend than we actually had. To eradicate the business cycle altogether, it would be necessary to subject the economy to much stronger regimentation than is acceptable. No doubt it would be possible to put the economy under intense inflationary pressure and at the same time try to suppress the symptoms of inflation by a multitude of direct controls over prices and wages. By this method, the method of a war or siege economy, employment could be stabilized to a greater degree and at a higher level of employment than actually has been possible in peace time. But the price would be high: repressed inflation, loss of economic freedom, lower efficiency and slower long-run growth.

I shall return later to the question of possible conflicts of stability and growth and the impact of inflation on growth in the following chapter.

THE "MONETARIST POSITION"

Does it follow that we should give up discretionary stabilization policies, monetary as well as fiscal, altogether and rely entire on the automatic stabilizers?

This question has been answered in the affirmative by M. Friedman and his followers. [21a] They believe that the best stabilization policy would be to aim at a steady "monetary growth," that is, a steady increase in the quantity of money by, say, 3 to 5 percent a year. What is important, according to the monetarist view, is the steadiness of monetary growth, not from month to month, but over somewhat longer periods, say over four to five months. The concrete magnitude of rate of monetary growth is of little importance, if it is within a range, say 3 percent to 5 percent, that permits GNP to grow along its normal long-run trend at approximately stable prices.[22]

If such a steady monetary growth is accomplished, monetarists think the economy would after a while settle down on a steady real growth path with approximately stable prices. Presumably there would remain mild ups and downs, but the attempt at suppressing and mitigating these mild fluctuations by means of discretionary monetary or fiscal measures would be counterproductive and lead to greater instability rather than less.

This view has gained considerable popularity in the last few years. For example, the majority and minority reports of the Joint Economic Committee of the United States Congress in 1967 have both recommended a policy of steady monetary growth.[23] The reason for its growing popularity was the adverse reaction to the erratic monetary policy pursued since 1965: Excessive monetary growth from April 1965 to April 1966 was followed by a sudden stoppage of monetary growth from May 1966 until the end of the year, which produced the "credit crunch" in the late summer of 1966. Tight money was followed, with a lag, by "a period of hesitancy" also called "mini-recession," just as monetary theory had predicted.[24] Monetary growth resumed in January 1967 and the ongoing explosion of government expenditures for the war in Vietnam and burgeoning "Great Society" purposes created huge deficits in the federal budget—$25.2 billion in the fiscal year 1968. Belatedly, the Johnson administration urged Congress to raise taxes. The tax increase, enacted retroactively in June 1968, brought the federal budget close to balance. But government economists, their eyes glued to fiscal policies and interest rates and neglecting the rapid monetary growth, completely misjudged the impact of the fiscal measures on the economy. Apprehensive that the swing in the federal budget toward balance would bring about a recession, the Federal Reserve in the summer of 1968 reduced the discount rate and accelerated monetary growth. As one would expect on the basis of monetary theory, and contrary to the expectations of government economists, the economy failed to slow down; price inflation continued unabated right through the year (and the election), despite the drastic fiscal medicine (tax increase) applied in June 1968. Toward the end of 1968 and early in 1969, the Federal Reserve realized the mistake it had made in the summer of 1968.[25] From January 1969 to February 1970 monetary growth was much slower than during the preceding three years. The fifth (very mild) postwar recession started around November 1969. As a reaction, monetary growth resumed in February 1970 and the recession ended in November of the same year. In 1971 until July the money stock rose at a rapid rate (almost 12 percent), and then growth was practically stopped for half a year—probably as a reaction to the dollar crisis which led to the adoption of the new economic policy of August 15, 1971. After the formal devaluation of the dollar in the Smithsonian Agreement of December 18, 1971, monetary growth resumed at a rapid pace.

The whole period from 1965 until now was, of course, one of rising prices (inflation) and rising monetary circulation. From 1965 to 1971 consumer prices rose at a compound annual rate of 4.2 percent and the money stock at 5.4 percent.[26]

The frequent and somewhat erratic changes and shifts in monetary and fiscal policy in recent years contrast unfavorably with the fairly steady monetary growth of about 3-1/2 percent from 1960 to 1965, a period characterized it will be recalled by practically stable prices. If financial policies had followed a more steady course, which should not have been beyond the wits of the money managers, there would have been less inflation and the growth of real GNP would have been steadier. To that extent the monetarist criticism of recent policies would seem to be justified.

But can we be sure that automatic stabilizers plus steady

monetary growth will always be able to do the whole job of stabilization? I doubt it. The effectiveness of automatic stabilizers depends, among other things, on the size of the budget and the structure of the tax system. Changes in war and defense expenditures, the vicissitude of the farflung activities of modern governments, are bound to change the strength and impact of the automatic stabilizers. Who can be sure that in a world subject to such changes the automatic stabilizers will always be of just the right strength? I am afraid that discretionary policies of stabilization cannot be ruled out once and for all.

THE KEYNESIAN POSITION

But this conclusion does not invalidate the proposition that an attempt to carry fine tuning beyond a certain point will result in greater instability. Nonetheless, many Keynesians continue to claim that the economy can be kept operating at full employment level by skillful monetary and fiscal management, sometimes called "functional finance." The idea is that whenever the economy shows signs of slack the spigot of effective demand will be opened a little by increasing government expenditures or reducing tax rates, and when signs of overheating appear the faucet will be closed. Some of the advocates of fine tuning think that the full employment objectives can be reached without inflation; others are not so sure about that but are quite willing to tolerate a considerable measure of inflation and direct controls in the form of guideposts or incomes policies.

Things are, however, not as simple as that. The analogy with the spigot is misleading for the reason that there is practically no lag between turning on and off the faucet and the changes in the flow of the water, while monetary and fiscal policies unfortunately are subject to the lags mentioned earlier which makes fine tuning beyond a certain point impossible.

The Keynesians have not come to grips with these strictures. In fact they have misunderstood the argument. Thus Abba P. Lerner[27] speaks of Friedman's "obsession" and "preoccupation" with the business cycle and charges that a policy that merely wants to "iron out the business cycle" does not aspire to more than stabilization of the economy on a trend through about the midpoints of the cycle between the upper and the lower turning points; this would imply stabilization of GNP on a level involving much unemployment.

Similarly, James Tobin calls the "preoccupation with the business cycle" an "intellectual obstacle" to expansionary policies. "For the true believer in cycles, equilibrium is roughly the median of the fluctuations; departures upward in booms and downward in recessions are symmetrical evils. . . . The task of policy is, so far as possible, to dampen these fluctuations both ways."[28]

Professor Tobin would find it difficult to name a single economist who believes that the midpoints of the cycle are either equilibrium positions[29] or mark a desirable level of economic activity which would furnish a reasonable target for economic policy. He, in fact, imputes to non-Keynesian economists the Keynesian notion that equilibrium is compatible with a great deal of unemployment.

To elaborate a little on the last point, classical or neoclassical economists assert that *competitive* equilibrium is incompatible with involuntary (nonfrictional) unemployment. If there is competition in the labor market, money wages would fall when there is unemployment and gradually full employment would be restored.[30] On the other hand, no neoclassical economist denies that there can be unemployment in equilibrium, if money wages are rigid and are prevented from falling by monopolistic labor unions. Similarly, a minimum wage set above the productivity of the lowest strata of unskilled workers will create unemployment among marginal[31] workers (e.g., teenagers, especially Negroes). But there is no presumption whatever that such an artifically created equilibrium with unemployment would be located at or near the "midpoint" of the cycle or be in any way systematically related to the "median of the fluctuations."

Inflation can improve employment if it is allowed to reduce real wage rates[32] and the real level of the minimum wage so as to make the employment of marginal workers possible. But this gain will be lost if unions succeed in pushing up money wages or if the minimum wage is from time to time raised in order to compensate for the loss of purchasing power of money through inflation.

THE CASE AGAINST FINE TUNING ONCE MORE

To summarize, "preoccupation with the cycle" does not signify, as the critics say, a wish to stabilize a high unemployment situation. What it implies is recognition of the existence of various lags, especially the virtually unavoidable administrative and diagnostic lag of fiscal and monetary measures, and the operational lag of monetary measures of expansion and contraction once they have been taken. It means, further, better realization that in the later phases of business cycle upswings a disequilibrium situation is likely to develop which often is described as "overfull employment" or an "unsustainable" level of employment; that is to say, a level of employment which, in view of the wage push exerted by labor unions and the tendency for minimum wages to be raised from time to time, can be maintained only by progressive inflation.

For these reasons, fine tuning beyond a certain point is, if not impossible, at any rate undesirable and counterproductive. Mild fluctuations of output and occasional small lapses from full employment are unavoidable, unless we are prepared to keep the economy under continuous strong inflationary pressure and accept, at the same time, tight control over wages, prices and international transactions so as to suppress some of the symptoms of inflation and prevent runaway open inflation.

This type of siege or war economy not only violates the objectives of free choice and free enterprise, but reduces efficiency and so conflicts with the objective of maximum long-run growth of GNP and real wages. The problem of conflicts of stability and growth will be taken up at greater length in the next chapter.

MONETARY VS. FISCAL POLICY

We have repeatedly referred to monetary and fiscal policy as joint or alternative devices for economic stabilization. But we have also stressed that fiscal policy to be effective presupposes certain monetary conditions. It makes all the difference whether a budget deficit is financed by the banking system or directly or indirectly by the Central Bank, or by borrowing from the public; similarly whether government surplus funds are recirculated by lending them out in the capital market or are "sterilized" by putting them on an inactive deposit with the Central Bank.

In the last few years the comparative merits of monetary and fiscal policy have lead to heated controversies. The battle between the "monetarists" and "fiscalists," the "new monetarism" and "Keynesian orthodoxy" has been raging in the learned journals and has spilled over into the financial sections of the daily press. The new monetarists are, of course, Milton Friedman and his numerous disciples and followers in many countries. The fiscalists are the innumerable Keynesians. The new monetarism is rooted in the classical quantity theory of money while fiscalism stems from Keynes' *General Theory*. [33]

As usually happens when economic issues enter popular policy discussions, the differences between two schools have been exaggerated. There was bound to be a reaction to the neglect, disuse and disrepute into which monetary policy had fallen during the Great Depression and immediately after World

War II. Under the influence of Keynesian thinking and the depressed conditions of the 1930s, much too little attention was paid to money and monetary policy. There was an urgent need for a "rediscovery of money"—a phrase coined by Howard Ellis and Michael Heilperin independently. In the United States the policy change came with the famous "accord" between the Treasury and the Federal Reserve of 1952. Throughout the war and until 1952, the Federal Reserve had been obliged to peg government bonds rigidly in order to stabilize interest rates. This policy, it was thought, was necessary to finance the war without pains. But it meant "monetizing" the public debt and it made the Federal Reserve an "engine of inflation." The change of 1952 marked the official rediscovery of money and the reinstatement of monetary policy as one of the most important policy instruments.[34]

Few would deny that the disuse of monetary policy had gone much too far and that the reinstatement of monetary policy was overdue and salutary. Keynes himself had never rejected monetary policy; he only expressed doubts about its quick effectiveness under certain circumstances, namely in a severe depression.[35] It should never be forgotten that Keynes wrote in the shadow of the Great Depression. It was Keynes' followers who went to extremes, took the existence of a liquidity trap seriously and declared monetary policy ineffective and unimportant. In recent years, however, Keynesians have become much more cautious than they were twenty years ago. They do not deny the importance of monetary policy any more. What they now insist on is that money is not the only thing that matters; fiscal policy is equally important.[36] Nor would even the most extreme monetarist say that monetary policy is all and fiscal policy is nothing.

First, from the point of view of *efficient allocation of resources* and of *growth* it makes a great deal of difference whether inflation is stopped by open market sales of government securities (monetary policy) or by raising taxes or cutting government expenditures (fiscal policy), keeping in mind that a

70

budget surplus (or reduced deficit) must be handled in such a way that it results in a net reduction in aggregate expenditures.[37] Similarly it makes a great deal of difference whether a recession is counteracted by open market operations (monetary policy) or a cut in taxes or an increase in government expenditure (fiscal policy).

Second, also from the short run *stabilization standpoint* it makes some difference whether inflation (booms) or deflation (recessions) are counteracted by monetary policy (open market operations) or by fiscal policy (tax or expenditure changes).

The monetarist is undoubtedly right when he says that for fiscal policy to be effective deficits must be financed and surpluses disposed of in such a way that a change in aggregate demand results. He is also right when he insists that this implies that money and monetary policy are essentially involved even if fiscal policy is used. On the other hand, the fiscalist is not prevented by the adoption of the Keynesian theory from recognizing the involvement of money. But in fact the Keynesian almost always slurs over the monetary issues involved. Thus it is usually assumed that public works automatically result in a *pro tanto* increase in aggregate expenditure and that it makes little difference whether the government borrows from the banks, the public or the Central Bank.[38]

How effective is monetary policy? Nobody would argue today, as many argued twenty or thirty years ago, that monetary policy is usually ineffective. It is always possible to tighten money sufficiently to raise interest rates, throttle investment and put the brakes on aggregate demand. This is possible even if the government budget shows a large deficit.[39] The converse question—whether making money easier and credit more readily available will always induce increased investment or in some other way stimulate aggregate demand—is not quite so easy to answer. Thirty years ago when money was in the eclipse many economists believed that aggregate expenditure in general and investment in particular were entirely unresponsive to lower interest rates and easier money. "You can take a horse to the water, but you cannot make him drink if he does not want to," or "You cannot push a string" were the standard phrases. In a depression, people just will not invest even with very low interest rates and easy availability of credit.

Few would take that position now. The theory of the absolute "credit deadlock" and "liquidity trap" was greatly exaggerated for the depressed conditions of the 1930s and is entirely wrong under conditions of high employment that have prevailed throughout the postwar period. The horse is ready to drink if you give him water—unless you frighten him by some foolish maneuvers.[40] Monetary policy is effective as a stabilization device.[41]

It does not follow, however, that it makes no difference whether monetary or fiscal policy is used to counteract recession or inflation, to reflate or to disinflate. Fiscal policy has one advantage over monetary policy which may be of crucial importance, namely that it acts faster. Its operational lag is shorter than that of monetary policy. An increase in government expenditures acts quickly on aggregate demand, and even a tax cut will result more quickly in increased expenditures than easier money brought about by open market operations. (Needless to repeat that public works may have anticipatory announcement effects and that a tax cut which is limited in time will have less, possibly much less, effect than an unlimited one.)

Quick action may be of great importance both in depression and inflation periods. The long and variable lag of monetary policy measures has been embarrassing on many occasions. It can be argued that the disadvantage of slow action of monetary policy will be outweighed by greater smoothness; that monetary policy will permit the economy to regain an equilibrium growth path, while fiscal policy, because it acts faster, runs the danger of overshooting the equilibrium position and bringing about a reaction in the opposite direction later. There may be some truth in this, but I am afraid we have to admit that we simply do not know enough to be sure that monetary policy, however smooth and gradual, will in fact put the economy smoothly on an equilibrium growth path. In fact it may be doubted whether it is at all possible, once the economy has strayed from the hypothetical equilibrium growth path, to lead it back, smoothly and without oscillation on to an equilibrium growth path. I find it more plausible, or at any rate safer, to assume that the economy is bound from time to time to stray from equilibrium in one direction or the other; and that all that skillful policy can do is to prevent expansion or contraction from spiraling into inflationary booms or serious recessions.

The upshot of this whole discussion is that both monetary and fiscal measures have their place in stabilization policy. Let us keep in mind, however, that legislative and administrative delays make discretionary fiscal policy a much less flexible instrument than monetary policy. (Built-in fiscal stabilizers do not suffer from this defect.) It is not possible to turn fiscal measures off and on at short intervals. Cutting government expenditures encounters massive resistance and easily becomes a major political operation. Public works once started cannot be interrupted or quickly scaled down without incurring great wastes and inefficiencies. Taxes cannot well be changed more than once a year. Frequent changes of business taxes in particular would lead to anticipatory and evasive actions, investment being rushed to beat a deadline or delayed to profit from an investment credit when it comes into force, thus producing erratic changes and promoting instability. This was demonstrated when, in 1966 in the United States, the investment credit scheme was first suspended for a year to "cool off the economy" and then after a few months was reinstated.

All this effectively rules out fiscal policy as an efficient instrument of fine tuning. But, let me repeat, we cannot be sure that in this unpredictable and changing world we shall be faced with nothing more serious than the problem of fine tuning, even if we are able to adhere to the policy of a fairly steady monetary growth. Something may go wrong and a situation more severe than a "short period of pause," or "mini-recession"

73

may develop. If that happens, it would be unwise to rule out discretionary fiscal measures.

It is often said that monetary measures to stop inflation, especially inflation of the cost-push type, have the disadvantage of producing unemployment and slack. Now there can hardly be a doubt that stopping an inflation which has been allowed to continue for some time will cause some transitional slack and unemployment. But substituting fiscal for monetary policy will not get us around that particular difficulty. Monetary and fiscal policy[42] are in the same boat as far as the problem of transitional unemployment is concerned. Whether wage or price guideposts or incomes policies can overcome that hurdle will be discussed in the next chapter.

Chapter 5

Stability, Growth, and Inflation

INTRODUCTION

For more than forty years now, and only with occasional pauses, prices have been rising in the United States, sometimes slowly, sometimes rather briskly. The same is true for other industrial countries; in many less-developed countries (LDC) the price rises have been much more rapid than in the highly industrialized countries.

We know that these price rises were only possible because governments permitted the necessary increases in the money supply. They could have prevented these increases. Our concern in this chapter is with the relationship between inflation and long-run growth. Does inflation promote or retard growth? Does the answer depend on the rate of inflation or on whether it is anticipated or unanticipated?

There will be general agreement that prolonged, severe depressions, such as the Great Depression of the 1930s or even somewhat milder ones, are not in the interest of long-run growth. A stabilization policy that prevents or cures such conditions, whether relying on automatic stabilizers or using discretionary policies, also serves to increase long-run growth.

From a narrow static standpoint, it is tempting to go on and to conclude that, to promote growth, any kind of unemployment ought to be prevented by expansionary measures because every hour lost in unemployment implies a reduction in output, and lost output is lost forever. This statement must, however, be severely qualified when we leave the static textbook world and consider the real world, especially a dynamic, rapidly growing free enterprise economy with large investment and technological change going on continuously. In such a world, it was stated earlier (Chapter 3), stabilization and full employment policies, if pushed too far, will come into conflict not only with the objective of price stability but will collide also with the objective of maximum long-run growth itself. Neither fiscal nor monetary policy can deal with all the varieties of unemployment found in the real world.

TYPES OF UNEMPLOYMENT

It is necessary, as has been mentioned in Chapter 3, to distinguish different types of unemployment although they shade into one another and it is often difficult or impossible to say exactly how much of the given total unemployment belongs to each category.

First, we must distinguish between voluntary and involuntary unemployment. What counts is *involuntary* unemployment, which may be defined as people unable to find work although they are able and willing to work at the wage ruling for the type of work for which they are qualified. We speak of *voluntary* unemployment if people do not care to work or would work only for a wage higher than the wage ruling for the kind of work they can do.[1] The distinction between voluntary and involuntary unemployment corresponds to the distinction between those individuals who are and those who are not in the labor force. The latter are people who could work, but for one reason or the other do not seek work. They are voluntarily "unemployed." People in the labor force are either employed or involuntarily unemployed.[2] When we speak of unemployment as an evil, we mean involuntary unemployment. But we cannot say that voluntary unemployment is *no* problem. Vagrants, hobos, hippies and similar types adorning the streets and squares of our cities constitute a serious social problem, although they clearly do not represent what economists have in mind when they speak of the problem of unemployment.

The borderline between voluntary and involuntary unemployment is not always well marked and often shifts. There are always people on the borderline who shift from one side to the other.[3] "Labor force participation," the percentage of the population of working age that "is in the labor force," that is, those who either are actually employed or seeking employment (involuntarily unemployed), changes according to circumstances.

All this makes the interpretation of unemployment figures difficult. The conceptual distinction is necessary nonetheless. But we cannot pursue this matter any further. From now on when we speak of unemployment, we mean involuntary unemployment.

There are four principal types of (involuntary) unemployment: (1) *frictional* or transitional, (2) *structural* or technological unemployment, (3) *institutional* and (4) *general* depression or recession unemployment, often called Keynesian unemployment. The four shade into one another, and it is often a matter of dispute how much of the statistically reported total unemployment belongs to each category. But for clear thinking, some such distinction must be made.

Frictional unemployment includes seasonal unemployment. It exists even in the best of times. There are always some workers who have lost their jobs or have quit and are looking for work. Transitional unemployment may be due to a great variety of factors—seasonal changes in demand (holiday seasons), production conditions (weather), and changes in the fortunes of the individuals concerned or of employing firms (production mishaps, mismanagement, etc.).

Unemployment is said to be *structural* or *technological* if it is concentrated in particular areas or occupations, workers having lost their jobs because of technological progress, or a shift in demand. In a dynamic economy, such changes are going on all the time. New products, better products, and cheaper products are introduced and firms that are not quick to change and adapt get hurt. Often the innovators themselves misjudge their chances and come to grief.

There is another important type of unemployment, often referred to as structural,[4] which should more accurately be called *institutional*. A legal minimum wage, higher than the wage in a free labor market, creates this type of unemployment.[5] Many economists believe that in the United States at the present time much unemployment among the lowest strata of the unskilled workers, particularly among the ethnic minorities, is due to the fact that the productivity of these people is below the statutory minimum. Private firms cannot afford to hire them.[6]

Obviously, frictional, technological and institutional unemployment shade into each other. The difference is that the latter two are concentrated and are more serious and longer lasting. But all three have this in common: They are partial, spotty unemployment, and are *not* due to a decline or insufficiency of aggregate demand (deflation), but to shifts and changes in technology and in relative demand or to artificial barriers to

78

wage adjustment. If in a changing economy some firms or groups of workers find that demand for their products has vanished or declined, causing idleness and overcapacity (under-utilization of plant and equipment), other sectors must experience brisk demand, labor shortages and strains on their capacity—unless there has been a decline in aggregate effective demand, either in absolute terms or, in a growing economy, relative to the normal upward trend.

The irreducible frictional unemployment is often assumed to be 3 to 4 percent. This includes a certain amount of voluntary as well as technological and institutional (involuntary) unemployment. Statistically, the three are not sharply separable. In the United States, it has been customary for a number of years to speak of full employment when unemployment is 4 percent or less of the labor force. Actually, frictional unemployment must be assumed to change from time to time according to circumstances, and the 4 percent normal cannot be taken as more than a very tentative and approximate guess. [6a] (Some recent developments in the theory of unemployment are discussed in Appendix B).

It is tempting to conclude that so long as unemployment is partial and spotty no global stabilization measures (strengthening of aggregate demand by monetary or fiscal policies) are indicated[7] and, conversely, that any general (widespread) unemployment can and should immediately be eliminated by global stabilization measures.

Unfortunately, things are not quite so simple. The dividing line between partial and general unemployment is not sharp. Even in depressions, except very severe ones, there exist, side by side with widespread unemployment and overcapacity, some production bottlenecks and shortages of certain types of specialized, skilled labor.

The magnitude of the employment problem arising out of technological progress tends to be exaggerated in popular discussion. Automation and other technological advances are alleged to have made large numbers of unskilled workers technologically unemployable. Much of the unemployment in the early sixties was said to be of this nature and beyond the reach of global expansionary monetary and fiscal measures. This surely was an exaggeration. The condition of generality of unemployment for the useful application of global expansionary measures must not be taken literally. It stands to reason, and has often been borne out by experience, that the absorption of pockets of unemployment and the dissolution of production bottlenecks can be speeded up by pressures of demand resulting from expansionary measures. If demand conditions are favorable and the outlook is good, it is easier and less risky than in times of recession and slack for workers to change jobs and locations, and for business to respond promptly by training and upgrading workers and by recruiting labor from other areas and occupations. Naturally there are limits to what expansionary measures can accomplish. At some point further, expansion will lead to inflation and a choice has to be made either to tolerate a certain amount of unemployment or to permit more inflation. To this problem we come presently.

Institutional unemployment caused by high minimum wages is a more serious matter than technological unemployment. It cannot be cured by global expansionary policies unless inflation is allowed to reduce the *real* level of the legal minimum wage sufficiently to permit the employment of even low quality workers.[8] The best solution to the problem of institutional unemployment is to abolish minimum wages. They serve no useful purpose. On the contrary, they are antisocial because they create unemployment among the poorest underprivileged workers (unskilled, teenagers, blacks). Some of the damage done by minimum wages could be avoided if a *lower* minimum were established for young inexperienced workers. Institutional unemployment can, of course, be reduced by better education and training; but this is inevitably a slow process which can be repeatedly frustrated by periodic upward revisions of the minimum wage.

CONFLICTS BETWEEN STABILITY AND GROWTH:
THE HIGH PRESSURE SYSTEM

Monetary and fiscal policies, aimed at creating and maintaining full employment, if pushed too far, lead to inflation and at some point collide with the long-run maximum growth objective. This is true despite the fact that there always is some unemployment and some slack in the economy which would seem to justify continued inflationary measures, or, to put it differently, to speak against an antiinflationary contractive financial policy. To reduce the pressure will almost always cause some temporary unemployment and hence bring about a short-run retardation of growth.

There are several reasons, nonetheless, why public policy should *not* aim at preventing any lapse whatsoever from full employment. First and foremost, if inflation goes beyond the creeping phase, a contagious "inflationary psychology" develops; people come to anticipate further price rises; inflation begins to "feed on itself." The price rise quickens. Larger and larger monetary injections are needed to forestall any slackening of real growth. This is bad in itself but even more serious is the virtual certainty that the government will step in with direct controls ranging from "guideposts" for wages and prices and "incomes policies" to fullfledged price and wage controls. The latter necessitate consumer rationing, material allocations, investment controls and the whole apparatus characteristic of socialist planning. These measures merely repress inflation[9] and are clearly inimical not only to the basic objectives of economic freedom and free enterprise but also to growth itself.

Apart from growth-reducing wastes and inefficiencies of excessive inflation, especially the repressed and government-controlled type, there is, second, the fact that during business cycle upswings and prolonged high-level activity, wastes and inefficiencies increase. When employment is full and jobs are easy to get, labor discipline deteriorates, absenteeism, excessive labor turnover and sloppy work increase rapidly. Management, too, takes it easy when demand is brisk. Bottlenecks, short supply and delays in the delivery of parts and material become frequent; all this reduces efficiency, raises cost and causes work stoppages.

These developments, which we find regularly during business expansions, have played a great role in earlier business cycle theories, notably those of W. C. Mitchell and his followers. Perhaps the idea was overplayed by some writers; toleration of long periods of depression or stagnation cannot be justified as necessary for the elimination of inefficiencies that have crept in during the preceding expansion. But the idea should not be dismissed altogether. Thus it is sometimes rejected on the ground that labor productivity (output per man-hour) does not, or at least does not regularly, show a decline toward the end of business cycle upswings. This is not a sufficient reason to doubt the decline in efficiency because output per man-hour is not by itself an adequate measure of efficiency; it is strongly influenced by other factors in addition to declining labor discipline, reduced efforts, absenteeism and the other inefficiencies that were just mentioned. One such factor is that in the course of cyclical expansion, when employment increases and labor shortages become frequent, "marginal" workers—less well-trained and unreliable men—are hired. This in itself cannot be called an inefficiency, but it operates in the same direction—raising marginal cost and reducing output per man-hour.

There is, furthermore, another factor at work that may operate powerfully to *increase* labor productivity (not efficiency): Cyclical expansions are usually characterized by heavy investment. Therefore, in the later stages of an upswing, new, more efficient plant and better equipment, the construction of which had been taken in hand earlier in the upswing, gradually come into operation and replace less efficient plant and equipment.[10] This increases output per man-hour; it may create unemployment but at any rate tends to compensate or possibly overcompensate productivity, reducing the effect of the mounting wastes and inefficiencies enumerated above.

A third reason for not aiming at literal and continuous full employment is, as mentioned earlier (Chapter 3), the possibility that "real maladjustments" may have developed during expansion periods—discrepancies, as it were—between the structure of demand and the structure of production. While these maladjustments by themselves would not be sufficient to explain a prolonged depression or to justify "letting the depression run its course," they may be sufficiently real to make an occasional pause in a business expansion advisable.

For all these reasons I conclude that occasional lapses from full employment (defined as above), making allowance for a certain amount of frictional, structural and institutional unemployment, will maximize long-run growth. During these periods of pause and recession inflation is checked, real maladjustments are corrected, labor discipline is tightened, numerous wastes and inefficiencies are eliminated and eventually output per man-hour (labor productivity) is raised. Conversely, running the economy at forced draft creates conditions inimical to long-run growth—inflation, wastes, inefficiencies. It makes the economy brittle and inflexible. Economists call it a state of "overfull employment," and practical businessmen and central bankers speak of "an unsustainable rate of growth."

INFLATION AND GROWTH: THE CASE OF THE LESS-DEVELOPED COUNTRIES

Debate regarding the relationship of inflation to growth has been especially lively throughout the postwar period. I shall review first the problem as it presents itself in the less-developed countries and then turn to the case of the developed countries.

Many of the less-developed countries suffer from chronic, severe inflation, ranging from rapid, more or less "open" inflation, especially in Latin America, to strongly repressed inflation elsewhere.

That rapid inflation (20 percent or more a year) is bad for growth can hardly be doubted. It discourages saving, drives past savings abroad and distorts investment. It is a constant complaint in poor countries that they have no efficient capital markets. But under highly inflationary conditions how could it be otherwise? Why should anyone buy bonds or put money in savings banks under chronic inflation? If there were no inflation, there would be no reason why a well-functioning capital market should not develop, capable of efficiently distributing among competing uses the supply of savings from domestic savers plus what can be borrowed from abroad. Under existing inflationary conditions, saving is discouraged and a large part of what is being saved goes abroad. Billions of dollars of residents of less-developed countries are hidden away in the United States and in numbered bank accounts in Europe.

The ravages caused by inflation are increased by governments trying to suppress some of the symptoms. Partly repressed inflation has become the rule, and open inflation the exception.

Suppression of symptoms implies a proliferation of controls, furthers the growth of red tape and bureaucracy and leads to more distortions. Import quotas, exchange control and bilateral trading are typical types of controls. In view of the high dependence on international division of labor of all less-developed countries, restriction and dislocation of international trade are very damaging. The other area where symptoms of inflation are typically suppressed and where controls do enormous damage is that of public utilities—railroads, electric power, telephone, telegraph, etc. When these industries are still in private hands rate control undermines their profitability, leads to underinvestment, undermaintenance and deterioration of service, thus preparing the ground for nationalization and expropriation, often with insufficient compensation, of foreign capital. This implies the loss of foreign know-how and makes foreign direct investment in the whole area of public utilities practically impossible. This is a great pity because in the past this type of foreign investment has made great contributions to the development of less-developed countries.

Once public utilities are operated as public enterprises, they often become one of the major sources of further inflation, thus closing the vicious circle. Inflation in those countries can in most cases be traced to large deficits in the government budget, and grossly inefficient and often grotesquely overstaffed government enterprises are one of the main reasons for the budget deficits.

Though the cause of rapid inflation (increase in the quantity of money and government deficit spending) as well as the adverse effects on growth are clear for anyone to see, there are economists (they call themselves "structuralists") both in the underdeveloped world and among Western advisers who deny both the cause and the deleterious effect on growth. They reject the "monetarist" explanation of inflation which stresses increases in the quantity of money, and the role played by monetary policy and government deficits. The structuralists treat monetary and fiscal factors as surface phenomena. Inflation is due, they say, to deep-seated structural defects and therefore requires structural reforms, such as land reform and measures to increase mobility of labor, to improve education, and strengthen the "infrastructure." Without these reforms, antiinflationary monetary and fiscal policies are ineffective and retard growth.

The structuralist school is strong in less-developed countries, especially in Latin America, but has also some adherents or apologists among economists in the industrial West. One of the most prominent among the latter is Dudley Seers who for some time held a high position in the British Ministry in charge of development aid.[11]

The "structuralist" theory of inflation has been refuted many times. Let me quote a well-known Argentinian economist,

Professor Julio H. G. Oliveira of the University of Buenos Aires:[12] "Underdeveloped economies ... show a chronic tendency to invest more than the amount of voluntary savings ... Yet however deep-rooted in their economic structure such propensity might be, the corresponding inflationary disturbances cannot be envisaged as structural inflation ... One thing is structural inflation and another structural proneness to inflation." Even if it were true that from a sociological or political point of view the deeper causes of inflation are rooted in nonfinancial structural defects, it does not follow that the cure, too, must be structural. "Structural reforms," however well conceived and efficiently carried out, cannot produce immediate results in the form of larger output and more rapid growth. Rapid inflation is too damaging to be allowed to go on until structural reforms bear fruit.

Structuralists and others who maintain that antiinflationary financial policies lead to stagnation try to support their case by pointing to countries that have progressed despite inflation and others whose economies have stagnated during periods when they had little or no inflation. It is easy to find such cases, but they do not prove that inflation is beneficial.

The truth of the matter is this: From an economic standpoint, assuming that a country conducts its affairs in a tolerably rational and efficient way, it is always possible to prevent or cure inflation with all the losses, distortions and misallocation of resources which inflation entails, without at the same time introducing other distortions. On the other hand, it is also possible, easy in fact, to eliminate inflation in such a way that other evils are simultaneously introduced. The "cure" may be, but need not be, worse than the disease, even if the latter is very serious indeed.

Let me give two typical examples. Suppose inflation was initially caused by excessive government spending and borrowing, and then is intensified by credit expansion for the benefit of the private sector of the economy. If now inflation is stopped or slowed down by restricting credit for the private sector and nothing is done to reduce government wastes and deficits, the result of the antiinflation policy will be to sacrifice the productive private sector for the benefit of government extravagance, entailing reduced efficiency, less growth and unemployment in the private sector.

Or suppose there are powerful and aggressive trade unions which exert a strong wage push, a condition usually present in an inflationary situation. If inflation is stopped by monetary and fiscal measures and the wage push continues, unemployment and stagnation will follow. Thus, in the short run, the cure may be worse than the disease if as frequently happens the wage push carries over into the noninflationary period. It must be remembered that we are still discussing the more rapid and cruder type of inflation found in less-developed countries. The problem of the wage push exists also in industrial countries, but in a much milder and hence less obvious form. In less-developed countries wage boosts of 50 percent or more are no rarity. Such increases clearly are a consequence of inflation and would subside when inflation comes to a halt.

Suppose that country A has a respectable growth under inflation, while country B is not doing so well although it has brought inflation under control. To draw from this observation the conclusion that inflation is good for economic growth would be like drawing the conclusion that heroin is healthy from the fact that some people have gotten into serious trouble through a too rapid withdrawal of the dope. However, the analogy must not be pressed too far. Fortunately, there is no physiological reason, unlike in the case of heroin, why the poison of inflation should not be withdrawn quickly. In fact, if properly done, there is much to be said for breaking the spiral of inflation and curbing inflationary psychology quickly and radically instead of slowing it down gradually.

In some less-developed countries where inflation has been endemic for many years, fairly rapid and automatic adjustment mechanisms have been recently developed. In Brazil for example very high interest rates (30 to 40 percent) reflect the accustomed and expected rate of inflation. The basic wage rate is automatically raised in step with the rise in the cost of living, thus avoiding numerous strikes. The exchange rate is frequently adjusted by small steps. This "trotting peg" system has worked quite well. It has largely eliminated disturbing speculation and has kept distorting controls to a minimum. "Purchasing power bonds" are issued, that is, bonds whose principal is routinely upvalued in line with the rise of the price level. [13]

By such measures some of the most glaring distortions, wastes and inequities produced by inflation can be eliminated or at least sharply reduced. They enable countries to "live better" with their inflation. But certain benefits claimed for inflation—for example, compulsory saving—are also sharply reduced.

If it were possible to achieve really continuous, complete adjustment—in the sense that all prices, wages, incomes, capital values, etc., rise continuously by roughly the same percentage, that interest rates reflect the price rise, bonds, etc., are indexed —it should not be difficult to adjust to a zero rate of inflation, in other words, to stop inflation altogether. But the fact of the matter is that complete, smooth adjustment is practically impossible.

The rate of inflation can never be correctly foreseen, if for no other reason than because the adjustment process itself is bound to influence the speed of inflation. There will thus be always numerous cases of incorrect adjustments (over- or under-correction) in different areas, causing distortions and inequities. There can be no compensation for the holders of money, and there are usually "old" contracts which are not adjusted. The first recipient of new money (usually the government) will always gain from inflation. Rapid adjustment to rising prices can never be more than a second-best solution. The ideal solution is still zero or near-zero inflation [14] and it cannot be repeated often enough that this solution, while it may be very difficult politically, is always economically possible and is in the general interest whatever the interests of special groups may be.

INFLATION AND GROWTH: THE CASE OF THE INDUSTRIAL COUNTRIES

The reason for considering inflation in less-developed and developed countries separately is not that inflation is qualitatively different in the two areas; nor is it that different principles of economics and of rational economic policy are applicable in developed and underdeveloped countries, which can almost be called the official doctrine of the United Nations.

Economics and the principles of rational economic policy are the same everywhere, and inflation is essentially a monetary phenomenon everywhere. The difference is one of quantity and degree, not of quality and principle. Inflation in mature industrial countries almost always is milder, at least in peacetimes. But they are more vulnerable to the distortions of inflation because of their complex financial structure, the large volume of fixed debt and contracts and their elaborate division of labor. On the other hand, the poor countries can less well afford any shortfall from the highest attainable level of output and rate of growth caused by inflation.

RAPID INFLATION

There is general agreement in mature industrial countries that rapid inflation (say a price rise of 6 to 7 percent per year for more than two or three years) is bad. It is bad for economic growth and even worse for social order and tranquility. And repressed inflation is still worse than open inflation as can be seen, for example, from a comparison between the open hyperinflation in Germany after World War I with the repressed inflation after World War II.[15] Output and growth suffered

89

much more during the period of repressed inflation (up to 1948 when the German economy, freed from the shackles of controls by the reforms introduced by Ludwig Erhard, began its phenomenal expansion) than during the open inflation from 1918 until 1922 when a new and stable mark was introduced. Both recoveries were very rapid, but the later one started from a much lower level caused by the enormous war destruction and the ravages of repressed inflation.

Some people may think that the Great Depression of the 1930s, which was in fact especially severe in Germany, can be regarded as a delayed aftereffect of the hyperinflation eight years earlier. Few economists would agree. The Great Depression can be fully explained by institutional weaknesses (especially of the banking system) and policy mistakes of commission and omission perpetrated during the depression or, at any rate, years after the inflation period.

Rapid inflation is bad, hyperinflation is a calamity, but even the latter cannot be held responsible for the hyperdeflation eight years later. If we wish to rank evils, there can be no doubt, in my opinion, that severe depressions are much worse than even hyperinflation. On the other hand, the choice between severe depressions and severely repressed and controlled inflation would be more difficult. Fortunately, no country need put itself in a position where it has to make that choice.

CREEPING INFLATION

The typical inflation problem of the modern industrial countries[16] is that of chronic creeping inflation. By that I mean an average annual price rise of, say, 3 to 5 percent proceeding intermittently over extended periods. It is mild enough to prevent serious inflationary psychology from developing; in technical terms "money illusion" survives for extended periods.

Hence, creeping inflation does not quickly accelerate or, if it does, acceleration can be easily stopped by monetary stringency, either automatic or contrived by policy. What we get is mild cyclical price swings along a rising trend with occasional periods of virtual price stability which tend to check inflationary psychology and to restore confidence in the purchasing power of money.

This definition is unavoidably not entirely precise, because the concept of price level is hazy and the borderline between creeping and rapid inflation or between creeping and no inflation[17] is somewhat fluid. It varies from country to country, because psychological reactions differ; people in some countries are more perceptive and sensitive than those in others to the actual or imagined danger of inflation, depending largely on past experience. Thus, the Germans are more sensitive to and fearful of inflation than the Americans because they have experienced two calamitous inflations in a single generation—one open (after World War I); one repressed (after World War II).

The question whether creeping inflation is good or bad for growth is still as controversial as it always was. Most economists would probably agree that ideally long-run stability of prices is the best condition for growth.[18] But many would add that, given certain unavoidable market imperfections such as wage rigidity and wage push, creeping inflation is the "lesser evil" or, as economists euphemistically express it, "the second or third best." It is again controversial how serious the "lesser evil" is.

On these questions the line-up of different economists is curiously mixed. Some laissez-faire liberals like Milton Friedman and good Keynesians like Paul Samuelson and Robert Solow take a relaxed view of creeping inflation while others, such as F. A. Hayek and some adherents of the "New Economics" (in the 1967 controversy over the tax increase) take it much more seriously.[19]

Defenders of creeping inflation are apt to claim that it was and is the price we have to pay for the good growth record of the postwar period. And indeed, if we compare the twenty-two years since World War II with the twenty-two years after World War I, the contrast is striking. From 1918 to 1940, the American economy and the world at large experienced two major depressions, the catastrophic Great Depression of the 1930s among them. Since 1945 there has been no deep depression at all, only mild recessions, and the rate of growth over the whole period, however measured, has been much greater than over the corresponding period after World War I.

I made it clear earlier that I do not question that creeping inflation per se is by far a lesser evil than severe depressions. But this does not tell us how high the cost of creeping inflation actually is. Is it possible that creeping inflation, if allowed to continue for a long time, brings with it some delayed dangers? Furthermore, is it necessary to pay any price at all in the form of inflation for the kind of growth we had during the postwar period? In other words, is growth without inflation altogether impossible?

Let us beware of exaggerations which so often spoil the best arguments. I do not say that creeping inflation must become sooner or later a trotting and then a galloping inflation. That would, of course, be a calamity. But the chances that in mature industrial countries, barring major wars and revolutions, creeping inflation will be allowed to accelerate into a prolonged, rapid price rise are small. At any rate, this development can easily be forestalled by not allowing the quantity of money to rise sufficiently. I cannot see the Federal Reserve manufacturing enough money to finance a prolonged, rapid price rise.

The danger is not, furthermore, that creeping inflation will lead to deep depressions. We have seen that even rapid inflation need not be and usually is not followed by deep depression. There is *a fortiori* no reason why creeping inflation should breed severe depressions.[20]

The real dangers of creeping inflation are less dramatic, but significant and real nonetheless. Before summarizing them, I must discuss a new sophisticated defense and apology of inflation.

FULLY ANTICIPATED INFLATION

In every period of inflation we can find experts who declare that inflation is unavoidable and not really so bad. Some regard inflation as the second-best choice (or lesser evil) which we have to accept because the first-best is a politically unattainable ideal. Others go further and regard mild inflation as the best policy for full employment and growth.

During the last great debate on inflation in the 1950s, the late Sumner H. Slichter took the position that we have to resign ourselves to continued creeping inflation of about 3 percent a year. He blamed it all on union power. In our "laboristic society," he said, an intolerable amount of unemployment would be required to bring the rate of inflation down to near zero. But he was confident that the Federal Reserve could and would prevent inflation from accelerating. He recommended the issue of government bonds with a purchasing power guarantee and the use of escalator clauses in labor and other contracts to minimize the bad social consequences of steady inflation.

Slichter's critics pointed out that unions would not be satisfied with, say, a 6 percent rise in money wages when they saw that half was lost in inflation. They would soon ask for, say, 9 percent and the monetary authorities would once again be faced with the dilemma of either permitting inflation to accelerate or "creating" unemployment. Given wage push and the fact that the so-called "fixed" incomes become flexible upward in a prolonged inflation, it was thought that the dilemma was inescapable. In other words, you cannot fool all the people all the time, and sooner or later—inexorably—"steady" inflation will accelerate or else unemployment will reappear.[21]

Naturally, with the advance of economic analysis the new versions of old theories become more and more sophisticated. Thus, Slichter's theory of permanent but harmless inflation has recently been revived, provided with new, up-to-date econometric foundations, and redecorated with Phillips curves, expectational analyses, cost-benefit computations and what not.[22] Where Slichter spoke modestly of 3 percent inflation, the new inflationists speak of 5 percent and mention no upper limit. They do not explicitly reject the theory of wage push, but cannot, in my opinion, accept it without ruining their case. However, they have not made their position quite clear; the possible exception is Tobin when he admits that his case depends on the assumption that *you can* fool all the people all the time.[23] Actually, Tobin puts it the other way around. The antiinflationist, i.e., "accelerationist" position, he says, "rests on an appealing but unverified assumption that you can't fool all the people all the time." Tobin does not exclude the possibility that "money illusion may be a transient phenomenon," but he thinks that "the period of adjustment is measured in decades." In other words, you can fool all the people for decades! This, it seems to me, grossly underestimates the intelligence of the common man. But Tobin is surely right that the speed of learning and reacting varies greatly from group to group and from individual to individual. However, this dispersion of anticipations and adjustments makes a shambles of the theory of "accurately anticipated inflation." Accurately anticipated inflation is practically impossible and inaccurately and not uniformly anticipated inflation is *not* harmless.

The new version of the theory of harmless inflation draws the crucially important distinction between anticipated and unanticipated inflation which Slichter failed to make explicit. Only an "accurately anticipated inflation" (Gordon) is claimed to be harmless. It is fully realized that full or sufficient anticipation requires that interest rates reflect inflation (which in turn implies legal reforms, e.g., abolition of using laws, authorization for banks to pay interest on demand deposits) and the introduction of exchange rate flexibility to avoid balance of payments difficulties.[24] It is also realized that wages, salaries, pensions, welfare payments, etc., are "indexed," and that medium and long-term bonds, securities, life insurance policies, mortgages, etc., carry purchasing power guarantees.

This is a tall order indeed. The apologists of inflation speak as if we had already gone very far in adjusting to a steady rate of inflation of, say, 5 percent. Gordon says "reducing the inflation rate below what people expect will cause an inequitable redistribution of income from borrowers to savers, just as increasing the rate above what is expected will redistribute in the opposite direction."[25] The implication is that since we have already gone very far in adjusting the economy to steady inflation, we might just as well go the whole way and adjust fully.

It is true that people generally do expect further inflation and there has been some adjustment to inflation, reflected in high interest rates, the inclusion of escalator clauses in some wage contracts and heavy pressures from unions for higher wages as protection for expected rises in the cost of living. Admittedly, therefore, a reduction in the rate of inflation may cause some pain, bankruptcies and unemployment. However, we are far from having already gone halfway or more to full adjustment. With hundreds of billions of dollars in old unadjusted contracts, bonds, mortgages and life insurance policies outstanding, with the expectation of future inflation varying a good deal as between different groups and persons, with escalator clauses in only a few contracts and with no agreement in sight on various reforms such as abolishing legal restrictions on interest payments and introducing flexible exchange rates (however desirable these reforms may be)—with all these adjustments still to come (or not to come), it is difficult to believe that it would be easier fully to adjust up to a 5 percent inflation than to adjust down to a lower rate.[26]

But let us assume that momentarily the economy has more or less fully adjusted to an inflation of 5 percent. Will it be a stable adjustment? There are compelling reasons to expect that the rate of inflation will not stay at the 5 percent level, particularly if there is an element of wage push behind it.[27] In today's world the unions will not let the fruits of their struggles be whittled away by inflation. They will raise their wage demands, and the monetary authorities will again have to choose between resisting the acceleration of inflation and "creating" unemployment or giving in and accelerating inflation. In other words, after a while, holding an inflation to a steady rate of, say, 5 percent causes the same difficulties as holding it to a lower rate (possible a zero rate) would have had earlier in the game.[28]

This raises once more the question of wage or cost inflation as against demand inflation, which will be discussed in greater detail in the next chapter.

SUMMARY

In the last chapter we showed that financial stabilization policies pushed beyond a certain point must fail because of unavoidable lags. In the present chapter we demonstrated why attempts to keep the economy continuously at very high levels of unemployment lead not only to price inflation but also cause more and more waste and inefficiency, thus reducing the rate of long-run growth. Different types of unemployment are distinguished, not all of which are amenable to amelioration by monetary and fiscal policies. The perennial question of the impact of inflation on growth is discussed at some length, from the point of view of the less-developed countries as well as from that of the mature industrial countries. For the latter in peacetimes, the problem is creeping rather than rapid or hyperinflation.

The conclusion is reached that ideally zero or near-zero inflation is best for growth. But this statement must be qualified; the cure may be worse than the disease—for example, if it produces a protracted deep depression or if an inflation that stems from government extravagance is stopped by monetary restriction at the expense of the productive private sector of the economy. This amounts to saying that some moderate and intermittent inflation may be a second-best solution or rather a lesser evil. But it never is the best solution. Finally, issue is taken with the modern theory that a fully anticipated inflation is harmless. It is shown that this is a chimera, because tolerably accurate and uniform anticipation is practically impossible.

Postscript on the 1973 Inflation [29]

This chapter was written before the inflationary explosion in 1973. By the fall of that year the rate of increase of consumer prices in all industrial countries had risen to levels unheard of in peacetime—to over 11.4 percent in the U.S., 12 percent in the U.K., 9 percent in Italy, 13 percent in Japan, 5.5 percent in Germany, and 10 percent in Switzerland and so on, in the three months ending October 1973.[30]

In the United States the acceleration of the price rise since March has been more precipitous than in other industrial countries. This difference must be attributed mainly to two factors: the exceptionally and unsustainably rapid cyclical expansion in the United States—real GNP grew by 8 percent from the first quarter of 1972 to the first quarter of 1973—and to the devaluation of the dollar. In the U.S. the price explosion was not foreseen by anybody. I do not claim that I foresaw it, but in retrospect it is fully explainable by what has been said in the present and earlier chapters. True, special factors were involved, notably the devaluation of the dollar and the spectacular rise of raw material on international markets. The shortfall in world output of grains (especially in Russia) contributed to the sharp rise in food prices. But it remains true that no *general* and sustained rise in prices would have been possible without an increase in the quantity of money. The 1973 inflation was no exception. In the United States monetary growth was very rapid in 1971 and 1972; in 1972 it was the highest since the Korean war. Similarly, in all the other industrial countries mentioned above (and elsewhere) the money supply rose sharply.

There is general agreement that in 1973 the speedup of the inflation was not due to cost or wage pressures. It was a clear case of a classical demand inflation. In fact, labor leaders were taken by surprise like everybody else and reacted slowly to rising prices. But, again, this does not mean that wage rigidities and wage push caused by labor unions has nothing to do with inflation. Under the inflationary conditions prevailing in 1973 a money-wage growth of 7½ percent was not excessive. But money wages are beginning to catch up with rising prices and, at any rate, a money-wage growth of 7 percent or more is entirely incompatible with a tolerable rate of inflation of, say, 2 percent or less. It will be very difficult to bring the money-wage rise down to a level of, say, 4 percent, which is probably the maximum compatible with reasonable price stability. Thus wage rigidity and wage push will remain the main stumbling blocks for regaining price stability. It remains true furthermore, that in the longer run *real* stability, in the sense of steady high employment and growth, is incompatible with inflation. After a while inflation will tend to accelerate or, if the acceleration of inflation is prevented by restrictive monetary or fiscal policies, employment and growth will decline, at least temporarily. Whether incomes policy offers a way out of this dilemma—either to permit accelerated inflation or "create" unemployment—will be discussed in Chapter 7.

Chapter 6

Demand Inflation and Cost Inflation

INTRODUCTION

In Chapter 4 it was shown that in a *competitive* free enterprise society, government can achieve price stability by monetary and fiscal measures. In Chapter 5 it was argued that over the long pull price stability (zero inflation) is the best way to achieve the continued growth most people seem to desire. Growth, as used here, it should be recalled, includes improvements in the quality of life and environment, much more than an increase in the GNP conventionally defined. The question arises why the governments of the mature industrial countries have done no better than to keep inflation at a creep until 1973 when the creep became a trot or gallop.

In the present chapter we examine the factor which an increasing number of economists of various persuasions regard as the main reason for that sorry state of affairs and set forth our own reasons for believing that we may be lucky to live with nothing worse than creeping failure if the general public cannot be made to realize three things: first, that the economy must be made much more competitive than it is at present; second, that this increased competitiveness can be accomplished by the withdrawal of the many special immunities granted to powerful occupational groups; and third, that these immunities, while alike in the price distortions and inequities they cause, differ quantitatively, though not qualitatively, in their impact on the general level of prices. We shall show that there is a significant difference between the powers of business and labor monopolies (unions). The term monopoly is used here loosely to avoid the more precise but forbidding terms dear to economic theorists—"duopoly," "oligopoly," monopolistic competition, etc.

Until fairly recently most economists could see no difference between the two types of monopoly. They were equally objectionable and equally related (or unrelated) to the problem of inflation. Monopoly was an evil. It permitted some unions to secure higher wages for their members and some businesses to charge higher prices and make larger profits for their owners. But their inflationary effect was doubtful. Resources (material and human) excluded from the monopolized sectors of the economy were supposed to gravitate to the competitive sectors, lowering rewards there, denying consumers an optimum assortment of goods and services, and creating greater personal inequalities than would prevail if competition were equally effective through all parts of the economy—except, of course, that part in which consumers are best served by a single supplier, the so-called public utilities.

This "a plague on both your houses" view no longer enjoys the wide support of earlier years. The appearance of powerful unions, able to bring the economic life of nations to a halt, as the strike of the British railroad workers in 1926 and of the miners in 1972 and 1973, amply demonstrated, has convinced increasing numbers that the nature of "the market power" possessed by these two types of monopoly is quantitatively though not qualitatively very different. According to this view, the "market power" of industrial monopolies is regarded as distorting but of limited inflationary impact. Union power, on the other hand, has a distorting and strongly inflationary effect, given permissive monetary policy.

To understand the reasoning behind this view, it is necessary to distinguish two different types of inflation and the reader has to familiarize himself with such concepts as "demand-pull" and "cost and wage push" which have spilled from the economic journals into popular discussions.

TWO TYPES OF INFLATION: DEMAND-PULL VS. COST-PUSH

. The distinction between demand-pull and cost-push inflation has become very popular. The first type, sometimes called "buyers" inflation and also known as the "classical type of inflation," is said to be due to an increase in monetary demand. The second type, frequently called "sellers" inflation and also known as the "new" type of inflation, is said to be caused by sellers pushing for higher prices. Cost-push inflation implies the existence of monopolies or oligopolies—in short "market power," that is to say, the power to set or to manipulate prices which is absent under competition. Cost-push inflation in practice becomes, as we shall see, wage-push inflation in the hands of powerful trade unions.

The distinction between demand and cost inflation strongly suggests, and many fall victim to that suggestion, that demand inflation is a monetary phenomenon while cost inflation is nonmonetary. In reality, both types of inflation are monetary in the important sense that they require monetary expansion. Either M, the quantity of money, or V, its velocity of circulation, must go up. Theoretically M may remain constant (or even decrease), and the rise in prices be entirely "financed" by an increase in V. But there has never, literally never as far as I know, been a case of sustained inflation without a rise in M. While V is not constant over a period of time—it usually rises during business cycle upswings and declines during downswings—it rarely moves out of a fairly narrow range. It did so during the hyperinflation in Germany after World War I when the velocity of circulation of money rose to fantastic heights.[1] During the 1930 Great Depression and during World War II, it fell to unusually low levels.[2]

Demand-push as well as wage-push inflations are monetary phenomena and both can be stopped or prevented by monetary restrictions. But there is a difference. Stopping a demand inflation by monetary measures has only a relatively slight and temporary adverse effect on output and employment, while stopping a cost-push inflation by monetary measures has a more lasting effect on both output and employment. This is because powerful trade unions are able to exercise such a continuing upward pressure on money wages by strikes, picketing and violence as to confront the monetary authorities with a disagreeable dilemma. They can create enough money to support the rise in prices along with the rise in wages, or they can prevent inflation by refusing to expand the monetary circulation, but at the cost of "creating" sufficient unemployment to stop the wage push. This very widely accepted theory implies the existence of a trade-off between inflation and unemployment. If we wish to keep unemployment low, we must accept a certain amount of inflation. This view has been formalized in the theory of the "Phillips Curve," which postulates a fairly stable relationship between unemployment, on the one hand, and the annual rise in money wage rates and the associated rise in the price level, on the other hand.[3]

The policy implications of the wage-push theory of inflation are quite straightforward. To eliminate the dilemma confronting monetary management, the rise in money wages must be kept in step with the general rise in labor productivity (output per man-hour). To achieve this result, "guideposts" or "guidelines for noninflationary wage changes" must be somehow enforced. In Europe this approach has gone under the name of "incomes policy"[4] a term that later gained acceptance also in the United States.

Incomes policy will be further discussed in the next chapter. First, we have to answer the question of how serious is the wage-push dilemma? Most economists regard it as real and serious. Milton Friedman and other monetarists disagree.[5] They believe that the power of trade unions to raise money wages has been greatly exaggerated. If the monetary authorities stand firm and keep the money supply sufficiently tight—that is to say, increase the money stock by as much as is needed to keep the price level stable by, say, 3 to 5 percent a year—labor unions will moderate their wage demands. The transition to a noninflationary price trend, they admit, might be attended by some temporary unemployment, but unions would soon realize that in the absence of inflation they could no longer expect the same annual increase in money wages as under inflation. Thereafter, the economy would settle down on substantially the same employment level and growth path at stable prices as under inflation. In the long run, growth would be even a little faster because the periodic disturbances caused by inflation, including those brought about by futile attempts of governments to suppress the symptoms of inflation, would be avoided.

This theory sounds too easy and comforting to be true. But let us carefully analyze it. I will first formulate a few propositions on which probably most economists could agree.

First, money wages were never very flexible, and the emergence of a strong trade union movement has certainly contributed greatly to the almost complete downward rigidity with which we are confronted today.[6] Downward rigidity of wages by itself can conceivably exert some inflationary influence but

103

is hardly a serious threat to price stability, although combined with an upward push exerted by unions it becomes a potent inflation-intensifying factor.[7]

Second, it is generally agreed that the replacement of competition by monopoly, be it in labor or commodity markets, will push up wages and prices. This is not denied by the critics of the cost-push theory of inflation. Thus, Milton Friedman himself has demonstrated convincingly that "from 1933 to 1937, the NIRA, AAA, Wagner Labor Act and the associated growth of union strength led to increasing market power of both industry and labor and thereby produced upward pressure on a wide range of wages and prices." He points out that "the concomitant rapid growth in nominal income at the average rate of 14 percent per year from 1933 to 1937 . . . reflected a rise in the quantity of money of 11 percent per year" and cannot be explained by the cost-push.[8] But "the cost-push does explain why so large a part of the growth in nominal income was absorbed by [higher] prices" and a comparatively small part reflected rising output and employment. "Despite unprecedented levels of unemployed resources, wholesale prices rose nearly 50 percent from 1933 to 1937 and the cost of living by 13 percent. Similarly, the wage cost-push helps to explain why unemployment was still so high in 1937 when monetary expansion was followed by another severe contraction."[9] This was, indeed, an extreme case of cost-push or "sellers" inflation.

Third, if unions were able in 1933-1937 to push up wages in the face of "unprecedented levels of unemployment," it would seem to follow that in periods of relatively full employment they are in an even stronger position to push up wages to higher levels *without any increase in market power.* Later developments confirm that conclusion.[10]

Fourth, increased market power of unions may be due to more complete unionization of labor, more aggressive union leadership, additional privileges and immunities conferred by law, more lenient administration of existing laws and regulations, and especially to financial help for striking unions through liberal welfare payments and unemployment benefits for the families of striking workers or the strikers themselves and nonstrikers who lose their jobs because of the strike. But even without any such increase in market power, the mere fact that unemployment has vanished or declined makes it much easier for unions to organize strikes and to hold out longer until demands for higher wages are met.[11]

CRITICISM OF THE MONETARIST POSITION

The core of the monetarist criticism of the theory of wage-push inflation is that the price and wage increases caused by monopolies (or oligopolies) in any market are strictly one-shot affairs which occur when the monopolies are first created or when their market power is strengthened. As a prominent monetarist put it, wage-push cannot explain "a general upward movement of wages and prices without a subsidiary assumption that the political process will not tolerate and live with the resulting unemployment," that governments will try to reduce unemployment "by inflationary policies to which the monopolies will react by raising [again] wages and prices."[12] In this formulation the monetarist position is not different from our own. What Johnson calls "a subsidiary assumption" about monetary implications has been made explicit in the present study right from the beginning.[13] But the monetarists clearly suggest more than that, namely that the unemployment which would result from monopolies, if the money supply were not expanded, would be moderate. They seem to envisage a few islands of monopoly in a vast competitive sea; where monopolies existed wages and prices would be higher, production and consumption lower, but unemployment would be transitory and moderate because the labor and other productive resources set free in the monopolized areas would find employment, at somewhat lower wages, in the large competitive sector. (This requires, of course, flexible wages in the competitive sector.) In support of this contention monetarist critics of the wage-push theory note that in the United States only a fraction of the labor force is unionized, that is, 20 to 25 percent. This makes it impossible, they think, to attribute to unions the power to push up the overall wage level.[14]

Actually, no such conclusion can be drawn. To begin with, it is not true of other industrial countries that only a fraction of the labor force is organized in unions. While the percentage of unionized labor in the private sector has not gone up in the United States, it has increased dramatically in the rapidly growing public sector—in all branches and on all levels of government. Teachers, firemen, civil servants, customs officials and in Sweden even army officers are organized in unions which often flex their muscles by calling strikes. This is a recent and an extremely important development. It has undoubtedly greatly intensified the wage-push. Finally, and most important, it can be shown that under American conditions of partial unionization, wage and salary increases pushed through by powerful unions in the private or public sector tend to spread throughout the system, even to nonunionized workers, although with a lag and incompletely. A favorable wage contract obtained by one union becomes a target and spur for others to do as well or better. Furthermore, in order to maintain morale, to preserve wage differentials between different skills, and to forestall further unionization, employers find it necessary to raise the wages and salaries of nonunionized personnel to match, at least approximately, the concessions they were forced to grant to union workers.

It is very important to realize and to keep firmly in mind that in our decentralized economy all these actions and reactions, including the monetary ones, are not simultaneous. They are spread out over time with lags of varying length. For example, the unemployment which unions cause among their own members and elsewhere by excessive wage boosts is usually much delayed. Unions are rarely confronted with a clear-cut choice between lower employment and higher wages; it is not surprising, therefore, that most labor leaders are unaware of the connection between wage increases and employment. At any rate, few will admit the connection. [15]

If nationwide organizations of labor and management bargained about the whole wage level, the connection between wages, prices and employment would be easier to see and one could reasonably expect greater moderation on the part of the labor representatives. Needless to add that such a system of nationwide collective bargaining is not only utopian, but also undesirable. But it is a useful mental experiment to compare a hypothetical centralized system, where the equilibrium relationship between wages and employment is almost instantaneously reached and clearly visible with our actual decentralized system, and where equilibrium is approached through a complicated, time-consuming, dynamic process of countless actions and reactions.

Monetarists like to postulate a "natural" or "equilibrium" rate of unemployment, whose magnitude is determined by the general characteristics of an economy including existing monopolistic organization of labor and commodity markets.[16] Equilibrium unemployment comprises both frictional unemployment (in the broadest sense) and monopoly unemployment caused by union wage-push and business monopolies. (The role of the latter is discussed in a later section). Equilibrium unemployment is a useful theoretical concept. But it would be wrong to assume that unions know the amount of unemployment which they create and that they can therefore be depended upon to be more moderate in their wage demands for fear of losing too many jobs.[17]

THE STRENGTH OF THE WAGE-PUSH: SOME RECENT DEVELOPMENTS IN THE U.S. AND GREAT BRITAIN

I conclude that wage-push does intensify inflation. Nobody knows what the final equilibrium unemployment would be if money were kept sufficiently tight to stop inflation. But given the low modern tolerance for unemployment, the chances are that the monetary authorities will not stand firm but give way before the final equilibrium has been reached. Some transitional unemployment after a prolonged inflation is unavoidable even under competition because inflationary expectations must be doused, which takes time, and unions must get used to the smaller wage increases they can look forward to in a non- or less-inflationary situation. This inevitably increases the transitional unemployment.[18]

The role of business monopolies is discussed in the concluding section of this chapter. In the next chapter, ways for making the economy more competitive are examined. Here some further reflections on the strength of the wage-push, based on recent developments in the United States and Great Britain, are in order.

The price organized workers have to pay for the right to engage in long strikes has been greatly reduced in recent years. The social cost of prolonged strikes is often very high, but the private cost to most of the strikers and their unions is frequently small. In the United States, the government in effect finances strikes by liberal welfare payments, and in some states by liberal unemployment benefits to the strikers themselves if the strike lasts longer than a few weeks; in all states workers thrown out of work as a result of a strike in which they were not involved are eligible for unemployment benefits. Unions have learned to conserve their financial resources by restricting strikes to certain strategically placed small groups.

In Great Britain similar developments have led to dramatic changes. Wage-push has caused a sharp intensification of the demand-pull inflation that had been going on almost uninterruptedly since the end of World War II. This has caused several prominent British economists to change their position. Professor Frank W. Paish, a close student of the working of the British economy, long rejected incomes policy on the ground that Britain was suffering from demand inflation caused by loose monetary policies rather than from cost or wage inflation. [19] In 1970 he changed his mind. To the second edition of his study (see note 19) he added a postscript: "Cost-push at last." On the basis of careful statistical analyses he concluded that since about 1969 a most dramatic change has taken place in the labor market. From mid-1969 to mid-1970 money earnings from employment increased by about 13.7 percent, whereas on the basis of earlier experience (1952-1966) one would have expected an increase of only 3.8 percent.[20]

Professor James E. Meade, in his study *Wages and Prices in a Mixed Economy,*[21] accepted Paish's conclusion that "a most dramatic and marked" change in the unemployment-wage relationship had taken place. Both economists now believe that tight monetary-fiscal policies, while essential, must be supplemented by "wage restraint" if inflation is to be curbed without creating more unemployment than modern society can tolerate.[22]

But why has the wage-push become so much stronger in recent years? Well-organized labor unions are not new in Great Britain. Monetarists, Harry G. Johnson and his followers, are surely right in holding that inflation itself and the resulting inflationary expectations are largely responsible. Britain had suffered from old-fashioned monetary demand inflation throughout the postwar period, and for this Johnson lays the blame squarely on the Keynesian disdainful rejection of monetary policy. The "rediscovery of money and monetary policy" has been particularly slow in coming there. The resulting demand inflation certainly greatly contributed to union strength and wage-push. But the British economists mentioned above (Paish, Meade and Robbins), while fully aware of the monetary background, believe that several other factors have helped to bring about such a dramatic and permanent change in union strength and attitudes. This, they insist, makes it imperative to supplement monetary restraint by some sort of incomes policy. In practice this means wage restraint, for, as we shall show in the next section, the impact of business monopolies on inflation is small compared with that of unions (labor monopolies).

"There have been in recent years," Meade writes, "two very important changes in the labor market—namely the institution of redundancy payments and of more generous income-related unemployment benefits—which have reduced the terror of temporary unemployment." This has greatly increased the power of unions to force up wages by crippling strikes.

Another important new development, Meade believes, is a change in the attitude of most wage earners toward higher taxes[23] and other deductions from gross wages, such as social security contributions and union dues. Workers are interested in their take-home pay, not their gross pay. They appear to regard as windfalls the social benefits for which they pay through social security contributions and general taxes. It is very important to realize that in the absence of unions endowed with monopoly power, there could be no wage pressure resulting from heavier taxes.[24]

Meade concludes that the factors he mentioned, and others including inflation itself, have given "trade unions an unexpected glimpse into the very large monopolistic powers which they possess for pushing money wage-rates up and which they have not fully exploited in the past. The consequences may have been a basic change in attitude. The order of magnitude of what is regarded as a reasonable annual claim may have been more or less permanently changed; and trade union leaders may have become much more acutely aware of their power to obtain concessions through the threat to disrupt basic economic activities" (ibid., p. 17).

Paish puts the same thought this way: "If it could be shown that the trade unions were in practice able and willing to use their monopoly power to hold the rest of the community to ransom, there could be no further argument about the desirability of a wage policy." A dock strike that threatens wide-spread power shortages, a subway strike that paralyzes a whole city, can surely be described as holding the rest of the society to ransom. As we have argued earlier, excessive wage settlements in important areas spur other unions to press for similar wage increases and spread, although with a lag and imperfectly, to nonunionized labor, tending to jack up the whole wage level. Thus, the monetary authorities are placed in the awkward dilemma: either permit inflation or "create" unemployment.[25]

We conclude that unions have the power to push up *money* wages. Whether they are in a position to influence *real* wage rates, *real* labor income or the share of labor in the national income is an entirely different question. They have certainly very little influence on the *general* level of real wages (including union and nonunion labor). On balance, their long-run effect on *real* income of labor as a whole is almost certainly nega-tive. Intensification of inflation provokes government attempts to restrain inflation either by monetary restrictions which create unemployment or by clumsy direct controls which reduce the efficiency of the economy. In addition, unions are responsible for numerous misallocations of resources, result-ing from inefficient wage differentials, costly work rules, reduced mobility of labor and excessive shortening of the workweek.[26] Then there are the direct losses from strikes and other work stoppages.

On the other hand, the influence of unions on the growth of real wages for unionized labor (as compared with labor as a whole) is a more difficult problem. There is evidence that unions create a permanent though changing wage differential in favor of unionized as against nonunionized labor.[27] But the pace of wage growth set by union wages tends to spread sooner or later to other areas and since the overall impact of unions is unfavorable for growth, it is very doubtful whether in the long run union wages in real terms are at all pushed up by union activities. This does not, of course, exclude the possibility that well-organized unions can secure substantial and lasting gains for certain relatively small groups of workers.[28]

LABOR MONOPOLIES AND BUSINESS MONOPOLIES

In principle the role of business monopolies and oligopolies in the inflation process is the same as that of labor monopolies (unions). The introduction of monopolies where there was competition before inevitably leads to higher prices. This happened on a large scale during the early New Deal. As Friedman pointed out (see note 8), the NIRA and Wagner Act greatly strengthened the monopoly power of both business and labor. The consequence was that from 1933 to 1937 unemployment remained high and that the sharp rise in money GNP reflected to an abnormal extent merely a rise in prices and to a correspondingly smaller extent an increase in real output and employment. But while the New Deal measures of fostering business monopolies (NIRA) were soon declared unconstitutional and the traditional antitrust policy against business monopolies was resumed, the immunities granted to unions were never revoked.[29]

The existence of business monopolies strengthens union power. This can be very clearly seen in public utilities, whether privately or publicly owned and operated. Unions quite naturally wish to capture some of the monopoly profits for labor. Thus, business and labor monopolies, despite frequent quarrels, conspire to push up prices of monopolized products.

But neither unions nor business monopolies can produce continuing inflation without the helping hand of the monetary authorities. To put it the other way around, by keeping money sufficiently tight it is always possible to stabilize prices despite monopoly pricing and wage-push, but only at the cost of creating slack and unemployment. If in addition to the unions which push up wages, there exist numerous business monopolies and oligopolies which keep many prices higher than they would be under competition, the hypothetical equilibrium unemployment will be higher than if there were only unions. But in our decentralized economy, as was shown in the preceding section, it takes considerable time to approach the equilibrium position. The chances are that long before equilibrium is reached unemployment will have reached a politically intolerable level and inflationary measures will be taken to reduce it.

Although in principle business monopolies and labor monopolies play the same role in the inflation process, there are compelling reasons for the proposition that the actual importance of business monopolies for inflation is quite small compared with that of labor unions.[30]

In the first place the American economy is highly competitive, much more so than most people, misled by slogans about the power of monopolies and oligopolies, realize. Where there exist "natural" monopolies as in the public utility area (communication, transportation, electric power transmission and the like), production is in public hands or, if still in private hands prices are controlled, usually overcontrolled. Outside the public utility field such power as monopolies or oligopolies possess is in most cases provided by government policies. There is ample evidence that governments through many of their policies raise prices more than private monopolies could. Examples are import restrictions by tariffs, quotas and especially by so-called "voluntary" export restrictions forced on foreign producers; farm price support policies; and in more direct fashion the notorious restrictions on production of oil in Texas by the Texas Railroad Commission. Also public utility regulations in practice often result in higher prices.[31] The overall unimportance for inflation of private business monopolies as compared with wage-push by labor unions is demonstrated by the fact that corporate profits, of which monopoly profits are just a fraction, are only about 10 percent of national income while compensation of employees is about 80 percent.[32]

No private business monopoly, producer organization or cartel wields the market (and physical) power or commands the discipline over its members which many unions have achieved. Unions can shut down whole industries, paralyze the economic life of the country, starve whole states (as the dockers in Hawaii did) in pursuit of higher wages. There is nothing like this on the other side, no "profit-push" corresponding to the wage-push.[33]

113

Public opinion is hostile to anything that looks like monopolies or excessive market power or disregard of consumer interests on the part of private business, but is lenient and not easily aroused as far as labor unions are concerned. Reflecting general public opinion, public laws and regulations and government policies treat unions and abuses of union power with kid gloves. [34]

What has been said should not be construed as an expression of "antilabor" sentiment—an attitude I regard as totally objectionable and absurd—or as implying that unions are intrinsically bad or that their leaders are wicked men and wild revolutionaries. In fact union leaders in most countries are politically conversative, sometimes to the point of being reactionary or stodgy. [35] Nor do I want to suggest that nothing should be done about business monopolies where they exist. Let us pursue antitrust policy as vigorously as possible and, above all, preserve and stimulate competition by free imports. But it would be utterly unrealistic to expect a quick impact on inflation from these measures. Intensified antitrust policy is necessarily a slow-acting reform. And trade liberalization, although highly desirable on general grounds and theoretically capable of quick implementation (formidable political hindrances apart), is a potent long-run antidote to monopolistic tendencies, but not a quick remedy for inflation. [36] There simply is no substitute for monetary restraint as a quick cure for acute inflation. Wage and price freezes as possible fast-acting stopgap measures are discussed in the next chapter.

Now let us look at the process of cost- and wage-push inflation once more from a slightly different angle. Economists have frequently visualized cost-push inflation as the consequence of the efforts of different monopolistic pressure groups—organized workers, farmers (who need, however, the help of governments to organize themselves), the government, business monopolies—to secure shares in national income that add up to more than the total. Inflation's function then is to scale down the inconsistent claims to the level that the available real national product permits, thus making them mutually

114

consistent. [36a] This is a fairly accurate picture of reality, provided it is firmly kept in mind that the inflation process is decentralized, dynamic and studded with lags of varying length. If all pressure groups were equally strong and if all adjustments were instantaneous, the futility of using inflation to bring rival claims in line with the available real national product would be apparent. In our decentralized economy this is not the case.

Some economists, the pessimists, regard the inflation method of adjusting inconsistent claims with alarm. Others, the optimists, take a relaxed view. Monetarists naturally are not worried. In their opinion labor monopolies and other pressure groups have nothing to do with inflation. But James Tobin, one of the foremost antimonetarists, is equally relaxed. Inflation works, he says, "blindly, impartially and nonpolitically," and he adds complacently, "there are worse methods of resolving group rivalries and social conflicts."[37] He is, of course, right. Detailed government regimentation is much worse than inflation as a method of adjusting inconsistent claims. But are there no better methods? Tobin visualizes a steady (or at least nonaccelerating) rate of inflation—how rapid he does not say—capable of keeping unemployment permanently at a level lower than would be possible with zero inflation. But it is difficult to believe that inflation would not accelerate if there is an element of wage-push. Would not unions and other pressure groups raise their claims when they saw their expectations again and again frustrated by inflation? And what happens when they become fully inflation-conscious, when "the money illusion" vanishes and they begin to bargain in real terms, and try to anticipate expected future price rises? Tobin does not face these questions squarely. Harry G. Johnson is somewhat less complaisant. He speaks, more realistically, of intermittent rather than of continuous inflation and says, cautiously, "it is not all that clear that stop-go involves much loss as compared with the alternative of steady growth."[38]

More and more economists who fear inflation are coming to the view that in our modern society, riddled as it is with monopolistic pressure groups, monetary-fiscal measures cannot stabilize prices. Thus, Friedrich Lutz after explaining inflation as the method of scaling down incompatible monetary claims, declares that the only way to solve the inflation problem would be to dissolve the pressure groups and make the economy more competitive. But only a strong government could do that, and democracy is likely to perish in the process. "Many will say that inflation could be stopped if the central bank simply refused to print the money that is necessary to transact the rising monetary demand. This method would work if it were true what the author formerly thought was true, that a weak labor market [i.e., some unemployment] would induce the unions to moderate their wage demands. But experience in many countries has shown that this is no longer the case if it ever was. Tight money does not prevent price increases but produces unemployment on top of inflation."[39]

This pessimism surely exaggerates the intensity of the wage push. We have not reached that stage yet. To illustrate that monetary restraint can only produce "stagflation"—stagnation and inflation—Lutz refers to what happened in the United States in 1969-1970. But the rate of inflation was substantially reduced from about 6 percent in 1969 to about 3 percent in 1972, and there is fairly general agreement that for various reasons the full employment target has to be revised; concretely, the figure of 4 percent unemployment that used to be regarded as the measure of unavoidable frictional unemployment must be replaced by a higher figure. In other words, the economy is at present (December 1972) much closer to full employment than the official unemployment figure of 5.2 percent suggests.

However, the pessimists are surely right to speak of a basic dilemma: Unless the power of unions and other pressure groups is curbed and the economy made more competitive, we have to accept a certain amount of unemployment. Inflation can alleviate the problem temporarily but offers no permanent solution.

How to deal with this problem is discussed in the following chapter.

Chapter 7

Wage Guideposts and Incomes Policies

INTRODUCTION

In recent years the standard approach in all Western industrial countries to the problem of cost-push inflation has become what in the United States used to be called guideposts or guidelines for noninflationary wage and price policy and what in Europe has for some time been known as incomes policy. Since about 1970 the term "incomes policy" has also become popular in the United States and has largely supplanted the term "guideposts." Incomes policy has indeed become a major issue in the fight against inflation. The question is whether antiinflationary monetary and fiscal policy should, or should not, be supplemented by incomes policy. Most economists are agreed that a tight rein on aggregate demand through an appropriate monetary and fiscal policy is a necessary condition for curbing inflation. Monetarists (Milton Friedman, Harry G.

Johnson and their followers) believe sufficiently tight money is not only a necessary but also a sufficient condition for stopping inflation. But an increasing number of economists as well as officials, bankers, economic journalists and others have become convinced that monetary-fiscal policy alone cannot do the job or can do it only at an intolerable price in terms of unemployment and slack. By 1970 demand inflation, they say, had been squeezed out of the system by tight money.[1] What remains is cost inflation which can be curbed only by incomes policy. (There is agreement however, that the resurgence of inflation in 1973 had nothing to do with wage or cost push.)

Although incomes policy has become a popular issue, as was to be expected, it has not contributed to precise thinking. Originally the term meant something like generalized guideposts. Now it means different things to different people.

I shall distinguish between incomes policy in the original sense as generalized guideposts—incomes policy I, for short—and incomes policy as an assortment of specialized measures designed to improve the working of the price mechanism and bring it closer to the competitive ideal—incomes policy II. The clearest description of incomes policy II has been formulated by Arthur Burns. In the past he had categorically rejected a "guideline" policy.[2] But when as chairman of the Federal Reserve Board he took charge of monetary policy, he soon came to the conclusion that the transition from an inflationary to a noninflationary growth path of the economy could be speeded up and made less painful by the adoption of a variety of measures which he calls "incomes policy." The new incomes policy includes abolishing or changing the minimum wage laws which keep marginal workers out of work; repeal (or suspension) of the Bacon-Davis Act which forces the government to pay highest union wages on its far-flung construction projects; compulsory arbitration of wage conflicts in certain areas (railroads, public utilities, shipping, etc.).

Burns also includes more vigorous antitrust action and import liberalization in his concept of incomes policy because these measures would tend to promote competition and keep down certain prices.[3] This list of measures he regards as illustrative rather than exhaustive.

I shall first discuss incomes policy in the original sense—incomes policy I—and then take up some of the measures of the new concept of incomes policy—incomes policy II.

To repeat, the almost universal approach in industrial countries to the problem of cost-push inflation has become the guideline policy for wages—incomes policy I. Concretely, the attempt is made to restrict wage increases to the rise in average productivity for the economy as a whole (output per man or man-hour). Guideposts and incomes policies are primarily concerned with incomes from employment—wages and salaries. This will also be the main subject of the present chapter. But we must first deal briefly with the tendency to extend incomes policy from wages and unions to profits, prices and business firms.

INCOMES POLICY I

Guideposts for Prices and Profits

In most countries governments and public opinion have been persuaded by social conscience and social impartiality, as well as by purely political consideration, that the policy of restraining and controlling the wage-push must be applied equally to profits and prices. Guideposts and incomes policies must deal with business firms, profits and prices as well as with labor unions, wages and salaries.

The equation of business monopolies and labor monopolies and their equal treatment leads, however, to most unfortunate results, because it completely misjudges the comparative strength of the two and ignores or misinterprets their very different natures which call for different methods of control.[4]

In Chapter 6 it was shown that industrial monopolies and oligopolies do not have the same strength and iron discipline over their members which many unions in most Western countries presently possess. The plain fact is that the American economy is much more competitive than most people realize.[5] The only really important exceptions are public utilities (transportation, communication, etc).[6] These industries are government owned and operated, or if still in private hands, prices are closely controlled, usually overcontrolled.

If public utility prices have become a problem for anti-inflation policy, it is because of the wage-push of powerful unions of labor in these industries. The monopolistic nature of the industry and essentiality of their services confers monopoly power on the unions. By shutting down vital services or threatening to do so, they obtain large wage increases and force the regulatory agencies to permit large price increases. In this way monopoly profits, which rate controls try to prevent, are effectively transferred to labor.

In the service and manufacturing industries, outside the area of natural monopolies, no price guidelines are needed. Free trade plus antitrust policy in the broad sense are sufficient safeguards against monopolies. Free trade is a very effective antimonopoly measure, particularly in small countries, but also in the United States, blessed though it is with a large internal free trade area. A steadily increasing volume of imports resulting from tariff reductions, cheaper transport, and the rise of competing industries in many foreign countries has made the economy increasingly competitive. Few monopolies can survive without government-imposed import restrictions. Quantitative restrictions, such as quotas, are even more damaging to competition than tariffs. Particularly detrimental and destructive are the so-called "voluntary" export restrictions imposed on foreign producers of steel, textiles and other products; for this policy induces or forces foreign producers to organize themselves in monopolistic cartels at the expense of the U.S. consumer. "Voluntary" import restrictions in effect allot the monopoly profits from imports to foreign exporters instead of capturing them for the home treasury, as in the case of tariffs.[7]

The upshot of this discussion is that the extension of the guideline policy to prices outside the area of "natural monopolies" (public utilities) involves either ineffective exhortation or detailed price controls, with all their invariable accompaniments. These include development of "black" or "gray" markets, creation of unearned profits for some people and losses for others, gradual destruction of the allocative function of the price mechanism and the substitution of formal or informal rationing for market forces, proliferation of red tape and bureaucracy, corruption and diversion of scarce high-powered skills from productive uses to the socially unproductive activities of complying with, or evading governmental regulations.

Wage Guidelines

A sharp distinction will be made in the following discussion between the objective and target of the guideposts, on the one hand, and the practical problem of implementation and enforcement on the other.

The objective

The purpose is to make the general level of money wages rise roughly in proportion to the long-run growth of average productivity (output per man-hour), say, 2.5 to 3 percent a year for the United States. The objective is laudable and sensible. If wage rates (more precisely the average wage level) could be made to behave in this fashion, the price level would remain approximately stable. This is what would happen under effective competition, if by appropriate monetary policy, the price level is kept stable. Average money wages would then actually rise approximately as the guidepost target postulates. In other words, the guidepost policy ideally seeks to make the economy as a whole and the labor market in particular behave as they would under perfect competition—an objective that should command general approval. We shall see, however, that this favorable conclusion has to be changed radically when problems of implementation are considered in detail. Let us consider first the rule as an ideal.

One objection is that, if wages actually rose in proportion to output per man-hour, all additional output would go to labor. This objection is not valid. If money wages rose according to the rule *and* prices remained constant, the proportion of wage income to other incomes would remain constant; labor and nonlabor incomes would share proportionately in any addition to the GNP.

Another objection to the rule is its alleged inflexibility. If strictly applied, it would rigidly fix the proportion of national income going to labor and nonlabor income including profits. There is more to this objection than to the first. But it should not be forgotten that if wages on the average rose in proportion to average productivity, the price level would remain only *approximately* stable. It can be shown that under certain circumstances the price level *may* have to change somewhat.[8] This is most easily seen by first considering the case of an individual industry which undergoes a rapid process of mechanization and automation; much capital equipment is installed and machines are substituted for labor. A few skilled men now operate an automated plant where formerly many less-skilled men worked with simpler tools. Output per man-hour goes up sharply. Clearly the whole increase in output cannot be attributed to labor, and the rule that the wage should go up in proportion to output per man could not be applied while leaving the price of the product unchanged. There would not be enough left to cover the greatly increased capital-cost. The distribution of income generated by the industry would have to be changed, more going to "capital" and less to labor. This could be accomplished by a higher price of the product if money wages rose in proportion to the larger physical output per man, or by money wages not rising in proportion to the rising output per man if the produce price remained unchanged.

The same may happen in the economy as a whole: When large sectors of the economy are rapidly mechanized and automated, it *may* become necessary that the share of national income going to labor be reduced and the share of nonlabor income including profits be increased.[9] But there is a difference: While for individual industries the equilibrium proportion of income going to labor and capital is often subject to fairly large and rapid changes, for the economy as a whole, as a matter of historical fact, the share of national income going to labor has remained fairly stable over time. It is not entirely constant over long periods (as some writers maintain), but it is not a magnitude that changes rapidly or exhibits large swings over protracted periods. It changes, of course, sharply in the short run; i.e., during the business cycle, profits rising more rapidly than labor income during cyclical expansions and falling more rapidly during contractions.

The empirical fact of the approximate stability in the long run of the share of wage income in national income makes the guidepost formula theoretically acceptable. Prices would remain approximately constant if wages behaved according to the formula.

If money wages rose according to the guidepost target, the small changes in labor's share in national income that may become necessary from time to time in order to maintain equilibrium would be brought about by slight variations in the price level. It can be shown that given the relative constancy of the wage share in national income, small price changes well inside the range of social tolerance would provide sufficient flexibility.[10]

The Implementation

The basic difficulty with the guideline policy of controlling wages lies in the fuzziness of "the average wage level" concept. It is very definitely not a policy variable. The wage *level*, as such, cannot directly be managed and changed by government action. It can be manipulated only indirectly by influencing wages in individual industries and locations.[11] The government can, of course, freeze all wages and permit only uniform percentage changes. But this is disastrous except as a short-run emergency measure and has in fact never been carried out successfully for any length of time.

Most economists agree that for the sake of efficiency *relative* wages must remain flexible. In other words, the relation of wages of workers of different skills and of workers in different localities, industries or even firms must be allowed to reflect changing conditions of demand and supply, expansion and contraction of different industries and firms. Such changes in fact go on ceaselessly. They provide incentives needed to bring about gradual and voluntary transfers of labor from industry to industry, from firm to firm, and to insure maximum employment during the process of adjustment. Governments cannot make the average wage level behave in accordance with the guidepost rule, without at the same time influencing and distorting relative wages. The government cannot simply decree the behavior of the wage level in the abstract. It can influence it only by influencing particular wage contracts. The attempt to manipulate the wage level, without eliminating the wage-push at its source by clipping the monopoly power of labor unions, remains ineffectual exhortation or degenerates into general wage and price control. To repeat, the wage level as such is not a policy variable.

This was implicitly recognized in the formulation of the guidepost policy in the United States.[12] Realizing that a strict mechanical application of the guidepost rule to all industries would be undesirable, it was conceded that for the sake of efficiency and equity a number of exceptions had to be permitted. Some of these were explicitly formulated, leaving others presumably to be spelled out from time to time.

Let me quote from the report of the Council of Economic Advisors for 1962.

The most important modifications are the following: (1) Wage rate increases would exceed the general guide rate in an industry which would otherwise be unable to attract sufficient labor; or in which wage rates are exceptionally low compared with the range of wages earned elsewhere by similar labor, because the bargaining position of workers has been weak in particular local labor markets. (2) Wage rate increases would fall short of the general guide rate in an industry which could not provide jobs for its entire labor force even in times of generally full employment; or in which wage rates are exceptionally high compared with the range of wages earned elsewhere by similar labor.[13]

These "modifications" are sensible, as far as they go. But they don't go far enough as the 1962 report recognized:

Even these complex guideposts leave out of account several important considerations. Although output per man-hour rises mainly in response to improvements in the quantity and quality of capital goods ... employees are often able to improve their performance by means within their own control. It is obviously in the public interest that incentives be preserved which would reward employees for such efforts.

Also ... it must be borne in mind that average hourly labor costs often change through the process of up- or down-grading, shifts between wage and salaries employment, and other forces. Such changes may either add to or subtract from the increment which is available for wage increases under the overall productivity guide. [op. cit. p. 190][14]

A little reflection should convince the reader that a serious attempt to apply these rules and exceptions must give rise to endless disputes. What are "exceptionally low wages" compared "with similar labor" elsewhere? Who is to decide whether alleged wage discrepancies are due to different "bargaining positions of workers" or to some other factors?[15] Who can determine whether "special incentives" are or are not required? Any attempt at consistent application must lead to general wage control, and wage control without price and profit control is politically not feasible.

Actually, little was heard about applying the wage guideposts in concrete cases until about the middle of 1965.[16] When the labor market tightened, attempts at application met with little success. For all practical purposes the guidepost policy was dead by 1966, although it was occasionally reaffirmed by the Council of Economic Advisors under the Johnson administration.[17]

The guidepost policy had to fail because the wage level is not amenable to direct manipulation. It invariably produces ineffectual exhortation or individual wages and price fixing, or both. In other words, it becomes the policy of repressed inflation, the most reprehensible and damaging kind of inflation.

The same is true, to an even greater degree, of guidelines for prices because outside the public utility area industrial monopolies are rare and of little worry as far as inflation is concerned. Wage guidelines, on the other hand, have at least the merit of calling attention to a serious problem—wage-push—and offering a sensible target. But it is one thing to describe in macroeconomic terms how wages and prices should behave; it is an entirely different thing to bring this about without prior restoration of sufficient competition in the labor market.

The truth is that the consequences of the wage-push have to be treated at the source. Excessive monopoly power of labor unions must be curbed somehow and a greater degree of competition restored in the labor market; there is no synthetic substitute for real competition. If union power is not curbed, we shall have to accept more inflation or unemployment or more likely more of both than is desirable from the point of view of stability and growth.

INCOMES POLICY II

The Problem of Restraining Union Power

How to restrain union power is a most intractable problem. No industrial country has found a satisfactory solution. Yet until one is found, there can be no solution of the problem of inflation at full employment. Inflationary wage pressures come only from organized labor. Nonunionized labor has no market power; wages in that area can safely be left to the forces of demand and supply.[18]

A radical solution of the problem would be to forbid industry-wide unions and industry-wide collective bargaining.[19] But in the present political and social environment, this solution is not practical. Is there nothing that can be done to prevent or at least sharply reduce excessive wage pressure by powerful unions? Some well-known economists have indeed reached the defeatist conclusion that nothing can be done and that we have to resign ourselves to the choice between perpetual inflation and substantial unemployment presumably in the form of a stop-go cycle around a rising price trend.

Fortunately there are many less-radical measures available which would help. They have been proposed many times, and some of them have recently found their way into the "new incomes policy." They have, however, never been applied systematically and consistently and should be tried out and given a chance before throwing in the sponge and accepting unpalatable alternatives.

To begin with, labor unions have acquired over the years, *de jure* or *de facto,* numerous important immunities and privileges which go far beyond anything accorded to business or other private associations.[20] Legal reforms designed to restore a more balanced power equilibrium between the parties in wage bargaining would surely have considerable effect in reducing the power of unions and relieving inflationary wage pressure. It should be possible in particular to force them to abstain from violence and intimidation. If unions and their leaders were held financially responsible for damages caused by breach of contracts, illegal strikes, intimidation and violence, considerable moderation in wage bargains could be expected.[21]

Repeal of minimum wage laws, or at least their modification by size-of-community differentials and by lower minimums for teenagers, would help. Size-of-community differentials would spur competition within the internal American market. Repeal, of course, would be still better, for any minimum wage creates unemployment among marginal workers (unskilled workers, the elderly, teenagers) and strengthens union power even though the minimum is well below prevailing union scales. This is because the minimum contributes to "the overpricing of unskilled labor relative to skilled labor."[22] This overpricing makes it profitable for employers, wherever possible, to substitute skilled labor for unskilled labor, sometimes directly, sometimes through the use of expensive capital equipment.

Repeal or a simple reinterpretation of "the prevailing wage" clauses in the Bacon-Davis and Walsh-Healey Acts, in the way the Congress presumably intended, would greatly strengthen competition. The Bacon-Davis Act is largely responsible for the "skyrocketing" of wages and costs in the construction industry.[23] The Walsh-Healey Act has channeled billions of dollars in federal funds to unionized firms located in the larger cities in the more industrialized parts of the country.[24] As matters now stand, the federal government is encouraging the very inflation it is trying to curb.

Equally important would be the repeal (or the reinterpretation) of laws which, as we have noted earlier, subsidized strikers and their dependents and nonstrikers thrown out of work (as a result of disputes of no concern to them), and subsidize them so generously as to remove what Professor Meade called "the terror of temporary unemployment." Withdrawal of these subsidies would make strikes much more costly and greatly reduce union power and wage pressure.[25]

An amendment of our social security laws to encourage the elderly to continue working without losing their pension rights would increase the labor supply, make the labor market more competitive, and would be a blessing to many who are forced or induced into unwilling retirement. Enforced idleness is a great social evil. The ideal solution would be to give those eligible for old age pensions the option to earn a larger pension in the future by continuing work. Such a reform would increase the money cost of social security but this would be offset to a considerable extent by the increased output of those electing to continue to work.

Just as repeal of the Fair Labor Standards Act, or its amendment by the introduction of regional or size-of-community differentials, and the reinterpretation of the "prevailing wage clauses" in the Bacon-Davis and Walsh-Healey Acts would increase the vigor of interstate competition in the American domestic market, so a further lowering of the tariff barriers around this market would enormously increase international competition. In brief, it would be very easy to increase vigorous competition in the product markets if the majority of the American people really wanted it. And increased competition in the product markets always weakens monopoly power in labor markets.

Wage and Price Freezes

Before summarizing the results of our analysis of guidelines and incomes policies, two related antiinflation measures should be mentioned. The first, a wage freeze and price stop has been tried out in many countries without success, except perhaps in the very short run; the second, tax measures against excessive wage or price increases, have been proposed as a substitute for guidelines and wage or price freezes.

A general or partial wage or price freeze is a radicalized version of the guidepost policy. As such, it has all the deleterious effects of the latter in pronounced form: It eliminates market forces, it quickly leads to distortions of the price and wage structure by making adjustment to changing conditions impossible, it creates gray or black markets. It is strictly a short-run emergency measure. If maintained for longer than a few months, it becomes necessary to make more and more exceptions in order to eliminate the most glaring distortions and inequities. Thus, it breaks down or degenerates quickly into general wage and price control.

A policy of general or partial wage and price freezes has a strong tendency to destabilize the economy. Since the freeze cannot be maintained for long, there is great danger that when it breaks down or is lifted, prices and wages will shoot up. The policy thus leads to instability or else it degenerates into general price and wage control. Emergency situations are conceivable in which short-run effects are the primary purpose. The outbreak of a war or revolution leading to panic buying, hoarding of goods and nonhoarding of money are examples. A decision to halt a raging wage-price spiral (a combination of demand and cost inflation) by a sharp step on the monetary brake may be another example of an acute emergency that could possibly justify a strictly temporary wage or price freeze until the monetary measures take hold. Still another purpose which cannot be excluded is to win an impending election; in the eyes of the government this may justify a temporary price stop, although hardly a wage freeze.

It should be clear, however, that cost-push inflation and the union wage pressure from which modern industrial countries suffer are definitely not acute emergency situations. They are on the contrary a chronic disease, especially "after excess demand has been eliminated," as the now often repeated phrase goes. These conditions cannot be dealt with by short-run emergency measures such as price stops and wage freezes which only suppress symptoms, produce instability and create inefficiencies and waste.

On August 15, 1971, in a complete reversal of its earlier policy the Nixon administration introduced a ninety-day wage and price freeze which was followed by fairly detailed wage and price controls. In a similar reversal of earlier professions the conservative British government of Edward Heath followed the American example in November 1972.

The American freeze came when inflation was already on the wane. The rise of the consumer price index had steadily decreased from over 6 percent in early 1970 to about 4 percent when the freeze was imposed. The deceleration of inflation continued under the freeze and the following period of controls.[26] The American policy thus was in step with the downward trend of inflation which had been brought about by earlier monetary and fiscal restraints.

It is possible to argue that the controls helped somewhat by moderating some excessively high wage settlements and keeping some price increases at a lower level. But against these modest gains must be set high administrative costs, some distortions of which have come to light[27] and which are bound to become more numerous with the passage of time and the probability that in the future, after the controls have expired, businessmen (reckoning with their possible reintroduction) will be reluctant to make price cuts which they otherwise would have made. In summary we may say that the American wage and price control program inaugurated in August 1971, since it went *with* the trend of disinflation produced by basic monetary policy, has not had much impact, possible modest gains being more or less offset by moderate damages.[28] (See postscript on the 1973 price freeze, Preface.)

The British freeze presents a very different picture. It was introduced in a period of accelerating inflation, explosive growth of money supply and excessive wage increases. It thus came at the time of an acute emergency. This makes the British move more defensible from the economic standpoint than the American freeze. But unless monetary support for the anti-inflation policy is forthcoming, the new start has no chance of success.

Tax Measures Against Wage-Push

Numerous suggestions have been made to impose tax penalties of some kind on price and wage increases. In the United States, Henry Wallich has proposed a special wage tax on employers who grant wage increases over and above a certain norm. In order to make a policy of wage restraint acceptable to labor, Sir Roy Harrod has proposed to supplement the excess-wage tax by a surtax on dividend payments exceeding the "normal" growth rate.[29]

The wage tax is supposed to stiffen the resistance of employers to wage demands. This approach is clearly superior to rigid guidelines or wage freezes because it does not destroy the price mechanism and leaves a certain elasticity in the structure of relative wages; for if it is necessary to attract additional labor, the employer can offer higher wages at the additional cost of the tax.

Naturally the higher the tax the greater the potential distortions and inequities. Thus, the administrative problems would become more and more serious especially if the wage tax were introduced (as in practice it would be) in the midst of an inflation, which has had an uneven impact on different industries and firms. Starting from a distorted situation it would be necessary from the outset to make numerous exceptions for industries and firms that had lagged behind in the inflation race. If no exceptions were made the "excess-wage tax" would have the same type of increasingly distorting effects as guidelines, although presumably to a somewhat lesser extent.

But why should such a complicated system of excess-wage and excess-profit taxes induce more resistance on the part of employers to excessive wage demands than would be induced, without any additional difficulties and administrative complications, by keeping a suitably tight rein on aggregate demand through an appropriate monetary and fiscal policy? The trouble with the monetary-fiscal approach during a cost-inflation is, as we have seen, that powerful labor unions by the strike threat force wage increases which the employers cannot absorb. If money is sufficiently tight to prevent employers from passing on the higher wage costs in the form of higher prices, a curtailment of production and rise in unemployment will result. There is no reason to believe that an excess-wage or excess-profit tax would change the dilemma in any way. If the employer cannot absorb the tax, he has to pass it on (together with the wage increase) in the form of higher prices or curtail output and employment. Similarly, there is no reason whatsoever to assume that unions would moderate their wage demands if the resistance of employers to higher wages stems from an excess-wage or profit tax, rather than being the result of tight aggregate demand.[30]

SUMMARY

The results of our analysis of guidelines and incomes policies can be summarized as follows: Both address themselves to the problem of wage-push inflation, supplementing basic monetary and fiscal restraints. Wage-push has become a very serious problem, jeopardizing stability, growth and employment.

We distinguish two policy types—incomes policy I, a generalized guidelines policy, and incomes policy II, an assortment of specialized measures designed to eliminate monopolistic restrictions and market imperfections in different sectors of the economy. Incomes policy II strengthens the market and works with and through the price mechanism. Incomes policy I seeks to create a substitute for market forces; while intentionally beneficial, it actually hinders and disorganizes the functioning of the market.

The generally accepted formula for wage guidelines—that the wage *level* should rise in proportion to the rise in *average* labor productivity (output per man-hour)—is a sensible and laudable objective; for in a smoothly working competitive economy, in which prices are kept stable by monetary management, the average wage would in fact rise approximately in proportion to the rise in labor productivity.

This favorable judgment must, however, be reversed when the problems of implementation are considered. The fact is that the *average* wage is not a policy variable. It cannot be manipulated by the government without affecting—freezing and distorting—*relative* wages. Economists agree that relative wages must be allowed to change in response to the changing pattern of demand and supply as it affects different types of labor. Such changes are, in fact, going on ceaselessly in our economy and are essential for its efficient working.

Incomes policy I has nowhere worked well for any length of time. Enforced, it either freezes the pattern of relative wages or else degenerates into detailed fixing of specific wages and prices. In either case the performance of the economy is progressively impaired.

Price stops and wage freezes are radical versions of the guideline policy. They quickly disorganize and destablize the economy. Emergencies are conceivable when short-run effects are of the essence. But wage-push is a chronic disease which cannot be treated with short-run emergency measures.

An "excess payroll tax" on wage increases above the guide-line norm has been proposed as a substitute for guidelines and wage freezes to stiffen employers' resistance to excessive wage demands. Such a tax would be preferable to the crudities of guidelines and wage freezes. But analysis reveals serious difficulties of implementation, and there are compelling reasons to doubt that the tax method of restraining the wage-push would be more effective than tight monetary management. The latter, too, stiffens employers' resistance, but it cannot prevent the wage-push from creating unemployment. It is not clear why tax measures would be more successful.

What shall we conclude? Is it that nothing can be done to check the wage-push? Definitely *not.* What we should conclude is that the problem of the wage-push has to be attacked at its source. The excessive power of labor unions should be curbed. There exists no synthetic substitute for restoring a greater measure of competition in the labor market and elsewhere.

Radical solutions, such as prohibition of industry-wide bargaining and dissolution of industry-wide unions, are politically impossible. Fortunately, there exist many other measures that would moderate the wage-push, if systematically applied. Examples are withdrawal of the special legal or de facto privileges which tilt the scale in collective bargaining heavily in favor of the unions; modification of minimum wage laws; and changes in policies which in effect subsidize strikes, such as unemployment and welfare payments to strikers.

Industrial monopolies or oligopolies are not much of a problem as far as inflation is concerned. Prices in the public utility area, "natural monopolies," are controlled, usually over-controlled, anyway. But measures that promote competition, e.g., more vigorous antitrust action or liberalization of imports, have not only a directly favorable effect on prices but also curb union power; for market power in product markets always strengthens the market power of labor unions.

These and other measures constitute incomes policy II. Any one of these measures in isolation, although desirable, would have no appreciable effect on inflation. But collectively they would have a strong impact.

If not enough is done along these lines, we will have to resign ourselves to more inflation and since inflation sooner or later must be restrained by monetary measures, the result will be more unemployment, lower output and slower growth. The suboptimal performance of the economy will take the form of an intensification of the familiar stop-go cycle, playing around a rising rather than horizontal price trend.

Postscript on the 1973 Price Freeze [31]

In January 1973, on the generally accepted but mistaken assumption that inflation would continue to abate, price and wage controls were greatly relaxed. Phase III was substituted for Phase II. This move unfortunately coincided with the resurgence of inflation. Journalists, politicians and many economists jumped to the conclusion that the relaxation of controls was responsible—*post hoc ergo propter hoc.* Actually the recrudescence of inflation had virtually nothing to do with the relaxation of controls. The spectacular price rise had already started and was largely concentrated in the uncontrolled agricultural and food sectors and the international markets for raw material. Nor had depreciation of the dollar anything to do with the relaxation of controls.

Nonetheless, the hysterical demand in the news media and in the Congress for immediate imposition of controls found such a ready echo in public opinion, particularly after the Watergate affair, as to make the demand politically irresistible. It was a good stick with which to beat the administration. The Democratic caucus in the Senate voted unanimously to press for a "90-day freeze on prices, profits, rents, wages and salaries, and consumer interest rates"; many Senators demanded a rollback of prices. In June the administration yielded to the pressure and imposed a sixty-day freeze on prices, but not on wages, followed in August by Phase IV.

The 1973 price stop ran into trouble right from the beginning. Serious shortages, especially of beef, developed quickly and the freeze had to be dismantled ahead of schedule.

It is not hard to understand why the seemingly successful

136

experiment of 1971 could not be repeated in 1973. In the first place, the success of the 1971 price freeze and the following Phase II was largely an illusion; the rate of inflation had been declining anyway because there was still unemployment and slack in the economy. The year 1973, in contrast, was a year of full employment and rapidly rising prices. In the second place, two years of controls had taught a lesson: people had learned how to anticipate and evade the controls. Let me mention only one perfectly legal method of evasion which has become increasingly important: Since export and import prices are uncontrolled, it often pays to export commodities and reimport them in processed or unprocessed form. Naturally no precise figures are available, but many cases have come to light involving important commodities such as aluminum, lumber, steel, even petroleum products. To close these leaks, the size of a barn door, would require detailed supervision of imports and exports.

The debacle of the 1973 freeze had a sobering effect on Congress and the public. Many of the senators who had demanded a general ninety-day freeze of everything, asked for the lifting of the price stop on beef when beef disappeared from the shelves. After termination of the freeze there came the expected price bulge. Phase IV continues; its purpose now is said to be to "stretch out" the price bulge created by the freeze, after which controls are to be phased out. But, in the meantime, controls have produced "scarcities" of dozens of commodities, which provoke revived demands for rationing. In a free market there can be no scarcities in the sense of actual excess demand, for the free-market price automatically allocates scarce supplies to competing demands.

The general disenchantment with controls is a most salutary development. But there is danger that it may go too far. The unfortunate thing was that controls were imposed indiscriminately on a largely competitive economy. The failure of this policy should not be allowed to compromise monopoly controls, especially of the monopoly power of labor unions. True, the 1973 inflationary spurt was a classical case of demand inflation. It was not brought about by wage pressures. Actually wages lagged behind prices. But they are now catching up. Workers' earnings (including fringe benefits) are rising by more than 7½ percent. This may not be excessive under rapid inflation. But can the money wage growth be reduced to, say, 3 or 4 percent, probably the maximum compatible with approximately stable prices? Wage push will be the main stumbling block for regaining price stability.

Chapter 8

International Aspects of Growth and Stability

INTRODUCTION

Until now we have discussed the problems of growth and stability from the point of view of a closed economy and have only hinted that impulses, favorable or unfavorable, for growth and stability may come from abroad. This neglect does not mean that the international influences are unimportant. On the contrary, all countries of the modern world are embedded in the world economy. They are more or less closely linked with one another through commodity trade, exchange of knowledge and ideas, international travels and migration, financial flows of money and capital. This interconnectedness is of paramount importance for growth and stability. Modern economic development cannot be fully understood and explained without reference to the currents of international trade, the flows of ideas and capital and the movements of men between nations.

Awareness of this has moved one of the wisest and most perceptive economists of all times, Alfred Marshall, to make the somewhat puzzling pronouncement that "the causes which determine the economic progress of nations belong to the study of international trade."[1]

Stability, too, is strongly influenced, favorably or unfavorably at times, from the outside. Especially price stability and inflation are for all countries—except the largest ones, the U.S. and the USSR—determined from the outside, at least under a regime of fixed exchange rates. Thus, the postwar inflation is essentially an international phenomenon and so were periods of inflation—and deflation—under the rule of the gold standard. Some countries, of course, inflate more than others. But then they have to devalue their currency. Under a regime of fixed exchange rates it is impossible for any one country to stay out of an inflationary (or deflationary) trend in the rest of the world. Whether and to what extent it is possible for any one country to maintain price stability and to ward off other threats to economic stability (e.g., to full employment) in an inflationary or deflationary world, by periodically changing or by floating its exchange rate, will be discussed in Section B of this chapter.

Nonetheless, the validity of the conclusions reached up to this point are not impaired by our failure to stress international influences. What we are trying to do in the present chapter is to apply what has been said about growth and stability in a "closed" economy to "open" and "interrelated" economies. The theory of international trade, in its monetary and non-monetary (real) aspects, is one of the most highly developed branches of economics. What we have to do is to apply it to the problem of growth and stability.

The subject divides quite naturally into two distinct, though interconnected parts. The first is the long-run influence on growth of the international division of labor and trade and of international transfers of real resources (labor, capital, know-how, ideas, entrepreneurship), *assuming that the international monetary mechanism works smoothly* and does not become the source of disruptions through the transmission of inflationary or deflationary disturbances and disequilibria from country to country. This assumption is made for purely expository purposes, namely to separate the long-run real contribution to growth that international trade can make from short-run monetary influences. Actually, malfunctioning of the international monetary mechanism often reduces the contribution to economic welfare and growth that international trade can make. But monetary disturbances can be prevented or minimized by appropriate monetary institutions and policies.

In Section A, *International Trade and Economic Growth,* we consider the contribution trade can make to long-run growth under the assumption that the monetary mechanism works smoothly and efficiently. Later in Section B, *International Aspects of Economic Stability and Stabilization Policies,* we discuss the functioning of the international monetary mechanisms under different institutional arrangements (gold standard, Bretton Woods system, flexible exchange rates, etc.) and consider methods of improving their operations.

SECTION A:
INTERNATIONAL TRADE AND ECONOMIC GROWTH

The Basic Facts

What contribution does international trade make to economic growth? The short answer is a tremendous contribution. Without international trade modern growth would be all but impossible. It is one of the weaknesses of Communist countries that centrally planned economies are congenitally incapable of taking full advantage of the opportunities for increasing productivity and stimulating growth offered by international trade and division of labor.[2]

The most conspicuous, physical fact underlying and necessitating international trade is the uneven geographical distribution of natural resources indispensable for economic growth—agricultural land, suitable climate, minerals, fuels, etc. Naturally, the smaller a country, the more dependent it is on imports. But even the largest—the United States, China and the USSR—lack vital ingredients of growth and are insufficiently supplied with others.

Moreover, even if two or more countries were fully endowed with all productive resources required for modern growth, it is inconceivable that their endowments would be the same. Each would be comparatively better supplied with some ingredients than others. This makes international trade privately profitable and socially productive. Thus, trade raises the level of output and, since part of the larger output will be saved and invested, increases also rates of growth.

Technological progress and discoveries of new methods and of hitherto unknown resources (fuels, minerals) sometimes increase, sometimes reduce, a nation's dependence on imports. Exhaustion of raw material deposits frequently increases dependence on imports. The unceasing progress of transportation and communication technology, which has been exceedingly fast in the last few decades, reduces the cost and increases the speed of transporting goods and transmitting communications, thus multiplying the opportunities for and the importance of international trade.

Technological knowledge and human skills are as important for economic growth as material means, and international trade is a provider of both. It transmits ideas, knowledge and skills from country to country. The less-developed countries stand to benefit most from international trade and exchange of knowledge and skills. But the industrially advanced countries are not equally developed, and the comparatively less advanced can learn from the more advanced ones. In fact, the learning process is multidirectional; people in all countries can learn from one another.

There is another very important way in which trade increases output and accelerates growth: It thwarts monopoly and promotes healthy competition. This is especially important for small and less-developed countries, because the domestic markets of even the largest among the latter are too restricted to permit full utilization of the advantages of large-scale production in many branches of industry. In many cases only international trade can provide such markets.

But even in a big country like the United States, endowed though it is with a large internal free trade area, imports have greatly helped maintain competition in many lines of industry and have much enlarged the available assortment of both consumer goods and capital equipment, thus contributing materially to consumer satisfaction and to the productivity of American industry.

Let me summarize: The short answer to our initial question is that international trade has made and is still making a tremendous contribution to economic growth, especially of the backward countries. Without the stimulus, resources and knowledge from the outside world, development and growth would have been immeasurably slower and in many cases might not have started at all. That the short answer holds true with only minor qualifications must not be obscured by the fact that a large part of the scientific and popular literature on the subject deals with real and imaginary exceptions to the rule, and that trade policy, especially in less-developed countries, often seems to be based on the conviction that trade as a rule is detrimental and not beneficial to prosperity and growth.

Free Trade and Protection

From what has just been said it does not follow, however, that literally free trade is necessarily the optimal policy for promoting rapid development and growth. Most economists, including those who are in principle free traders,[3] concede that judicious deviations from the free trade policy may, in many cases, accelerate growth, especially in industrially and technologically less-developed countries. To what extent this is possible and under what conditions is an enormously complicated and controversial question.

Here is not the place for a thorough discussion of the ancient problem of free trade and protection or, as it is now euphemistically called, the policy of "import substitution" (substitution of domestic production for imports) by means of tariffs, quotas, import prohibition and many other types of measures. I must confine myself to basic principles.

It should be recalled that in this section we discuss deviations from free trade, that is protection or import substitution, designed to stimulate growth of the *economy as a whole* and not merely to protect or promote the development of any particular industry irrespective of what this policy does to overall growth. Furthermore, we abstract in this section from monetary disturbances caused by malfunctioning of the international monetary mechanism. These assumptions rule out (1) protection for the purpose of warding off deflationary influences from abroad ("protecting the balance of payments"), (2) protection as an antidepression measure to simulate aggregate effective demand, and (3) protection to prevent or alleviate unemployment in particular industries threatened or damaged by foreign competition. Historically, balance-of-payments difficulties and general depressions or recessions, as well as unemployment in particular industries, have often been extremely important motives for general or selective protection.

In case (1) and (2) we obviously have problems of economic stability of the kind we discussed in earlier chapters. There we saw that these problems, especially the problems of preventing or alleviating depressions and recessions, have to be dealt with by general monetary and fiscal policies. In the next section it will be shown that if internal policies of stabilization are impeded by international factors (balance-of-payments difficulties) or if stability is threatened by inflationary or deflationary impulses from abroad (via the balance of payments), the proper and effective response is exchange rate changes combined with appropriate domestic monetary and fiscal policies and *not* import restrictions or export subsidies.

In the third case—unemployment in particular industries caused by imports—measures to hasten and facilitate the transfer of labor and other productive resources to other industries can be justified. Examples are retraining of workers and unemployment relief measures to reduce the pains of adjustment and transition. But a policy of protection to keep alive firms or industries whose products can be imported more cheaply from abroad has no economic justification; it would be an antigrowth and not a growth policy. Exactly the same has to be said about subsidies and tax measures to keep those export industries that have lost their competitiveness in the world market alive.

However, the problem of governmental assistance in the process of industrial adjustment is not easy. There are very serious administrative difficulties, and there is always the danger that generous assistance to reduce the pains of adjustment will indefinitely postpone the transition to a more efficient allocation of resources and thus reduce the rate of growth.

Fortunately experience has demonstrated many times that, especially in the industrial area, the transitional difficulties of adjustment to freer trade have been greatly exaggerated. The adjustment has been smooth and often almost painless whenever deficiencies in aggregate effective demand (deflation and general unemployment) have been avoided by appropriate monetary and fiscal policies. For example, when the European Economic Community (EEC or European Common Market) was formed in the 1950s there was much apprehension that the rapid reductions in tariffs between the six original member countries might cause serious dislocations in the industrially weaker members (Italy, France). Actually there were no serious adjustment difficulties, and the complete elimination of tariffs on industrial products was accomplished ahead of schedule.[4]

To summarize, protection to alleviate a recession or depression or to remove a deficit in the balance of payments, as well as protection to prevent transitional unemployment caused by imports, cannot be justified as growth measures. As far as growth is concerned, it is the so-called "infant industry" type of protection that is relevant.

The Infant Industry Argument for Protection

The infant industry theory of protection goes back almost to the beginning of man's theorizing about international trade. It was popular in the late eighteenth and early nineteenth centuries in the United States and Germany, which were underdeveloped countries at that time as compared with Great Britain.[5] Many "free trade" economists accept the infant industry argument at least in principle as an exception to the free trade rule particularly in the case of industrially less-developed countries. The postwar period has seen a great revival of interest in the infant industry idea in connection with the pressing problem of development of less-developed countries. In the modern literature the theoretical analysis has been greatly elaborated and refined. The new versions of essentially the old idea come now in new terminologies such as "disguised unemployment," "lower wages and lower productivity of labor in agriculture than in industry," "dynamic external economies" and the like.[6]

The basic idea is that new ("infant") industries in less-developed countries are handicapped vis-à-vis their established competitors abroad because they have to work with inexperienced, untrained, inefficient and hence—despite low wages—expensive labor. The concept "labor" is to be understood in the broadest sense including labor of management and entrepreneurship. But these inexperienced and untrained workers and managers, if given a chance by protection from imports or by direct subsidies, will gradually acquire experience and skills, their efficiency will increase and labor costs will decline; thus in due time infant industries will "grow up" and eventually be able to meet foreign competition without protective crutches.

The analysis could be indefinitely elaborated and refined, different methods of giving encouragement to new industries (e.g., import restrictions vs. cash subsidies) could be compared,[7] chances of success, failure and misuse could be evaluated. But space permits only a few remarks. Most economists agree that there is a kernel of truth in the infant industry idea. What should be kept in mind, however, is that even successful infant industry protection implies a temporary, possibly heavy, sacrifice in the form of higher prices and heavier real cost of the previously imported and now locally produced commodities. Infant industry protection thus implies compulsory saving. It is a case of what is now often called "investment in human beings," investment in human skills, training and experiences. (The old infant industry idea is also linked with the modern theory of "on-the-job training.") Like any other investment this type too, even if eventually successful, involves a temporary but possibly severe reduction in the standard of living.[8]

Lessons of History

Let us now ask the question of how successful infant industry protection has been. What contribution has it actually made to economic growth of less-developed countries in different parts of the world, in our time and in former periods?

It is easy to find examples of apparently successful infant industry protection. There exist in many countries industries that have enjoyed protection from imports in their formative years and have eventually become viable and competitive, some even to the point of becoming exporters themselves. But there is always the question whether they would not have grown up, perhaps more slowly but with less temporary pain and deprivation, if protection had been withheld. And whether long-run growth of GNP of the economy as a whole has really been accelerated by protection is an entirely different question which cannot be answered by pointing to particular industries that have grown up under tariff protection.

Proponents of infant industry protection and "import substitution" almost invariably claim that the now developed countries—the United States, Germany, France, Japan, etc.—owe their development in the nineteenth century to protection from the overpowering competition of the old established British industries. Actually the verdict of history is very different.

The German Case

German industry in its formative years had very little protection until the end of the 1870s. Duties under the German Zollverein (Customs Union) which preceded the creation of the German Reich in 1871 were very low, and during the first eight years of its existence imperial Germany pursued what by modern standards can only be described as free trade policy. The protectionist policy which Bismarck inaugurated in 1879 and which his successors continued and intensified was the opposite of infant industry protection. High duties on food imports slowed industrialization, while high duties on iron and steel was a handicap for manufacturing, especially the engineering, machinery, and electrical equipment industries on which German's economic future was largely based.

The French Case

French policy in the post-Napoleonic period was highly protectionist. Economic historians are unanimous in their opinion that it was very poorly conceived and held up French industrialization and economic development. In 1860 France concluded the famous Cobden-Chevalier treaty of commerce with Great Britain. It put France on something close to a free trade basis and led to rapid industrialization. During the 1880s France gradually returned to highly protectionist policies. Just

148

as in Germany these policies which included high protection for agriculture were definitely not of the infant industry type; they slowed the pace of industrialization and reduced the rate of growth.

The Japanese Case

The conclusions to be drawn from the rapid industrialization of Japan are not much different from those for Germany and France. True, from the time Japan was forced out of its long isolation the government actively sponsored industries, but it soon turned them over to private enterprise. In the nineteenth century import restrictions through tariffs played a minor role because international treaties imposed by the Western powers prohibited their use. According to Professor Rosovsky, one of the most knowledgeable experts on Japanese industrial development, "the policy of enforced free trade had very beneficial effects. It made the private sector concentrate its efforts along the line of comparative advantage—and with considerable success. The government's efforts emphasized the rapid development of exports in the areas in which it had a true comparative advantage, especially textiles." Later "the Japanese textile industry became the perfect example of private entrepreneurial success."[9]

In the twentieth century, after the ending of the international treaty restrictions, Japanese policy turned protectionist and in recent years there have been many complaints about Japanese protectionism in connection with Japan's strong balance of payments and the undervaluations of the yen. But Japanese industry has long ago passed the infant industry stage.

The American Case

As mentioned above, the infant industry idea found an early, able and eloquent expression in Alexander Hamilton's famous *Report on Manufactures* (1791); it had wide popular appeal and has strongly influenced U.S. tariff history. The United States

149

became, indeed, the classical country of infant industry protection in the nineteenth century.

What was the contribution of protection to the enormous growth of the American economy in the nineteenth century? Fortunately we have Frank W. Taussig's careful and extensive studies of U.S. tariff policies and their bearing on the development of the economy as a whole, and that of particular industries.[10] These studies give little support to the infant industry thesis.

The broad fact is that in the United States the conditions for economic and industrial development were so favorable that tariff protection cannot have been more than a comparatively minor element in the whole picture. It surely has speeded up the growth of particular industries in certain locations, but the great sweep of overall growth was shaped by other more basic factors, especially the successive waves of immigrants from Europe, and was only marginally influenced, favorably or unfavorably, by tariff policies. These policies, it should be noted, have not been uniformly protectionist; periods of high protection alternated with periods of comparatively low duties.[11] But whatever the overall impact of protection, which certainly was not profound and may well have been unfavorable both quantitatively (reducing the secular growth rate of GNP) and qualitatively (fostering the growth of urban slums), more important are the lessons taught by certain internal developments inside the U.S. economy.

Taussig drew attention to the fact that inside the United States industrial centers sprang up, in the Middle West, later in the Far West and South, although these regions lacked tariff protection from the competition of the old established industries on the Atlantic Seaboard. This was contrary to what one would have expected on infant industry grounds.

The rapid industrial development of the Old South which got underway around 1900 despite lack of tariff protection is all the more remarkable because the region was subjected to a number of handicaps, imposed or tolerated by the federal government. These included an unduly burdensome fiscal system, discriminatory freight rate structure and later minimum wages and similar burdens tailored to the needs of the more highly developed North.[12]

The Case of Modern Less-Developed Countries

None of the examples cited above offers much comfort to the advocates of "infant industry" protection. Does the extreme protectionism pursued by many of the underdeveloped countries of our times call for a different conclusion? True, many new industries have been created in a number of countries, but the fruits of industrialization at breakneck speed have rapidly acquired a bitter taste. Some of the by-products have been rapid growth of mammoth cities entailing the spread of urban slums and ghettos, monumental pollution in many places, not to mention bureaucratic blight, corruption and trotting or galloping inflation. Even many former enthusiastic advocates of the policy of "import substitution" now recognize that the policy has gone far beyond what can conceivably be justified on infant industry grounds; many have become thoroughly disenchanted by the results.[13] In the last two years two comprehensive statistical studies of the results of forced industrialization by protection in poor countries have been made and several well-known experts have tried to appraise the results of those studies and to sum up the lessons "of empirical observations of twenty-five years of effort to promote economic development in various parts of the world."[14] The picture that emerges is one of complete failure of the policy of extreme protection. A striking example involving gross misallocation and waste of resources and a heavy burden on the economies concerned is the automobile industry in Latin America. This case has attracted wide attention and has been carefully analyzed.[15] By means of sky-high protection and large subsidies through tax privileges and import licences for intermediate goods and equipment, several Latin American countries have attracted automobile firms from Europe, Japan and the

151

United States to set up branches. In 1967 Brazil had ten automobile firms operating; Argentina, eleven; Mexico, eight; Venezuela, thirteen; Chile, ten—compared with four automobile firms in the whole of the United States! Even compared with Europe where the scale of operations is much smaller than in the United States, the output per firm in Latin America is ridiculously small, often less than one-tenth of the average output of European firms. The most amazing waste and inefficiency is in Chile where automobile production is located in a depressed area (Arica) 1,000 miles away from the chief market (Santiago), and is literally a seasonal industry: six months a year are spent in collecting parts which are then assembled in the following six months!

It should be stressed that none of the critics of protectionism cited above, nor the present writer, questions the desirability of diversification through the growth of "secondary" (manufacturing) and "tertiary" (service) industries. Industrialization is a necessary and desirable concomitant of development. What is criticized is the far-reaching substitution of central planning and control for market forces, the disregard of the principle of comparative advantage, the excessive speed of industrialization, the almost exclusive emphasis on manufacturing, especially on heavy industries and neglect of agriculture—all entailed by the policy of extreme protection ("import substitution").

Fortunately the overall picture is not one of universal gloom. There exist a number of developing countries that have *not* pursued the policy of extreme protectionism, and others have turned away from it. It is gratifying, but not unexpected, to find that the countries with moderate tariffs have consistently outperformed the highly protectionist ones. The former exhibit a much higher rate of growth in per capita income, agricultural production has grown faster and their exports, also of manufactured products, have flourished better than in the highly protectionist countries. Outstanding success stories are those of Taiwan, South Korea, Hong Kong, Malaysia, Singapore and Brazil (after she changed her policies).[16]

That éxtreme protectionism is very bad for economic development is easy to prove. But whether moderate tariffs have somewhat accelerated the growth of GNP is still a moot question. It can be shown that moderate tariffs—say, 10-20 percent *ad valorem*—if they do no good could not do much harm, especially if the rates are stable and uniform. It is therefore not unreasonable to advocate a strategy of moderate import duties, especially because import duties are a very convenient source of government revenue. But such duties should not only be low but also stable over time and uniform ("across the board"), leaving it to market forces to determine which industries will profit most.

It should be kept in mind, however, that once a policy of protection is started the temptation is almost irresistible to escalate the policy, to raise and differentiate the rates of duty under pressure of the special interests concerned and according to the whims and fancies of the planners. The temptation is so strong because the first steps of "import substitution" are easy; textiles, shoe and other light industries which are especially suited for poor countries may have developed anyway. Lured by early successes—or what appeared as a success of the policy of protection—it is therefore very tempting to go on and protect by higher duties other industries which become a heavy burden on the economy, drain away resources from agriculture and potential export industries. Many countries have succumbed to this temptation with disastrous results. Moreover experience has shown many times that even if protection has been successful in nurturing some industry to a stage where it could stand up to foreign competition, it is extremely difficult to put the experiment of infant industry protection to the ultimate test of removing the crutches—tariffs—to see whether the infant has really grown up.[17]

In *summary,* the case of the less-developed countries of our times, as documented in recent studies, demonstrates the folly and destructiveness of *high* protection. Nonetheless, *moderate* protection judiciously applied may speed up development. But infant industry protection is a delicate operation. The early steps of import substitution are deceptively easy, and few countries have resisted the temptation to go down the road of excessive protection. Those countries that have kept their tariffs at a moderate level have been rewarded by higher rates of growth of GNP as well as of exports and less inflation compared with the highly protectionist countries. But many of the moderates may well have gone beyond the optimum.

Conclusion

The overall answer to the questions posed in this section is that international trade has made and is still making a tremendous contribution to economic growth and welfare of all countries, rich and poor; and that the less-developed countries stand to gain most from free trade. If the governments of these latter countries allow market forces to price their resources, if in Harry Johnson's words they make "competition" rather than government planning and controls the basic principle of their economic order, they will find that they can produce goods and services saleable in world markets. This will enable them not only to buy in world markets consumer goods, materials and equipment beyond their present capacities to produce, but also to procure know-how and to borrow abroad savings and capital indispensable for rapid growth.

All this is not to deny that moderate import duties may somewhat speed up economic growth. There is a grain of truth in the infant industry argument for protection. But not much should be expected. The history of the now developed industrial countries in their formative years in the nineteenth century suggests that protection was a minor factor in their economic development. The historical record of development of the poor countries in our age is full of examples of countries that have overdone protection with disastrous consequences for growth and prosperity. Countries with moderate protection have consistently outperformed those which have gone further in their policy of import substitution; GNP as well as exports have grown faster in the low tariff countries than in the highly protectionist ones. But it is politically and sociologically extremely difficult to hold the line of moderation. Special interests in the protected industries and the inclinations of government planners conspire to escalate the policy of protection and to substitute the visions of the planners for the forces of the markets.

SECTION B:
INTERNATIONAL ASPECTS OF ECONOMIC STABILITY AND STABILIZATION POLICIES

Introduction

In the preceding section we reached the conclusion that international trade has a powerful favorable effect on long-run growth, and nowhere more so than in the less-developed countries. We assumed, however, that the monetary mechanism works smoothly and permits full realization of the growth-promoting opportunities offered by international trade. While this is generally true for the long run, it is not always true for the short run.

In the present section we discuss these international aspects of stability and note how national stabilization policies are affected by international monetary arrangements.

It will be recalled that by economic stability we do not mean stability of individual firms or industries or regions, but generalized stability of the economy as a whole; in other words, the business cycle in the broad sense of pervasive processes of expansion and contraction of aggregate demand, output and employment accompanied by more or less parallel fluctuations

155

in price levels, nowadays usually around a rising (rather than a horizontal) trend. In the present section we study the international effects, favorable or unfavorable, on stability in that sense.

This analysis is conducted in three stages. *First,* we present a brief and highly idealized picture—a model—of the *gold standard* and of the way it was supposed to function (and to a considerable extent did function in its heydays). Admittedly, there was always a gap between the model and reality. Nonetheless, an understanding of the model will make it easier for the reader to understand the alternative monetary arrangements. Under the gold standard, exchange rates were credibly fixed by the gold parities of the various currencies. The rates were sacrosanct and were changed only in extreme emergencies—wars and revolutions.

The *second* stage is the *Bretton Woods* system, the so-called "par-value system" administered by the International Monetary Fund (IMF) which was set up by an international conference at Bretton Woods (N.H.) at the end of World War II. It was conceived in the shadows of the Great Depression and the international disorders of the 1930s and reflects the thinking of that period.

Under that system, too, exchange rates—"par values"—are fixed. Countries are obligated to peg their currencies to the official par expressed in terms of gold. But the peg is subject to occasional adjustment whenever there exists a "fundamental disequilibrium." Hence, it is often referred to as "the adjustable or jumping peg" system.

The Bretton Woods system has been in force until recently, but it has been raked by a succession of increasingly frequent and violent confidence crises involving all major currencies. This has led to urgent calls for a basic reform in the direction of greater flexibility of exchange rates. The Bretton Woods system finally broke down in March 1973 when extensive floating of all major currencies started. Needless to add, that the International Monetary Fund as a bureaucratic institution continues to function—international institutions may change their names or lose their function but they never die.[17a]

The *third* stage in our analysis is the system of flexible exchange rates. Under this arrangement exchange rates are either determined by demand and supply in free markets like other prices, "floating rates" or "gliding parities," or are subject to frequent small adjustment—in contrast to the prevailing par-value system with its relatively infrequent, discontinuous adjustment of the peg by large jumps.

Historically the three systems—gold standard, Bretton Woods system, and flexible exchange rates—are not sharply separated; one has grown out of the other and there has been considerable overlapping, with different countries adhering to different systems.

In all three cases we shall assume, as a rule, full market convertibility of the various currencies into each other at uniform exchange rates: Under the gold standard at fixed rates; under the Bretton Woods system at fixed parities with occasional, discontinuous jumps; and under flexibility at the prevailing but ever-changing market rates. In other words we assume competitive exchange markets, free of exchange controls imposed by the government.

This is, unfortunately, an increasingly unrealistic assumption. Nowadays few governments refrain entirely from imposing controls. An almost infinite variety exists, ranging from mild controls of capital flows to comprehensive rationing of foreign exchange. A detailed description and analysis of the various control systems is beyond the scope of this study, but some basic principles will have to be discussed.

The Gold Standard

During the rule of the international gold standard in the late nineteenth century until 1914 most currencies were rigidly linked together through their general convertibility into gold.

Bank notes could be exchanged for gold without charge. But currencies could also be converted directly into each other on the exchange market without the intervention of gold. If the market rate between any two deviated slightly from the gold par it became profitable for private traders to present bank notes of the currency below par to the Central Bank for conversion into gold (at face value), and to ship the gold abroad for conversion into the strong currency (at par). Exchange rates could fluctuate slightly between the so-called "gold points" which were determined by the cost of shipping gold from country to country. Thus, the international gold standard provided in effect a common international money. In the last years of the gold standard monetary gold shipments were taken over entirely by official agencies. Under the Bretton Woods agreement the range of permissible fluctuations of exchange rates was fixed at 1 percent on each side of parity and (after 1971) at 2¼ percent.

How the Gold Standard Functioned

If a disequilibrium in international payments developed, corrective forces and policy responses were set in motion. Gold would flow from deficit to the surplus countries, reducing money supply in the former and expanding it in the latter. Prices and costs including wages fell in the deficit countries relatively to the surplus countries which stimulated exports from the deficit countries and checked its imports. The gold flow also tended to raise interest rates in the deficit countries relatively to those in the surplus countries, thus inducing equilibrating capital flows from the surplus countries to the deficit countries.

The smooth functioning of this mechanism, sketched here in barest and idealized outline, clearly depended on several conditions which were more or less fulfilled at the time but were gradually eroded later on.

First, the gold standard had to be accepted in principle. In particular, it had to be taken on faith that the gold supply would remain broadly adequate, neither grossly superabundant or excessively scarce. The gold mystique was indeed very strong. Now it has disappeared, although there still exists a few fervent believers in the gold standard.

Second, gold parities and exchange rates must be credibly fixed and free convertibility (absence of controls) must be assured. This was the case under the rule of the gold standard. As a consequence slight interest differentials were usually enough to bring about equilibrating capital flows which facilitated the adjustment of disequilibria and enabled the system to function with a surprisingly small amount of international reserves (gold stock). A country that developed a deficit in its balance of payments and saw its gold reserve shrink, could stop the gold drain by stepping mildly on the monetary brake; this would attract funds from abroad and enable the country to spread out and make less painful the process of final adjustment by a gradual improvement in the trade balance.

Third, confidence in the fixity of exchange rates and free convertibility required strict observance of appropriate monetary and fiscal policies known as "the rules of the game." Deficit countries must not expand monetary circulation, surplus countries must allow a modest monetary expansion. Under the gold standard these rules were on the whole observed, but later on, for reasons to be given presently, violations became more and more numerous.

Fourth, for governments to observe the rules of the gold standard game it was necessary that prices and money wages should be neither rigid downward nor forced continuously upward by powerful labor unions. Otherwise monetary restraints in deficit countries would produce intolerable unemployment. Actually during the gold standard era money wages, although not as flexible as often pictured in theoretical models, were not so rigid as they became later and there was no wage-push. It was therefore possible, if necessary, to reduce labor costs and prices without creating too much unemployment.

159

The Passing of the Gold Standard

The soil in which the gold standard flourished has been gradually eroded. It was finally swept away in the Great Depression of the 1930s. The gold mystique is gone. Today few experts seriously propose to entrust the international monetary system to the vagaries of gold production in two countries, Russia and South Africa, to the whims of gold hoarders and to the unpredictable changes in demand for gold for industrial uses. Exchange rates are no longer credibly fixed, so that we can no longer count on the help of equilibrating capital movements which was essential for the working of the gold standard. Even large interest differentials will not induce capital flows from surplus to deficit countries, if there is danger that the currency of the deficit country may be drastically devalued or tight controls be imposed. Wages have become totally rigid downward in most countries, and in many countries a strong and continuous upward wage-push is exerted by aggressive labor unions. And most important, partly because of the changed wage situation, violations of the rules of the gold standard game have become more and more numerous. Stable exchange rates and convertibility of the currency are no longer the overriding objective of economic policy. Priorities have changed. Tolerance for unemployment has become very low and whenever there is, or appears to be, a conflict between external and internal equilibrium, internal policy objectives—employment, growth or price stability—take precedence over external policy objectives—payments equilibrium and stable exchange rates. Moreover, the propensity is very strong everywhere to impose direct controls to solve real or imagined conflicts between internal and external equilibrium.

The theory of the international money mechanism, too, has changed profoundly, partly to take account of the changed situation and the new priorities. Economists have had their full share in changing the objectives and priorities of policy makers. The "Keynesian revolution" had a strong impact in the international sphere. But the difference between the Keynesians and their monetarist antagonists is much smaller in the international than in the domestic area. Almost all economists in *both* camps reject the gold standard, and a growing number prefer flexible exchange rates.

Rising dissatisfaction with the working of the gold standard actually antedates Keynes. This was not surprising, for the economic consequences of the gold standard were not always satisfactory, not even with respect to price stability. Price levels were not stable under the gold standard. There were the so-called "long waves" of rising and falling prices (which many economists attributed to changes in gold production due to new discoveries of gold-bearing ore and better methods of extraction),[18] and there were the short-run business cycles with their sharp price fluctuations. In fact, the cyclical fluctuations in price levels were more pronounced under the gold standard than since 1945. The gold standard did not prevent severe depressions in the late nineteenth century, nor the outbreak of the Great Depression of the 1930s.

Economists and policy makers had become cycle conscious long before Keynes and monetary policy was increasingly used to counteract cyclical expansions and contractions.[19] Vigorous anticyclical policies inevitably led to sharp conflicts between the requirements of internal and external equilibrium and to frequent violations of the rules of the gold standard. Although under the gold standard the cyclical movements were roughly synchronous in the countries on the gold standard, the timing and the intensity of the impact of the cycle on different countries was uneven and, most important, the policy reactions to cyclical movements varied greatly from country to country.

Whenever a deficit country suffers from recession and unemployment, there is a clash between the requirements of internal and external equilibrium: unemployment and recession call for expansionary policies, a deficit in the balance of payments requires the opposite. With the growing sensitivity to unemployment, governments of deficit countries give increasing priority to domestic objectives. Similarly, governments of surplus countries suffering from overfull employment and rising prices try to counteract the inflationary effects of their surpluses. How such conflicts can, and actually are, resolved will be discussed presently. Here we note that such conflicts had appeared during the rule of the gold standard and became much more pronounced as policy makers shifted their priorities. Employment, growth and sometimes internal price stability became more important than the fixed exchange rates and equilibrium in balances of payments.

The gold standard broke down with the outbreak of the war in 1914. It was superficially restored in the early 1920s but was definitively swept away and abandoned in the Great Depression. There is now no chance that it will be resurrected, although gold still plays a role, albeit a diminishing one, in the international monetary system because it constitutes a large component of the international reserves of many countries. Even if gold were generously revalued—if its price were doubled or quadrupled which seems very unlikely, but cannot be entirely excluded—it would not mean resurrection of the gold standard. Raising the price of gold would intensify worldwide inflation, but countries surely would not faithfully respect the rules of the gold standard. Deficit countries would not permit contraction of their monetary circulation because such a policy would spell depression and unemployment; nor would surplus countries cheerfully submit to inflation (although this reaction of the surplus countries is perhaps less unlikely than observance of the rules by deficit countries because countries are generally more sensitive to unemployment than to inflation).

The Bretton Woods System
or
The Adjustable Peg

Introduction

The international monetary system of the postwar period, the "Bretton Woods system," differs from the gold standard in two main respects. The *first* "functional" difference is that exchange rates, although fixed in principle, are subject to occasional changes—hence, "adjustable peg"—reflecting the shift in policy objectives which we just discussed. The *second* "institutional" difference is that, while under the gold standard, the international reserves of the participating countries consisted of gold; in the postwar period the role of dollar balances as liquid international reserve assets has steadily grown and come to overshadow gold. From that standpoint the postwar system can be characterized as "the dollar standard" or "the gold-dollar standard." Since 1968 an artificial international reserve asset, "Special Drawing Rights," SDRs—popularly called "paper gold"—has been created and is being issued by the International Monetary Fund. We can therefore speak of a "dollar-gold-SDR standard." There is presently a widespread demand that the role of the dollar be reduced and that of SDRs expanded. The world may be moving in the direction of a SDR or gold-SDR standard. But that is still in the future, and uncertain, although a recent high-level conference of the ministers of finance of the leading countries declared that "the Special Drawing Rights should become the principle reserve asset of the reformed [international monetary] system," replacing gold and dollars.[20] Ministers and governors propose, but in the end the logic of the market may dispose differently.

The first functional aspect of the present system, the adjustable-peg aspect, is more basic than the second institutional aspect that dollars have taken the place of gold. It is, at any rate, more akin to the subject of the present volume and will be the main subject of the next section. But a few words should first be said about the dollar standard and the prospective SDR standard because this issue looms so large in current discussions on the evolving international monetary order.

From the Gold Exchange Standard to the Dollar Standard

The practice of substituting national currencies for gold as an international reserve had already started in the late years of the nineteenth century. Some continental European central banks, notably the Austro-Hungarian National Bank, found it advantageous to hold balances in London and later in New York in addition to gold in their vaults. These balances, fully convertible into gold, yielded interest, something gold did not, and provided an equally easy access to the major financial centers and capital markets of the world. This came to be known as "the gold exchange standard" system. After World War I the practice spread and was actually encouraged in order to economize gold which was widely feared to be insufficient to support the growing needs of world trade.

These fears were not unfounded. Prices in the United States, the dominant economic power, had about doubled since 1914, while the price of gold in terms of dollars—and even in terms of the pound sterling[21]—remained unchanged. The spread of the gold exchange standard certainly was an antideflationist or, in other words, an expansionist factor because it involved an increase in international liquidity and provided the basis for an expansion of the money supply. Thus, it helped sustain the growth of world trade at fairly stable prices in the 1920s. But already at that time there were warnings of the dangers inherent in the pyramiding of credit made possible by the gold exchange standard. Critics later blamed the gold exchange standard for the severity of the Great Depression of the 1930s. In the post World War II period the criticism became much louder. Before examining this criticism we must sketch the later evolution of the system.

In the 1940s and 1950s the gold exchange standard or rather the dollar standard came into its own.[22] The United States had emerged from the war as the undisputed leading economic power and the dollar, which at that time had a large gold backing, was far and away the dominant currency in the whole world. Understandably, the war-torn countries found it cheaper and easier to rebuild their international reserves in interest-yielding dollars rather than in gold. The whole development was unplanned. The dollar standard was not forced on the world by the United States—except in the sense that massive American aid and loans to foreign countries helped them to rebuild their economies and to accumulate dollar balances. Later when foreign countries became worried about their growing dollar reserves, the American attitude also changed. Long before the dollar was formally declared inconvertible into gold on August 15, 1971, the U.S. government encouraged or even pressured foreign governments to take dollars rather than gold and to abstain from asking for their conversion into gold.

It should be stressed, however, that "convertibility" has two different meanings: (a) *asset convertibility,* i.e., convertibility into gold (or SDRs or some other "ultimate" reserve medium); and (b) *market convertibility,* i.e., freedom to exchange dollars for other currencies in the market. While the dollar has been inconvertible in the asset sense for sometime, it has remained fully convertible in the market sense (apart from some restrictions on Americans, not foreigners, as far as investments abroad are concerned). Anyone can use his dollars to buy anything he wants, to invest in the United States or to disinvest, and to convert his dollars into any other currency in the exchange market thus "taking them out of the country." Most other countries have numerous restrictions of varying stringency on the use of their currencies. Only a few countries keep their currencies as fully and freely convertible as the dollar. It is market convertibility, and not gold or asset convertibility, that is important for world trade.

Thus, in the postwar period the dollar has provided the world with an efficient international monetary medium that made possible the spectacular growth of world trade. International trade has grown by leaps and bounds throughout the postwar period. It is a remarkable but widely overlooked and ignored fact that this growth was *not* interrupted nor visibly slowed by the series of recent currency crises. The fact that the dollar, although no longer convertible into gold, has remained fully convertible in the market surely has greatly contributed to that happy outcome.

Critique and Defense of the Dollar Standard

Nonetheless, the gold exchange and the dollar standards have been subjected to increasingly sharp criticism from old-fashioned gold standard advocates such as Jacques Rueff, on the right, and from Professor Robert Triffin, on the left, who recommend turning the IMF into a world central bank with broad money-creating power. Both regard the gold exchange standard as an engine of inflation and hold it largely responsible for the Great Depression. Unless the world monetary system is radically reformed and the dollar replaced by gold (the Rueff position), or by SDRs or some type of world fiat money (the Triffin position), it is bound to collapse with the same disastrous consequences as the collapse of the gold exchange standard in the 1930s.

This impassioned indictment is based on facts and fantasies, actually more on fancy than on fact. Let us try to separate fact from fancy. To make the gold exchange standard responsible for the Great Depression is a gross exaggeration. The liquidation of the gold-exchange standard in the 1930s was an intensifying factor of limited importance compared with the major policy mistakes on the national and international levels which were detailed earlier. The main focal point of the world depression was the catastrophic slump of the American economy and that was due almost entirely to *domestic* American policy mistakes of commission and omission. In view of the great weight of the American economy in the world and given the system of *fixed* exchanges, no matter whether a gold, a gold exchange or a dollar standard, the American depression was bound to spread to the rest of the world.[23] This is, however, not to deny that in many other countries, in Germany for example, similar policy mistakes contributed to making the depression worldwide and catastrophic in its dimensions.

It is true that the dollar standard has inflationary implication for the world if the reserve currency, the dollar, suffers from inflation. Countries on the dollar standard (i.e., that peg their currencies to the dollar) must participate in the U.S. inflation or

166

accumulate indefinite amounts of dollars. Thus, the U.S. inflation since 1965 has embarrassed some countries. The only way
for any country to escape the American inflation was to appreciate its currency or let it float—that is, break away from the
dollar standard or apply severe controls which in effect amount
to disguised appreciation.

A sense of proportion is needed here. The plain fact is that
while many countries complain about imported inflation, most
cheerfully accept it or even inflate more than the United States.
Only a few have been seriously embarrassed. And very few of
these, notably Germany on several occasions, had the insight
and courage to do what needs to be done to escape the
dilemma—namely, to let their currencies float up.[24]

The critics were right, however, when they predicted that the
dollar standard would become increasingly unpopular. As dollar
balances in foreign central banks piled up from about $10
billion in 1959 to $60 billion in July 1972, and to over $70
billion early in 1973, swelled by successive U.S. balance-of-
payments deficits and waves of speculative capital flows from
the U.S., foreign dollar holders became more and more restive.
U.S. inflation, of course, greatly contributed to their discom-
forts. There is now a widespread demand, shared by American
officials, that the role of the dollar as an international reserve
currency should be reduced. Many foreigners regard the dollar
standard as an "exorbitant privilege" (General de Gaulle's
words) for the United States and American officials see in it an
embarrassing burden. There exist innumerable plans for its
replacement by an SDR standard or something similar. This is
not the place for a detailed analysis of these issues and plans. I
must confine myself to a few observations on certain basic facts
and prospects on which we can be fairly certain.

The world-wide dollar standard has gradually been phased
out as more and more countries stopped pegging to the dollar
and let their currencies float. The dollar standard can be said to
have finally passed away when the currencies of the major
European countries and Japan were set afloat in March 1973.

Its demise was accompanied by much financial pyrotechnics, currency crises precipitated by massive speculation, countless emergency meetings of ministers of finance and even heads of state, etc. But what is important for world welfare is the growth of world trade and investment, not the financial firework. Fortunately the end of the dollar standard and its replacement by widespread floating, has not even caused a ripple in the growth of world trade; contrary to the prophecies of doom it came with a whimper and not with a bang.

The demise of the world-wide dollar standard, however, does not signal the end of the role of the dollar in the world economy. Many countries continue to peg their currencies to the dollar and to keep a large part of their international reserves in dollars. We can therefore speak of a "dollar bloc." There are furthermore, as a legacy of the past, the huge official dollar balances—"dollar overhang"—of countries such as Germany, Japan, France, etc., whose currencies are now floating. Thus the dollar is still the world's foremost reserve currency although the role of reserves under floating has diminished.

If in the future the dollar is replaced wholly or in part by SDRs or something like that, and if the main features of the Bretton Woods adjustable-peg system, are retained, the new system would be faced with essentially the same problems as the dollar standard was, including the inflationary bias which under modern conditions any system of fixed or semi-fixed exchange rates is bound to have. We come now to an analysis of these problems.

Parity Changes Under the Bretton Woods System

Under the gold standard exchange rates (parities) were fixed, under the Bretton Woods adjustable-peg system they are subject to change in case of a "fundamental disequilibrium," in the language of the IMF charter.

There have indeed been innumerable parity changes during the IMF era. The relative values of all major currencies have been changed several times, mostly by devaluation of the currencies of more inflationary deficit countries. Parity changes have become the major balance-of-payments adjust-ment instrument. Another method is that of differential infla-tion, surplus countries inflating faster than they really wish to, so as to keep their surpluses in check. There has been no case of real deflation in any deficit country, as under the gold standard, but direct controls were used during the first years after the war on a large scale by deficit countries (e.g., by Great Britain) to keep down imports. The fact that in the modern world defla-tion is out has a very important implication which is not generally recognized. If prices in deficit countries are never allowed to fall and exchange rates are fixed, balance of pay-ments adjustment can be achieved only by inflation in the surplus countries. [24a] It follows that under modern conditions a fixed rate system necessarily has a strong inflationary bias for the world as a whole.

Now under the Bretton Woods system exchange rates were not completely fixed, but they were by no means sufficiently flexible to eliminate the inflationary bias. Let me now trace some of the major parity changes.

After the wholesale realignment of exchange rates of 1949, which brought a drastic devaluation of the British pound and many other currencies vis-à-vis the dollar (and gold), controls were progressively relaxed and the market convertibility of many currencies largely restored.

There followed a period of stable exchanges of the major currencies—except for the French franc which was repeatedly devalued until 1958 when de Gaulle put it on a firm basis, and the Canadian dollar which has floated from 1950-1962 and again since June 1970.

Since 1967 there have been again numerous changes in exchange rates, punctuated by currency crises—speculative capital flights on an increasingly large scale. In August 1971 the dollar was officially declared inconvertible into gold and the "Smithsonian agreement" of December 18, 1971, devalued the mighty dollar and many other currencies in terms of gold and effected a general realignment of parities.

However, the new pattern of exchange rates soon proved to

be inappropriate. In June 1972 sterling was set afloat and there was a speculative attack on the dollar. Late in 1972 the Italian lira came under pressure, and in January 1973 it was allowed to float.

This triggered a chain reaction which in a few weeks led to extensive floating. Speculative funds flowed into Switzerland and the Swiss let the franc float. Thereupon huge sums of dollars rushed into Germany and the Bundesbank (the German Central Bank) bought $6 billion in one week to prevent the mark from going through the roof. On a smaller scale, the same thing happened to Japan and some other countries. Since Germany and Japan refused to appreciate or to float, the United States broke the logjam by offering to devalue the dollar, the second time in fourteen months. The American action (February 12, 1973) brought about a general realignment of parities; numerous currencies were appreciated by different margins vis-à-vis the dollar, but many others were maintained at their former parities.

Contrary to general expectation, the new pattern of parities did not inspire confidence. Another wave of speculation forced the German Central Bank to buy on one day (March 1, 1973) a record $2.7 billion in a vain attempt to keep the rate fixed. The German authorities were forced to let the mark float. After frantic negotiations a decision was reached to let the currencies of Germany, France, Belgium and the Netherlands float jointly against the dollar, as well as against sterling, the lira and the yen.

These events mark the end of the Bretton Woods era, though not in the sense that the IMF as an international institution is finished—international agencies never die—but in the sense that the rigid par-value system has been shattered. It has been superseded by extensive floating, its benefits and limitations will be discussed in the next section on Flexible Exchange Rates, below.

During the recent period of crises the use of direct controls has again been on the increase, largely in the form of capital import controls by surplus countries. Fortunately, unlike what happened in the 1930s, deficit countries have on the whole abstained from restricting imports of goods and services and have relied primarily on parity changes. Thus, international trade and payments are not nearly as tightly controlled as they were in the 1930s and after the war up to the early 1950s.

On the whole the Bretton Woods system, in effect a dollar standard, served the world well. It has permitted a fairly quick resumption of world trade by a gradual removal of the shackles of wartime controls and the restoration of currency convertibility in the market. To repeat, the expansion of world trade has continued in the last few years despite a succession of currency crises. The rash of new control measures have on the whole affected capital movements, especially speculative capital flows rather than current transactions.

Saying that the system on the whole has worked well does not mean that it was perfect. Far from it. There is in fact, widespread agreement that it needs to be reformed and that the main trouble is with the balance-of-payments adjustment mechanism. Exchange rates have been much less rigid than in the 1930s. Therefore the Bretton Woods system has worked much better than the gold standard in its dying days. But parity changes have been jerky and much too slow. Deficit countries and especially surplus countries practically always waited much too long before they changed their parties.

WHY THE ADJUSTMENT IS NOT SMOOTH UNDER THE ADJUSTABLE PEG

How does the mechanism work under the adjustable peg? How does it affect internal stability in the participating countries? An understanding of the basic principles, to be discussed in the following pages, will remain valid and useful whatever the shape of the future reform of the international monetary system.

Why has the system become so crisis-prone? To answer the question, we must *first* explain why balance-of-payments difficulties—in other words, why the fundamental disequilibria which necessitate parity changes—arise so frequently and *secondly* why, under the (adjustable-peg) system, parity changes cannot be made smoothly. Why are they almost always attended by spectacular currency crises, by flows of funds from country to country so massive as to threaten to disrupt international trade? (An exception was the devaluation of the French franc in the summer of 1969; it came unexpectedly during the vacation period.)

The first problem is rooted in the changed objectives (priorities) and methods of macroeconomic policies since the gold standard days which we discussed earlier, and in the fact that the Western world still consists of sovereign states with different, or at any rate insufficiently coordinated, national policies. The result is significant differences in price-level stability and inflation rates in different countries.

The crucial factors can best be identified by asking why there are no balance-of-payments troubles inside a country between its regions while they are so conspicuous between countries? Nobody ever speaks of California or the Middle West or the U.S. South getting into a deficit vis-à-vis the Northeast of the United States, while the payments balance between Europe and the United States has become a serious problem. In striking contrast the U.S. balance-of-payments with Canada, its most important trade partner, has most of the time not caused any trouble. This is largely due to the Canadian policy of letting the Canadian dollar float. Troubles arose only when Canada had a fixed rate before 1950 and again from 1962 until June 1970 when the float was resumed.

The contrast between the smooth intranational (interregional) and the troublesome international balance-of-payments adjustment has puzzled economists for a long time. Many reasons have been given. The most important one surely is that inside any modern country, monetary, fiscal and incomes or wage policies (if any) are automatically unified, while internationally they are not.[25] A central bank pursues the same policy in all parts of a country. If it is inflationary, it is the same in California as in New York and Texas. Internationally, the propensity to inflate is often not the same. The comparative weight that national policies give to the objective of price stability, on the one hand, and full employment and growth, on the other, differs in different countries, nor is the strength and aggressiveness of labor unions the same everywhere. Equally important, in all countries, priorities accorded to internal and external policy objectives have changed since the gold standard days. Whenever there is a conflict between the two, *internal* policy objectives—full employment or price stability or whatever they are—take precedence over *external* policy objectives that is, equilibrium in the balance of payments. Thus, deficit countries suffering from unemployment refuse to tighten the monetary and fiscal policies although this course of action would be required to correct the deficit. Similarly surplus countries suffering from inflation refuse to loosen monetary and fiscal restraints, although it would be required to eliminate or reduce their surpluses.

The straightforward resolution of such policy conflicts or dilemmas is parity changes: A deficit country suffering from unemployment can counteract the deficit and recession at the same time by letting its currency depreciate.

Similarly, a surplus country suffering from inflation can reduce the surplus and inflationary pressure at the same time by letting its currency appreciate.

The existence of a conflict between the requirements of internal and external equilibrium constitutes what the IMF charter calls a "fundamental disequilibrium." A nonfundamental disequilibrium, on the other hand, is one involving no such conflict. If a deficit country suffers from inflation (rather than unemployment), antiinflationary measures (tighter monetary and fiscal policies) counteract the deficit and the inflation. Similarly a surplus country suffering from recession (rather than inflation) can apply expansionary monetary and fiscal measures which will alleviate the recession and, at the same time, reduce the surplus.

Needless to add, governments often find it difficult to follow these prescriptions. For example, deficit countries often fail to stop inflation because it may create unemployment. Such internal policy dilemmas as those between price stability and full employment can, of course, not be resolved by exchange rate changes. Moreover if an inflation has gone on for some time, merely stopping inflation may not be enough to eliminate the deficit. Thus, a nondilemma situation can easily turn into a dilemma situation which requires a parity change.

Having explained why in the modern world we have to expect the frequent occurrence of fundamental disequilibria—dilemma situations which require parity changes—we now ask why these changes cannot be made smoothly. Why is it that these changes, especially when major currencies are involved, are almost always preceded and accompanied by more or less violent currency crises, by massive flows of funds from deficit to surplus countries? Furthermore, why have these crises become more and more spectacular in recent years? (Later we shall ask what can be done to make the changes smoother.)

It is easy to explain why smooth parity changes are rare exceptions under the adjustable-peg system. If a country has a deficit and has for some time been losing reserves, more and more people expect that the country will be forced to devalue, and this expectation induces actions to avoid losses or to make profits. Importers speed up imports, place orders earlier than they usually do, try to prepay foreign deliveries or pay promptly to anticipate the expected rise of the value of the foreign currency. Similarly exporters with receipts falling due in foreign currencies tend to postpone collections in expectation of higher prices for their foreign currencies. These reactions of exporters and importers are called "leads and lags," and they often run into many billions of dollars. Furthermore, treasurers of large corporations, especially the multinationals, shift available funds out of currencies that are expected to depreciate into currencies that are likely to appreciate. "Pure speculators"—that is to say, people who have no regular foreign business—get into the act, selling weak currencies short and buying strong currencies.

Under the adjustable peg the dice is heavily loaded in favor of the speculators—using now the term in the broadest sense to cover the various groups mentioned in the preceding paragraph. The fixed par-value system discourages frequent parity changes and hence gives plenty of time for pressure to build up. Since it is impossible to know exactly what the new equilibrium rate will be, a deficit country tends to depreciate by a large percentage to avoid going through the same painful process in the near future.[26] Thus, the speculator will make a large gain if he guessed right and parities are changed. If he guessed wrong— that is to say, if the parity change does not materialize—his loss will be small (transactions costs and interest), since the currency of a deficit country cannot go up and the currency of a surplus country cannot go down. Heads the speculator gains a lot, tails he loses little or nothing.

Why is it that in the last few years the crises preceding and accompanying parity changes have become more and more spectacular as measured by the increasingly huge sums, some-times several billion dollars a day, rushing into countries whose currencies are expected to appreciate? Surely the basic reasons are, first, the tremendous growth of world trade and trans-actions; second, the increasing international mobility of capital; and last but not least, the fact that numerous parity changes have alerted more and more business firms and individuals to the profit opportunities offered by exchange speculation.

HOW TO MAKE THE ADJUSTMENT SMOOTHER

We can distinguish three types of policy reactions to this state of affairs—controls, creation of a new type of world money, and greater flexibility of exchange rates.

Controls, both those designed to correct or suppress a fundamental disequilibrium and those to prevent speculation, will be discussed later.

Plans to create a new kind of international money have been proposed by the dozen. Here is not the place to discuss them in detail. I must confine myself to two observations on fundamentals.

First, substituting for the dollar, gold or SDRs or some other newly created international fiat money would be a major operation for which the time has hardly come. More important even if the dollar were replaced by gold or SDRs, it would not change anything essential unless the underlying factors requiring frequent parity changes were removed. The only result would be that gold and SDRs would flow into countries whose currencies are expected to appreciate. Since the dollar would in any case continue to be an important private transactions currency in the world and since the United States will remain the world's leading economic power, dollar balances along with gold and SDRs would move in the direction of the surplus countries in search of profits from expected parity changes. The replacement of the dollar by some other international money would by itself accomplish little if anything. It would not make the system less crisis-prone than it is now and would not remove the inflationary bias from which any system of fixed or semi-fixed rates suffers under modern conditions.

Second, it follows that reforming the international monetary system to make it work smoothly requires much more than replacing the dollar by some other international money—nothing less than creating internationally the conditions that make the smooth interregional (intranational) functioning of the balance-of-payments mechanism possible. This in turn requires as we have seen, as a minimum, centralization or at least very tight coordination of monetary, fiscal and wage policies.[27] The magnitude of the job is thrown into high relief by the fact that the enlarged European Common Market has been trying for years to achieve for Europe monetary unification, but so far without success. The floating of sterling in June 1972 and of the Italian lira in January 1973 have been major setbacks, and the goal of a unified European monetary system is not yet in sight. If it is not yet possible to unify the currencies of the politically and economically closely knit European countries, it follows *a fortiori* that the time has not come to attempt it on an international scale.

Before going on to the *third* approach, greater flexibility of

176

exchange rates, let us have one more look at the problem of monetary integration from a slightly different angle. It could be argued that the goal could be achieved by the following simple arrangement: The monetary authorities of a group of countries agree to support each other's currencies unconditionally and without limit; surplus countries would buy any amount of the currencies of the deficit countries. Technically there is nothing wrong with this scheme, for each country has an unlimited supply of its own currency. But it would require the less inflationary members of the group to underwrite, finance and eventually join in the inflation of the less-disciplined members. Thus, the most inflationary countries would set the pace of inflation for the whole group. [28] To make such a scheme acceptable, all members would have to follow a common line in their macroeconomic policies or make appropriate parity changes if and when large imbalances arose. This brings us back to where we were: sufficient coordination or centralization of economic policies requires far-reaching political unification. If this goal has so far eluded the European Economic Community, it surely is premature on the international level. Parity changes, on the other hand, raise the issue of the adjustable peg versus flexible exchange rates. To this problem we turn now.

Flexible Exchange Rates

We have seen why it is that under modern conditions, i.e., since the days of the gold standard, frequent parity changes have become necessary. We have also seen why such changes are usually preceded or accompanied by acute currency crises, loss of confidence in the currencies of deficit countries and massive flows of speculative funds into strong currencies. The increasing inability to effect parity changes smoothly is the great flaw in the par-value system (adjustable peg). The system of flexible exchange rates, contrary to what its critics often say, does *not* suffer from his defect.

Consider the situation in a country with a freely floating

exchange rate, in other words, in a country that does not stabilize the exchange value of its currency by buying and selling gold or dollars at a given par value (or within a narrow margin or "band") but allows the rate to be determined by the forces of demand and supply in a free, untrammeled market. What happens if such a country experiences an adverse change in its balance of payments for any reason whatever—e.g., because it pursues a more inflationary policy than its neighbors? It cannot lose reserves because it does not peg its currency to gold or dollars or anything else. Instead the exchange value of its currency will decline; it will float down, until equilibrium is reached.

Will that not give rise to adverse speculation? It surely may; if people expect rightly or wrongly that inflation will continue they will try to get rid of that currency. But the difference is this: Under the adjustable peg the authorities encourage speculation by selling speculators all the marks or dollars or gold they want at the fixed parity and thereby eliminate the speculative risk. For the speculator knows that a currency under pressure is likely to go down but never can go up. Under a flexible regime, on the other hand, the exchange value of the currency will immediately decline; the speculator can never be quite sure whether it will go further down or whether it may not have gone down too far and will rise again. Speculation becomes a risky business with the chances of loss and gain evenly distributed. The dice is no longer loaded in favor of the speculator. Under floating speculators speculate against each other rather than against the central bank as under pegging. Such speculation manifests itself in movements of the exchange rate. It can no longer take the form of massive additions to the official reserves of surplus countries imposing on them an unwanted monetary growth, nor massive subtractions from the reserves of deficit countries imposing monetary contraction.

The difference was dramatically illustrated by events in Germany in the fall of 1969. Throughout the year the German mark was expected to be appreciated and billions of dollars of hot money from all over the world (not only from the United States) flowed into Germany. During the summer appreciation became an election issue in Germany, and the flood of hot money rose enormously. A few days before the election the exchange market was closed. On Monday, September 29 (the day after the election), the market was opened at the old rate. In a few hours huge sums poured into Germany. At noon the market was closed again and the decision was reached to let the mark float (no more pegging). The next morning when the market was reopened the value of the mark shot up, but—lo and behold—speculation had practically vanished. It simply became too risky to push up the rate any further. Even more interesting, speculation was not revived, at least not on a substantial scale, when a public debate got underway as to whether the mark should be allowed to go up by 6 percent or 10 percent or more.

The advocates of the fixed rate system will say that the German case was a special one and indeed it was. To discuss in public, government officials and central bankers participating, how far a currency should be allowed to appreciate is an awkward method of changing an exchange rate. But the point is that one should have expected under these circumstances that there would be a lot of speculation. In fact, there was none or very little; the flexible rate had made speculation too risky.

There is another aspect of the German case which deserves mention. After the restabilization of the mark, speculators realized their gains by buying back at a reduced price the dollars the Central Bank had bought before the mark was set afloat. These gains amounting to many hundred million marks were a clear loss of the German Central Bank.[29] One would think that the German authorities had learned their lesson. But they made exactly the same mistake in 1971 and 1973. In May 1971 the mark was allowed to float, but only after the Central Bank had bought several billion dollars in the vain attempt to keep the exchange rate fixed. The 1973 experience was especially spectacular. In January the Italian lira got into trouble and was

179

allowed to float down. Thereupon speculative funds poured into Switzerland. But the Swiss had learned their lesson and let their franc float up when they saw the avalanche coming. This deflected the dollar flood to Germany. The German authorities refused to budge and bought $6 billion in one week to stem the tide. Then the exchange market was closed for one week during which Germany accepted an appreciation of the mark in the form of a 10 percent devaluation of the dollar; meantime the Japanese yen was allowed to float up and numerous other currencies appreciated vis-à-vis the dollar. When the exchange market was opened again the speculators showed no confidence in the new rate. On March 1, the Central Bank again had to buy a record amount of almost $3 billion. Then the decision was reached to let the mark float. (The authorities did not call it a float, they called it again "a closing of the market," but unlike the earlier occasion it only meant that the Central Bank stopped buying dollars and stayed out of the market, while private trading continued as usual.)

When, as in 1969 and in 1971, the market was left alone and the exchange rate was allowed to be determined by demand and supply, speculation stopped, or at any rate it did not push up the rate of the mark to an uncomfortable level as the opponents of floating had predicted.

A little later Germany, France, Belgium, the Netherlands and Denmark agreed on a common float against the dollar and all other currencies, but only after the Germans had consented to an additional 3 percent appreciation of the mark. The German Central Bank lost several billion marks in the process.

Among the industrial countries the best-known and best-managed example of extended floating is Canada. The Canadian dollar floated from 1950 to 1962 and again since June 1970. There has been no trouble at all with speculation during these periods of floating. Again Canada is a "special case." It pursued responsible internal monetary and fiscal policies, and consequently the floating rate was actually quite stable; there were no violent fluctuations, only mild undulations.[30]

180

A counterexample of a country with not so responsible monetary policies is Brazil. The country has lived under rapid inflation for many years. During the last five years the rate of inflation, as measured by the consumer price index, has declined from 25 percent to about 12 percent per annum. Before 1968 the rate of inflation was much higher and the Brazilian exchange system was that of a "jumping peg." Every six months or so the cruzeiro was devalued by a large amount. In between, the rate was kept nominally stable with a battery of controls, special rates for different types of transactions and black markets in full swing—an extremely messy and grossly inefficient system. In September 1968 the system was changed. Brazil adopted what has come to be known as "trotting peg" under which the cruzeiro is devalued every five or six weeks by "small" amounts, 1½ or 2 percent. The new method has worked very well. There has been very little speculation. With interest rates as high as 30 to 40 percent because of inflation, it does not pay to speculate on a depreciation of 1½ or 2 percent if the precise date and magnitude of the next change are not known. There is a black market for dollars because access to the official market is not entirely free. But the black market rates are only moderately higher than the official rates.

The trotting peg has been a great improvement over the adjustable peg. It has allowed trade to grow rapidly and has thus contributed to the excellent overall growth performance of the Brazilian economy. This does not mean that inflation of 20 percent is harmless. The country would certainly be much better off if it were able to reduce the rate of inflation to near zero without causing more than temporary unemployment. The point is, however, that given the inflation, its adverse effects on foreign trade can be minimized and the very costly and inefficient policy of tight controls over trade and payments can be avoided by means of frequent small but uncertain changes in the exchange rate.

For the industrial countries where inflation is much less virulent, the main lesson taught by the Brazilian system is to confirm the conclusion drawn from the Canadian and German examples—namely, that contrary to what is widely believed, exchange flexibility is not liable to induce disruptive speculation. If speculation is no serious problem for a regime of flexible rates under conditions of rapid inflation when everybody knows that the exchange value of the currency will be reduced again and again, we can confidently conclude that it will be no problem under the much more favorable condition of slow, creeping inflation. [31]

Flexible Exchange Rates and Economic Stability

Until a few years ago the idea of freely fluctuating exchange rates had been associated with financial instability and disorder by the general public as well as by bankers, practitioners in international finance and many academic economists. Flexible rates were thought to be unstable rates, jumping wildly about under the influence of destabilizing speculation, thereby causing internal instability and inflation or deflation, depending on circumstances.

This argument mixes up cause and effect. Obviously financial disorders, especially high inflation (or deflation) at different rates in different countries, make stable exchange rates impossible and lead inevitably to violent exchange fluctuations. It is true, once an inflationary (or deflationary) spiral has got underway there may be a feedback from the changed external value of the currency to its internal purchasing power. This has happened or was thought to have happened in many countries during the turbulent period of high and hyperinflation after World War I, and again on the deflationary sides during the Great Depression of the 1930s. These experiences and their misinterpretations have conditioned the thinking of a whole generation. But clearly internal monetary and fiscal policies—the inability to resist inflationary forces, whether from the demand or cost side, and the lack of sufficient coordination of policies between countries—are the causes of violent exchange fluctuations and not the other way around. The experience of the last twenty years—in Canada, Germany, Brazil and other countries—made it quite clear that a floating exchange rate need not be a very unstable rate. If the internal policies of the countries concerned avoid inflationary excesses and do not diverge too much, exchange rates will exhibit only moderate movements. Thus, the fluctuations of the Canadian dollar vis-à-vis the U.S. dollar were very mild during the periods of clean float, 1950 to 1960,[32] and again since June 1970. Canada has thus been spared the numerous balance-of-payments crises which shook many other countries. The United States, too, has greatly profited from the financial order and tranquility reigning along its long northern borders. The huge U.S.-Canadian trade remained undisturbed.

We can say, then, that flexible exchange rates do promote economic stability. If a surplus country lets its currency float up in the exchange market, it avoids or at least mitigates inflationary impulses from abroad. If a deficit country lets its currency float down it avoids or mitigates deflationary influences from abroad and can maintain a high level of employment.

The Danger of Controls

Flexible exchange rates do more than promote the smooth parity adjustments and minimize disruptive speculation and thus contribute to stability and growth. They remove a strong incentive for the imposition of controls. Under fixed rates the propensity to impose controls is very great. There exists an almost infinite variety of controls, ranging from mild controls on capital flows, to uniform taxes on imports and subsidies for exports which amount to a thinly disguised form of depreciation (or appreciation) of the currency, to full-fledged exchange control involving detailed supervision and centralization of the exchange market and rationing of foreign exchange. A detailed description and analysis of the controls is beyond the scops of the present study. I confine myself to giving a few examples.

The first reaction to a loss of reserves is usually to apply gimmicks such as the so-called "operation mix." Under this policy an attempt is made to change the "mix" of fiscal and monetary policy. Deficit countries in recession are urged to shift emphasis from monetary to fiscal policy, to use tax reductions or increases in government expenditures rather than easy money to stimulate the economy and counteract recessive tendencies. The theory behind this prescription, on which much analytic ingenuity has been lavished, is that fiscal policy has a comparatively stronger impact on internal equilibrium and monetary policy a comparatively stronger impact on the balance of payments. The reason is that an easy money policy operating as it does through lower interest rates, although it tends to counteract the recession, also tends to cause a deterioration of the balance of international payments by encouraging capital outflows and discouraging capital inflows. An equally expansive fiscal policy, on the other hand, will result in higher interest rates which will induce capital inflows or check capital outflows. If it works, this policy is not much different from financing an external deficit by ad hoc borrowing abroad from the IMF or from a foreign central bank, except that the attraction of private foreign capital by higher interest rates is conventionally treated as "autonomous" while borrowing from the official agencies is regarded as "accommodating." In the conventional balance-of-payments accounting the former is entered "above the line," the latter "below the line." In other words, the former is part of the deficit, the latter not.

Actually the chances of dealing successfully with a recession and a weak balance of payments by means of a different monetary-fiscal policy mix has been greatly exaggerated. The usefullness of such methods is in reality very limited. It is essentially a cosmetic device to make the balance of payments look better.[33]

When such stratagems fail as they usually do, deficit countries often resort to the dangerous device of direct controls. They restrict imports usually by quotas (i.e., quantitative restriction), impose limits on what tourists are allowed to spend abroad and apply many other restrictive measures which cannot be further discussed here.

During the Great Depression of the 1930s most countries made extensive use of restrictive controls. The consequence was a catastrophic contraction of world trade which fell much more sharply than GNP in most countries.[33a]

During most of the post-World War II period, from about the middle 1950s on, the use of direct controls by deficit countries, especially among the industrial countries, has sharply declined. Currency devaluations have come to be preferred. Greater flexibility and freely floating rates would further discourage the use of direct controls.[34]

Controls on the part of the deficit countries are potentially much more dangerous than controls by surplus countries for the reason that import-restricting controls in deficit countries play into the hands of the ever-present protectionist forces and create vested interests which make their eventual elimination very difficult. In surplus countries, on the other hand, import-restricting controls would make the embarrassing surplus even larger. Surplus countries would have to use "negative controls," that is to say, import-stimulating (or export-restricting) measures which are just as unpopular as currency appreciations.[35]

Surplus countries are not likely to behave in such an irrational manner.[36] What they actually often do is to erect a variety of barriers against the inflow of speculative capital: Banks are prohibited to pay interest on deposits by foreigners or have to charge a "negative" interest; foreigners are not allowed to buy securities or to acquire real estate; the exchange market is split into a pegged one for current transactions and a free one for capital transaction. This is known as "dirty floating"; it implies a partial appreciation of the currency. If deficit countries make use of such devices, the result is a partial devaluation of the currencies.

All these methods have this in common: they cause high administrative cost, and they give rise to wasteful methods of evasion which the authorities then try to counteract by further tightening of controls. If applied for any length of time and if the underlying disequilibrium is severe, full-fledged control of international payments will be needed to separate current from capital transactions. At this stage capital controls by surplus countries become destructive of trade. But in milder forms controls by surplus countries are less dangerous than trade-restricting controls imposed by deficit countries because they create no vested interests for their perpetuation (except those of the controlling bureaucracy itself) as trade controls invariably do.

To sum up, by keeping countries out of the morass of trade and capital controls, exchange flexibility makes a great contribution to economic stability and growth.

Limits of Effectiveness of Floating

Under modern conditions, flexible exchange rates are an indispensable method for a smooth balance-of-payments adjustment and for eliminating or at least alleviating the inflationary bias inherent in any fixed parity system. They are not, however, a panacea for other difficulties often associated with balance-of-payments problems. They cannot resolve, for example, internal policy dilemmas such as the one between price stability and full employment (or growth). It would not be necessary to stress this, were it not for the fact that the opponents of flexibility often point with relish to such dilemmas as if anybody had claimed that they can be resolved by floating.[37]

Exchange flexibility can shield a country from inflationary or deflationary effects from abroad via the balance of payments. [38] Only by floating is it possible for a country to stay out of an inflationary (or deflationary) trend in the rest of the world. In an inflationary world floating is a *necessary* but not a sufficient condition to protect a country from inflation. This rather obvious point must be stressed because advocates of fixed exchanges have criticized floating on the ground that in 1973 it did not provide a reprieve from inflation for Germany, Japan, Switzerland, etc., when they allowed their currencies to float up. But to stop inflation it is clearly not enough, by letting the currency float, to stop the monetary growth that results from an external surplus ("imported inflation") it is also essential to stop monetary growth that results from domestic sources ("home-made inflation"). This the countries mentioned above failed to do.

But exchange flexibility cannot protect a country against what economists call (real) shifts in international demand: From the loss of foreign markets of a particular industry or group of industries due to rising foreign competition (for any reason whatsoever, protectionist measures of the foreign country or "natural" development of foreign industries), rising imports of particular commodities (again for any reason), changes in the terms of trade, etc. What is very important to realize is that inflation and especially deflation (and depression)[39] abroad are usually accompanied by, or may be the cause of, (real) shifts in international demand. Monetary and real factors are often inextricably intertwined. Floating protects only from the *monetary,* and not the *real* deflationary effects from abroad via the balance of payments from the *general* price rise (inflation) or price decline (deflation), but not from shifts in relative demand and relative prices.

The spread of the American depression in the early 1930s to the rest of the world illustrates the point. By letting their currency depreciate vis-à-vis the dollar, foreign countries could have avoided a decline in their price level parallel with that in the United States. But the depression in the United States caused not only a contraction of U.S. international demand (of exports and imports) but also changes in its composition; it further induced a violent protectionist reaction, the imposition of skyscraper duties imposed by the famous, or rather infamous, Smoot-Hawley terriff of 1930. (Apart from that the precipitous decline of prices involved a sharp increase in the incidence of specific, as against ad valorem, duties.) Felxible rates could not afford any protection against these *real* changes in international demand caused by the American depression.

187

But in most cases the damage done by inflationary and especially deflationary impulses from abroad, which can be avoided by floating, is probably greater than the associated real dislocations which floating cannot prevent.

The plea for greater flexibility of exchange rates should not be interpreted to mean that each of the over 120 members of the IMF should let its currency float against all the others. Even if floating becomes and remains very popular many smaller countries will peg their currencies to that of some large country with which they have especially close economic ties. If that can be done without submitting to damaging deflation (unemployment) or inflation and without imposing direct controls, the policy of exchange stabilization is unobjectionable and should be applauded by advocates of floating.

Furthermore, in some cases, groups of countries will form currency blocks with mutually pegged exchange rates and common float against the outside. If the currencies in such a group are tied together closely and irrevocably with no or only a narrow band of permissible fluctuations, we speak of "monetary integration." The nine members of the European Economic Community have long been trying to establish such a monetary union, so far without success because they have been unable to achieve the necessary degree of harmonization and coordination of economic policies. And it is very doubtful whether it can be done without a high degree of political unification.

The proponents of fixed exchanges stress the importance of an international money—gold and sterling in the past, dollars in the postwar period. Under a system of exchange flexibility, they say, this great advantage for the world economy is lost. [40] They rightly emphasize the enormous economic benefits that the United States, and every other country, derives from the existence of a single currency on its territory. They are also right in pointing out that the larger the area the greater the benefits of a single unified currency, from which it follows that any two or more countries would benefit greatly by establishing a monetary union with permanently fixed exchange rates, *pro-*

vided they can do it without imposing controls and *without* being forced from time to time to submit to *damaging deflation or inflation.* Unfortunately in the modern world these conditions are rarely fulfilled by sovereign states. Disregard or insufficient realization of this fact is the basic mistake of the uncompromising advocates of fixed exchange rates.[41]

Limited Flexibility

Much ingenuity has been lavished on inventing schemes of limited flexibility. The purpose of these proposals is, by limiting the variability of the rates, to allay lingering fears that unlimited flexibility may give rise to destabilizing speculation. Such concessions to fixity, it is hoped, will make flexibility more acceptable to central bankers and to policy makers generally.

The most popular proposal is to widen the band of permissible fluctuations to 3 or 4 percent from the 1 percent on each side of parity as presently laid down in the Articles of Agreement of the IMF. A widening of the band to 4½ percent has recently been authorized by the IMF and accepted by many countries.

This is a useful reform as far as it goes. It increases the risks of speculation and gives the monetary authorities a little more leeway for internal demand management, because it makes possible a somewhat larger spread of interest rates between countries without running the risk of inducing massive arbitrage flows. But the importance of the wider band should not be exaggerated. In many cases larger changes than the band permits will be needed to restore equilibrium with the result that the exchange rate stays glued to one edge of the band and the flexibility is lost.

More important than the wider band is what has become known as the "crawling peg" or, in more dignified language, a "gliding parity." Under this arrangement the exchange rate can be changed if necessary at short intervals (monthly or weekly) by small steps cumulating, if the movement was all in one direction, to not more than 2½ or 3 percent a year. The basic idea behind these proposals is that if exchange rate changes were confined to that order of magnitude (2½ or 3 percent per annum), the danger of disruptive speculation could be eliminated or sharply reduced because it would always be possible to remove any inducement for such speculation—arbitrage might be a better term—by creating a sufficient interest differential. The gliding parity can, of course, be combined with a wider band. We would then speak of a crawling or gliding band.

There exist many proposals which differ in various details. Some envisage *automatic* changes according to some statistical formula. Some would let the change in the exchange rate be determined by the average of the spot rate over some past interval. This scheme presupposes the existence of a free market operating within the confines of a fairly wide band. In other proposals, the glide would be triggered by changes in international reserves. If a country lost reserves, the parity would glide down. Others have proposed a discretionary or managed crawl, leaving it to the judgment of the authorities when the glide should be operated. A compromise between an automatic and a discretionary glide is a "presumptive glide"; that is to say, the glide is *presumed* to take place if either the reserve position changes or the spot rate moves in a certain way. But the presumptive glide can be suspended by the authorities for good cause, which would, however, be subject to international surveillance presumably by the IMF.

It would lead too far to discuss these schemes in greater detail. None of them has been adopted anywhere, and there is little chance that any will be adopted. There are technical objections and difficulties which cannot be discussed here, and the schemes are probably too complicated for practical adoption in the sense that it is hard to imagine an international conference agreeing on any of them.

The fear of disruptive speculation in case of an unlimited float is greatly exaggerated anyway. On the other hand, balance-of-payments disequilibriums are often greater than a slow crawl could handle, even if we disregard rapid inflation as in Brazil. If the crawl is insufficient and the country loses, reserves, the gliding parity scheme will lose credibility; people will expect a larger parity change and the country will be back at the adjustable-peg system with its proneness to destabilizing speculation.

The conclusion is that the practical value of these complicated schemes is doubtful. . This is especially true of the automatic schemes. Hardly any country will entrust its exchange rate to an "objective," statistical formula and, if it did, it would be hard to assure its adherence to the policy. International agreement on the general adoption of schemes as complicated as these is difficult to envisage.

Unlimited flexibility as in the case of Canada, a wider band and ad hoc-managed flexibility or a "trotting peg" in case of a rapid inflation (as in Brazil) are all that would seem to be needed for efficient balance-of-payments adjustment. [42]

SUMMARY AND CONCLUDING REMARKS

In the section on the international aspects of economic and financial stability we first discussed the working of the international gold standard until 1914. The gold standard gave the world an international money—a service of utmost importance comparable to what a unified monetary system does for the national economy of each country. But the gold standard could function only so long as there existed a modicum of wage flexibility downward and the participating countries observed certain rules in their economic policies, especially in the monetary area. The fulfillment of these conditions had become more and more problematic. Wages are now almost totally rigid downward and violations of the rules of gold standard policies have become more and more numerous and blatant; domestic policy objectives—full employment, growth, price stability in combinations differing from country to country—everywhere take precedence over the requirements of external equilibrium (balance of payments adjustment at stable exchange rates). The gold standard finally broke down in the Great Depression of the 1930s. There is no chance whatever that it will be resurrected.

After World War II the Bretton Woods system replaced the gold standard. While under the gold standard exchange rates were rigidly fixed by the gold parities of the various currencies, under the Bretton Woods system par values could be changed in case of a "fundamental disequilibrium." The system can therefore be described as one of the "adjustable peg." It differs from the gold standard also by the fact that dollar balances were increasingly used as international reserves. The system could therefore be characterized as a gold-exchange standard so long as the dollar was convertible into gold, and as a dollar standard after the gold convertibility of the dollar was suspended in August 1971.

The Bretton Woods—adjustable peg—dollar standard came to an end in 1973 when it was replaced by widespread floating. The demise of the Bretton Woods system was due to two interrelated developments: First, the system became increasingly crisis-prone and developed a strong inflationary bias. Each parity change was preceded and accompanied by increasingly massive speculation. Second, under modern conditions every fixed or semi-fixed rate system is bound to have an inflationary bias. This follows from the fact that nowadays no country is willing to tolerate a deflation. The consequence is that with fixed parities a disequilibrium in the balance of payments can be eliminated only by inflation in the surplus countries—or by controls. But controls are not only destructive of trade and undesirable in themselves, they are in reality nothing but a messy, inefficient and wasteful method of changing exchange rates.

The chances are that widespread floating is here to stay for the foreseeable future. Since its inception in March 1973 it has worked quite well. Many skeptical central bankers and other practitioners of international finance have come to admit that floating has worked much better than they had anticipated. Comparatively mild fluctuations of exchange rates involving all major currencies, have taken care of serious disturbances, including those resulting from the energy crisis, which under the old system would have produced massive speculation, violent currency crises and stringent controls. It is true that there have been some official interventions in the dollar market on the part of the Federal Reserve and some foreign central banks, but they have been miniscule compared with the enormous volume of private transactions. At times they may have had a reassuring psychological influence, but they were a factor of minor importance.

It is possible, however, that if the dollar remains strong in the market as it is at present (December 1973), there may come a period of *de facto* stabilization as far as a few major currencies are concerned. The Germans, Swiss, French and a few other large dollar holders may decide—as the Japanese have done for some time—to stabilize their currencies by selling dollars from their swollen reserves with a view of curbing their inflation by keeping import prices a little lower. By the same token such a *de facto* stabilization would be mildly inflationary in the U.S. But there is nothing the U.S. could do about it. We cannot forbid others to use their dollars and we would not want to make the dollar inconvertible in the market.

It would be a great mistake, however, to regard such a *de facto* stability as permanent and to try to formalize and perpetuate it by returning to an adjustable peg system. So long as inflation rates are as high as they are now it would be a miracle if the major countries were able to find a combination of inflation rates that would suit them all and make parity changes unnecessary. In other words the *de facto* stability of exchange rates would not last long. If inflation rates came down to near zero—without recession—it is conceivable that some major countries could find a mutually acceptable pattern of exchange rates, because in that case no country would have to accept a high rate of inflation. But even in that case stable exchange rates would require formal or *de facto* coordination of monetary and possibly other policies. If such a high degree of harmonizations of policies could be achieved, floating rates would automatically be stabilized by the market, as they were in the case of the Canadian dollar. It would be safer not to formalize such a state of affair. A return to "stable but adjustable" parities would at any rate be out of the question for countries with a chronically weak balance of payments such as Great Britain, not to mention scores of highly inflationary less developed countries.

Widespread floating does not mean, however, that each of 120 odd currencies of the Western world will fluctuate with respect to all the others. There will always be, as there are now, many small or even medium-sized or possibly large countries that will peg their currency to the currency of some major economic power—to the U.S. dollar, the German mark, the yen, etc. It does not violate the spirit of floating and is in no way objectionable if a country pegs its currency to another, or if several countries form a currency bloc (monetary union) by tying their currencies closely together—*provided* the pegged rates need not be propped up by direct controls and no participant country is subjected to excessive inflation or unemployment. But in the modern world these conditions are not often fulfilled by sovereign countries.

The floating will certainly not always be "clean" and unmanaged. But that does not matter too much unless the floats became very dirty. If the growth of world trade has not been stopped or visibly slowed by the violent currency crises under the Bretton Woods system, it surely can stand a good deal of managed or even dirty floating. Optimism in this respect, however, does not imply complacency about the current galloping world inflation, exacerbated as it is by the energy crisis. On the contrary there is great danger that rapid inflation will lead to a world recession when several important countries at long last step hard on the monetary brake.

A recession will greatly strengthen protectionist tendencies everywhere, no matter what the exchange rate regime, floating or stable and adjustable. Moreover a world recession will produce shifts in international demand and relative prices (terms of trade), even if a protectionist explosion can be averted.

Floating is not a panacea. It can shield a country from imported inflation or deflation, but it cannot protect it from (real) changes in international demand and changes in relative prices of exports and imports (terms of trade) which are likely to be associated with inflation and deflation. Protectionist reactions of other countries to a recession (deflation) are a case in point. Floating can not protect a country from the impact of other countries' protectionist measures on its export industries.

This does not mean, however, that floating is less important or less desirable in a recessionary environment than in an inflationary one. On the contrary, if anything it is even more important, for three reasons:

First, floating can protect a country from the deflationary pressures associated with shifts in international demand (including those caused by foreign protectionist measures). Secondly, floating reduces the temptation for any country to resort to protectionist policies in a recession, because it greatly facilitates the adoption of alternative, non-protectionist policies to achieve the same purpose: Under fixed exchange rates a country must watch its balance of payments and is therefore constrained in the application of expansionary internal policies designed to fight unemployment and recession. This was one of the main reasons why during the Great Depression of the 1930s most countries resorted to import restriction for the purpose of reflating their economy.

Floating liberates economic policy from the balance-of-payments constraint and therefore makes the adoption of non-protectionist, anti-recession policies much easier. This does not mean that in a recession there will be *no* protectionist tendencies under floating. To deal with *specific* unemployment in particular import industries by import restrictions will remain a

195

temptation. But countries will not be tempted to use protectionist measures as a shield for *general* reflationary policies as was the case in the 1930s.

Third, under floating any country can protect itself against aggressive exchange rate manipulations of others—frequently called "competitive depreciation." It is true that, contrary to what is often said by advocates of fixed parities, competitive depreciation is *not* a consequence of floating. If a country deliberately depreciates its currency by selling it in the exchange market it does the very opposite of floating. But it cannot be excluded that *managed* floating (as distinguished from unmanaged, free floating) could be misused by some countries to depress the value of their currencies for the purpose of snatching a trade advantage. But if country A sells its currency in the market to stimulate its exports, country B can easily neutralize A's move by buying A's currency, in other words by selling its own currency. Under fixed parities countries were restrained from doing that. Thus in the 1930s gold standard mentality prevented countries from countering promptly beggar-my-neighbor depreciations of others by depreciating their own currencies. Instead they reacted by tightening monetary policy—in the midst of a depression—and by imposing quotas and tariffs on imports. Exchange rates were changed only after long delays *in extremis*. The result was a vicious spiral of competitive depreciations and deflation. This was the consequence of rigid parities and not of floating. (But one should not make the perversions of the gold standard in its dying days the basis for an indictment of the classical gold standard in its prime.)

To sum up, there can be no doubt that economic stability and growth are best served by fixed exchange rates, *provided* the fixed rates need not be propped up by controls and do not impose on any country excessive inflation or deflation (unemployment.) Unfortunately in the modern world these conditions are rarely fulfilled by sovereign countries. They do obtain, however, inside each country; if a country suffers from inflation or deflation, it is the same in all parts of the country, so that the unified currency is not in danger. On the international level this is rarely the case. Therefore, parity changes have to be made from time to time. It is then much better to bring them about by floating than by occasional large appreciations or depreciations as was the procedure under the Bretton Woods adjustable peg system.

Appendix A

Appendix to Chapter 2

Why Growth Policy?*

In the text, the question was raised whether it is at all necessary for the government to have a growth policy. Why not leave the rate of growth to be determined by the relevant decisions of private individuals such as the decisions to save, to invest, to spend money on education, research and development? It was shown that these doubts concern only one type of growth policy, namely policies that attempt to accelerate long-run growth by stimulating saving and investment at the expense of current consumption.

---

*In the economic literature these questions have been discussed on two levels. First, there exists an extensive, highly abstract and largely mathematical theory of "optimum investment and saving." Second, the question is often raised in the literature on growth. The latter is well sampled in *The Goal of Economic Growth,* a collection of essays edited with an introduction by E. S. Phelps (New York, 1969, rev.). There is little rapport between the two bodies of literature.

I argued that there are grounds on which such a growth policy can be justified, even if one accepts, as the present writer does, the principle that the government should respect consumer preferences and the decisions of private individuals and business firms on how to spend their income.

It was stressed, however, that such a policy of induced or compulsory saving must not be interpreted to mean substituting government command for the capital market and the price mechanism which, in a free enterprise economy, have the indispensible function of allocating the scarce supply of saving (capital) among the practically unlimited investment opportunities. The idea is not to replace or restructure the capital market and price-interest mechanism by government regulations, but to work with and through the market. The supply of saving (capital) would be supplemented and increased by appropriate tax measures. The additional capital would be made available for private (or public) investment by channeling it through the capital market.

Even with all these precautions a growth policy of this kind does involve a deviation from pure laissez-faire. But this can be justified on two grounds: *First,* it should be remembered that in this essay the problem of growth and stability is being discussed in the framework of the present Western economies with their large public sectors, numerous government activities and growing government budgets. All this makes it virtually impossible for the government to remain neutral with respect to growth. For better or worse, government activities do have a strong impact on economic stability and growth. Can there be any doubt that many government activities, for example highly progressive income taxes and some of the social welfare measures, retard growth? It is then quite possible that the financial policies which may be used to stimulate growth or other growth-promoting policies that might be adopted will do no more than partly offset growth-retarding effects of other government activities. In other words, the growth-promoting policies may well, on balance, bring the total government

200

impact on growth closer to "neutrality" than it would be in the absence of conscious growth policy, in accordance with the principle of noninterference in private decisions.

Second, it may be almost impossible to decide objectively whether conscious growth policy pushes the total government impact on growth beyond the point of neutrality. Let us assume (although I would regard it as unlikely) that the total impact was positive; in other words, that because of government policies more is saved and invested and growth is faster than would be the case if all this were determined by the individuals' decisions alone. I would not regard that outcome in any way alarming or even undesirable; for it must be doubted whether the government should remain entirely neutral with respect to growth, even if it could. Granted, we wish as a matter of principle to preserve freedom of consumer choice, but even in the area of current consumption certain limitations are unavoidable and are generally accepted. Let me mention restrictions of certain types of consumption (alcohol) by minors, restrictions on the use of narcotics and drugs, compulsory expenditures on education, liability insurance and other things. No doubt present practices in most countries restrict consumer choice and prescribe certain expenditures much more than many of us would regard as defensible. But it is a question of more or less. The radical solution—no government influence at all—seems to me impossible of consistent application.

When it comes to decisions involving investment, in other words, decisions that imply choices between consumption and economic welfare in the present and in the future, possibly in the distant future, the individualistic postulate that all decisions should be left to individual choices and market forces must be more severely qualified than in the case where only choices between different types of present consumption are involved. The main reason is that in the case of intertemporal choices generations as yet unborn are involved. They cannot speak for themselves. When decisions are made on what types of goods should be produced for *current* consumption, it makes sense (with minor limitations) to let the market decide, on the grounds that the market gives everybody the same weight, dollar per dollar, provided that we accept the prevailing income distribution (as modified by the existing tax system and welfare policies). When future generations and children are involved, the situation seems to me essentially different.

There are conceptual difficulties connected with intertemporal choices, even if we disregard the problem of future generations—difficulties which make it impossible, in some cases, to attach unambiguous meaning to the postulate that individual choices ought to be respected and should be the only criterion of public policy.

Suppose the government embarks on a policy of compulsory or induced saving. By suitable taxes consumption is reduced and the revenue is plowed back through the capital market into private investment. The result is a larger income and consumption in the future.

Forced savings goes against the *present* wishes of the individuals. But it is quite possible that in the future, when the fruits of the present abstinence from consumption mature, the same individuals may be glad to have been compelled in the past, against their wishes at that time, to restrain their consumption. There may, thus, exist a conflict between the present and future preference system of the same individuals. Which preference should the government respect, the present or the future?

Clearly, the postulate "respect the individual preferences" has no clear meaning in such cases; it is impossible for the policy maker to avoid a value decision of his own. He needs a value judgment, a "social welfare function," to guide him; he cannot shirk it by saying, "I accept the individual preferences" because these preferences may be inconsistent over a period of time. A hands-off, laissez-faire policy could conflict with the individual preferences as of the later period. Not to tax for investment would be a possible decision for the policy maker to make, but as far as individual preferences are concerned, it would imply an arbitrary value judgment—arbitrary because it is not clear why the individual preference system of period one should take precedence over that of period two.

However, rejection of the simple solution to throw out all growth policy on the grounds that the problem of growth can be left to market forces does not imply endorsement of all policies that sail under the flag of growth and development. Much that goes as growth policy in many countries, developed as well as underdeveloped, is poorly conceived, inefficient, does not promote growth at all or violates other policy objectives. To be sure, growth policy is often highly interventionist, but then it need not be. The simplest, most efficient, relatively noninterventionist growth policy would be to tax consumption and channel the tax proceeds through the capital market into private (or public) investment, leaving the choice of the most promising investment opportunities to market forces and private enterprise. Care has to be taken, of course, that the method of taxing does not undo what the tax-financed investment achieves. A highly progressive income tax which stifles the spirit of enterprise, discourages effort and reduces saving, would obviously not be an effective engine of growth even if the tax revenue were channeled through the capital market into private productive investment.

Quite apart from technical mistakes (in the choice of taxes and the methods used in the selection of the investments to be undertaken) there is a basic limitation: At a certain point reduction of current consumption will result in a reduction in the quantity or quality of work put in by the labor force and, hence, at some point a "growth policy" will produce a lower rather than a higher rate of growth. Where this absolute limit lies, in other words by how much current consumption can be compressed without reducing current effort (quantity and quality of labor input), depends on the level of income and on social and political factors and psychological attitudes too numerous and complicated for discussion at this point. Naturally, for poor countries the scope for accelerating growth by restraining current consumption is severely limited, resembling the effort to pull oneself up by one's own bootstraps.

There is furthermore no doubt that in many countries preoccupation with growth (and employment) has stoked the fires of inflation. (The relation of inflation to growth and employment is fully discussed in Chapter 5.) So some may feel that admitting growth as a legitimate objective of policy is like letting a camel push its nose into the free enterprise tent; sooner or later the hump will follow.

The danger undoubtedly exists. Any policy, however beneficial it may be in moderate doses, becomes detrimental when overdone. The fact is that we live in a dangerous world full of temptation. A large part of life, especially of economic life, consists of resisting the temptation to go too far in one direction. This is one aspect of what is generally regarded as the essence of economic behavior—to allocate scarce resources to different uses so as to equalize marginal benefits and thereby maximize total utility. When the time factor is involved, in other words when it comes to equalizing benefits over extended periods of time, maximizing welfare becomes a very complicated business.

Appendix B

Some Recent Developments in the Theory of Unemployment

In recent years great progress has been made with what is called microeconomic analysis of the labor market, unemployment and inflation.[1] It is a theory of what I call "frictional" and "structural" unemployment. It describes in detail the process of finding suitable jobs on the part of employees and of finding suitable candidates for job openings (vacancies) on the part of employers. Stress is laid on the costs of gathering information, in other words, the investment of time and money (income foregone by not accepting second- or third-best options which may present themselves). All this is very important and interesting. Alchian and Allen in *University Economics* (p. 507) emphasize that frictional and structural unemployment often coexist with what they call "aggregate demand unemployment," which is our fourth category, "general depression or recession unemployment" (often called "Keynesian unemployment"). The authors say we do not know precisely at any moment how much there is of each of these two types of unemployment.

This certainly is a valid and fruitful theory. It explains why in case of a contraction of aggregate demand there will be a certain amount of unemployment even if people act rationally without any money illusion and in the absence of unions. The picture of a perfectly competitive labor market in which wages immediately adjust to the market-clearing levels so that full employment is continuously preserved—this idealized picture does not correspond to reality. People usually take their time to look for the right job and prefer to remain unemployed for a while rather than accept a wage cut in their old employment (if that is an option) or take some other inferior job offer. It stands to reason that generous unemployment benefits and welfare payments enable workers to search for the right job much longer. All this can be expressed by saying that frictional unemployment shades off into depression and recession unemployment. (Alchian speaks of "massive frictional" unemployment.) In still other words, the labor market is never perfect—strictly speaking no market is perfect, the labor market less so than most others. Has anybody ever doubted this?

Let me repeat, spelling out all these frictions and imperfections enriches our understanding and is very useful. But there is the danger that too much attention to the details blots out the vision of the whole. There is a strong tendency completely to obliterate the distinction between *general* depression unemployment on the one hand and *partial,* frictional and structural unemployment on the other; to deny the importance of money illusion and to play down the importance of labor unions and the almost complete wage rigidity which unionization has created.

This is a most unfortunate exaggeration. Prolonged inflation has weakened money illusion, but it is not yet dead. Even if there is a certain amount of wage rigidity in the absence of labor unions, there can be no doubt that unions have made rigidity almost complete. In addition, unions exert a strong wage push. These are developments of greatest importance. (The role of monopolistic labor unions and of business monopolies in the inflation process is analyzed in greater detail in Chapter 6.)

The new microeconomic theory of inflation and unemployment has led to a reinterpretation of Keynes' theory of unemployment. Axel Leijonhufvud in his brilliant book *On Keynesian Economics and the Economics of Keynes* (New York, 1968, page 38) says: "Alchian has shown that the emergence of unemployed resources is a predictable consequence of a decline in demand when traders do not have perfect information on what the new market-clearing price would be. No other assumption, we argue, needs to be relinquished in order to get from the classical to Keynes' Theory of Markets." Wage rigidity, labor unions and money illusion have nothing to do with depression unemployment.

Leijonhufvud's interpretation of Keynes has been accepted by Alchian and Tobin. If workers do not accept a reduction in their *real* wage when it comes in the form of a reduction of the *money* wage, while they do accept it when it comes in the form of a rise in the price level, it is not because unions simply do not permit the money wages to be reduced or because of money illusion (on the part of the unions or their members). The real reason is different: Workers accept a fall in their real wage in the form of a price rise, because a rise in the price level "conveys" the information that "money wages everywhere have fallen relative to prices." They reject an equal cut in their real wage in the form of a money wage reduction because "a cut in one's own money does not imply options elsewhere have fallen" (Alchian, op. cit., p. 44). Tobin expresses the same thought by saying, "Rigidities . . . of money wages can be explained by workers' preoccupation with relative wages and the absence of any central economy-wide mechanism for altering all money wages together" (op. cit. p. 5).

In other words workers and their unions do not accept a reduction of their money wages because they are not sure that other groups are called upon to make the same concessions. It would seem to follow from Tobin's formulation that money wages could be reduced if it were done across the board.

In my opinion this is entirely unconvincing both as an interpretation of what Keynes really had in mind and, what is even more important, as an explanation of reality. Keynes was confronted with the mass unemployment and misery of the Great Depression. He surely did not want to explain that kind of unemployment and the stickiness of wages by suggesting that workers were refusing to accept jobs at lower wages because they were shopping around for better options or because they were not sure that other groups did not have to make the same sacrifice. Such considerations make more sense in the context of today's mild unemployment when liberal unemployment and welfare payments have taken out much of the terror of idleness than at the time when Keynes wrote his *General Theory*. But the suggestion implied by Tobin that unions might accept a reduction of money wages if it were offered as a result "of any central economy-wide mechanism for altering all money wages together" strikes me as unrealistic. Are we really supposed to believe that in the United States, the United Kingdom or in any other democratic country unions would accept a general across-the-board wage cut or ceiling on money wage increases? Even temporary freezes or limitations on increases are strenuously resisted.

The discussion could be continued for a long time, and it would not be hard to quote passages from the *General Theory* that are quite inconsistent with the new interpretation. But the readers surely are already weary and doubtful about the relevance of the dispute.

Let me then try to indicate briefly what, in my opinion, are the important and unimportant issues.

(1) That general unemployment should be attacked by general wage cutting is not an issue. It is well known that Keynes admitted that competition in the labor market and falling money wages would eventually restore full employment via an increase in the real money stock and the consequential fall in interest rates.[2] He gave good reason why this should not be the main line of attack. But this is not controversial anymore, if it ever was. Let me recall that Pigou made it quite clear that he was not "in favor of attacking the problem of unemployment by manipulating wages rather than by manipulating demand" through monetary and fiscal policies.[3]

(2) While nobody recommends *general* wage cutting as antirecession policy, most economists would agree that *relative* wages (in the sense of the wage structure—in other words, the relative level of wages of labor of different skills, different geographic areas, and so on) should have a certain flexibility in the interest of a proper allocation of resources and speedy adjustment to changing conditions of demand and supply.

Actually, changes in relative wages are going on continuously even in our times of almost complete downward rigidity of money wages. But the changes in relative wages are effected almost entirely by differential wage *increases* and only in exceptional cases by money wage reductions. It stands to reason that the downward rigidity produces an inflationary bias. On the other hand, the more rapid the productivity growth the easier it is to overcome the inflationary bias.

(3) It is clear that even in the absence of unions (labor monopolies) the labor market cannot possibly be as perfect as markets of standardized commodities, that competition is not of the pure, atomistic type, and that wages are usually somewhat sticky in the sense that they do not adjust immediately to changes in demand. The consequence is that a contraction of aggregate demand causes a certain amount of unemployment

even if there were no unions which tend to make the wage completely rigid in the downward direction. Economists have been aware of all this, but it has been more fully analyzed by the modern microeconomic theory of inflation and unemployment.

Although they shade into each other, it is nonetheless important to distinguish between frictional and structural unemployment, on the one hand, and general depression or recession unemployment on the other. Also it must not be overlooked that the development of powerful labor unions, the almost complete downward rigidity of money wages, and the upward wage push resulting from unionization have profoundly changed the problem of inflation and unemployment. In Chapter 6 we grapple with the impact of labor unions and business monopolies on inflation and unemployment.

Appendix C

Appendix to Chapter 6

The Phillips Curve

The relation between price inflation and unemployment, more precisely between the rise in money wages and the level of unemployment, the existence of a trade-off between unemployment and inflation, and how much unemployment is required to stop inflation—these problems have been discussed in recent years in a rapidly growing literature. The strongest impetus came from an economic and statistical study by Professor A.W. Phillips: "The Relation Between Unemployment and Rate of Change of Money Wage Rates in the United Kingdom, 1861-1957."[1] Phillips seemed to offer a simple and elegant solution and his paper immediately acquired the general recognition and fame which it fully deserved.[2]

The results of Phillips' work are epitomized in the "Phillips Curve" which has become a household word in modern macroeconomics. The curve depicts the relation between (a) the level of unemployment as measured by the unemployment percentage and (b) the rate of change of money wages (in percent per year), or, at one remove, the rate of change of prices. In a diagram with the unemployment percentage plotted on the horizontal axis and the wage or price change plotted on the vertical axis, the Phillips curve slopes down from left to right: The higher the unemployment the smaller the rise in money wages and prices. At some level of unemployment money wages would remain stable and at some (lower) level of unemployment prices would be stabilized.[3] At that point the Phillips curve cuts the horizontal axis. At higher levels of unemployment money wages and prices would decline.

For the United Kingdom, Phillips estimated that, assuming an increase in productivity of 2 percent per year, it would take a little less than 2½ percent of unemployment to keep product prices stable. To maintain wage rates stable would require 5½ percent unemployment.

The economic theory on which Phillips' empirical work is based is extremely simple and suggestive:

When the demand for a commodity or service is high relatively to the supply of it we expect the price to rise, the rate of rise being greater the greater the excess demand. Conversely when the demand is low relatively to the supply we expect the price to fall, the rate of fall being greater the greater the deficiency of demand. It seems plausible that this principle should operate as one of the factors determining the rate of change of money wage rates, which are the price of labour services. When the demand for labor is high and there are a very few unemployed we should expect employers to bid wage rates up quite rapidly, each firm and each industry being continually tempted to offer a little above the prevailing rates

212

to attract the most suitable labour from the other firms and industries. On the other hand it appears that workers are reluctant to offer their services at less than the pre-vailing rates when the demand for labour is low and unemployment is high so that wage rates fall only very slowly. The relation between unemployment and the rate of change of wage rates is therefore likely to be highly nonlinear.[4]

On the left the curve is steep, reflecting the fact that in order to depress unemployment to very low levels (frictional unemployment) increasingly higher money wage and price boosts would be required. Toward the right the curve eventually flattens out because larger and larger levels of unemployment are necessary to reduce wages and prices still further.[5]

In addition to the main determinant of the change in money wages, that is, the level of unemployment ("excess supply"), Phillips mentions two other factors: (a) The rate of change of demand for labor and so of unemployment" and (b) "the rate of change of retail prices." But these two factors he considers merely subsidiary; they do not substantially change the picture resulting from the operation of the principal factor.

Contrary to what is often assumed, Phillips' own theory of inflation is that of the demand-pull and not cost-push type. He clearly regards his statistical findings as evidence in favor of the demand-pull hypothesis. Actually, the postulated relation between unemployment and the rate of change of wages and prices would seem to be perfectly compatible with attributing wage pushing power to labor unions. Clearly, other things being equal, the greater the level of unemployment, the weaker the position of labor unions and the weaker the wage-push; conversely, the lower the level of unemployment the stronger the position of labor unions and the stronger the wage push. Hence, even if labor is organized in well-disciplined trade unions there will exist a level of unemployment, presumably a higher level than under competition in the labor market, at which labor unions are sufficiently weakened to assure stable prices (and a still higher level of unemployment which would stabilize the level of money wages).[6]

So much about Phillips' theory. It is only fair to add that he calls his conclusions "tentative." "There is need," he emphasized, "for much more detailed research into the relations between unemployment, wage rates, prices and productivity" (op. cit. p. 299).

The call for more research has been answered in abundance. The theory has been extensively discussed and refined and innumerable Phillips' curves have been constructed for many countries. For the United States, pessimistic conclusions have been reached: 6 or 8 percent unemployment would be required to maintain price stability. Surveying this literature one cannot help getting the impression that the idea of a unique and stable Phillips curve has been gradually discussed to death. The conclusion reached in a careful study on "The Wage-Price-Productivity Perplex" by Albert Rees and Mary T. Hamilton (*The Journal of Political Economy,* vol. 75, Feb. 1967, p. 70) sums up the situation:

> . . . We have been astounded by how many very different Phillips curves can be constructed on reasonable assumptions from the same body of data. The nature of the relationship between wage changes and unemployment is highly sensitive to the exact choice of the other variables that enter the regression and to the forms of all the variables. For this reason, the authors of Phillips curves would do well to label them conspicuously: *Unstable! Apply with extreme care!*

We should be quite sure, however, what the negative verdict about the Phillips curve means and what it does not mean. It does *not* mean that the fundamental idea from which Phillips starts is wrong: It remains true that at any point in time and over the short run the higher the unemployment is, the slower will be the rise in (money) wages and prices; it also would seem to be plausible to assume there always exists a level of unemployment that is compatible with stable prices and another, higher level of unemployment that would stabilize money wages although it may well be a socially and politically intolerable level. Furthermore, rejection of the Phillips curve does not contradict the proposition that there is a wage-push in the sense explained earlier. It is one thing to say that powerful trade unions are capable of pushing up money wages and thus putting the monetary authorities before the nasty dilemma of either allowing prices to rise or stopping inflation by creating a sufficient amount of unemployment. It is an entirely different thing to postulate, cautiously as Phillips did or incautiously as many others do, a stable, long-lasting relationship between the level of unemployment and the rate of change of wages and prices. What the negative judgment of the Phillips curve does mean is that there does not exist a *stable, long-run* relationship between unemployment and the rate of change of prices (or wages); in other words, there is no long-lasting *constant* trade-off of inflation and unemployment. The curve, if it is more or less well defined at any moment of time, is subject to rapid shifts over time.

This conclusion is based on the following considerations: Phillips derives his curve from annual British figures for the whole period 1861 to 1957. It is true he does study subperiods separately. But his final (tentative) conclusion—that for the United Kingdom about 2½ percent unemployment would be required to assure price stability—is derived from the figures for the whole period of almost 100 years.

This is a highly implausible theory on the face of it. It implies that the far-reaching changes in the structure of the labor market that have taken place during those almost 100 years—the rise of the labor movement, the tremendous increase in the power of trade unions, and profound shifts in government policy and public attitudes with respect to labor relations—that these and other structural changes have had no influence on the power of labor unions to push up wages and the interrelation between inflation and unemployment.[7] But even for shorter, more homogenous periods the search for a unique, statistically meaningful and stable Phillips curve has not been successful. Let us recall the conclusion which has been reached by Rees and Hamilton after a careful and comprehensive study: Many different relations between unemployment and wage changes can be derived from the same statistical data by adopting alternative, perfectly plausible assumptions.

THE "TRADE-OFF" VERSUS "EQUILIBRIUM" VIEW

A seemingly more radical rejection of the theory underlying the Phillips curve has come to be known as the (long run) "equilibrium" view. The best-known representative of the latter is Milton Friedman.[8] The "basic defect" of the Phillips construction is, according to Friedman, "the failure to distinguish between *nominal* wages and *real* wages." Friedman does not deny that it is possible in the very short run to reduce unemployment by means of inflationary policies, in other words, that in the very short run there is a trade-off between inflation and unemployment. But he regards the success of such a policy as strictly temporary. For high rates of inflation, this is a familiar proposition which is undoubtedly true. Suppose the Phillips curve for a particular country tells us that in order to reduce unemployment to, say, 2 percent (of the labor force) inflation has to be stepped up to, say, 10 percent (per year). Few would regard this as a stable situation. Inflation at that speed would soon affect expectations. Further inflation would be anticipated; in other words, "inflationary psychology" would develop, workers would ask for higher (money) wages and lenders for higher (nominal) interest rates in compensation for the expected rise in prices. Thus, a more rapid inflation, say, of

15 percent, would soon be required to maintain the real position, the existing level of output and the low unemployment percentage. This can be conceived of as an upward shift of the Phillips curve; the curve will not stay put for any length of time.[9]

In other words, inflation has its favorable effect on unemployment only so long as it is not generally anticipated. Usually, prices rise faster than wages. This enables the employers to hire more labor and to step up production. This implies that real wage *rates* decline or at least fall short of expectations; the workers' expectations are disappointed. Similarly, savers and money lenders will be shortchanged. But you cannot fool people all the time. "Money illusion," that is, the belief that stable money wages and nominal interests reflect real wages and real interests over a long time to come, is bound to be eroded and sooner or later destroyed. When that happens nominal wages and nominal interests will rise to catch up with the expected rate of inflation. Then inflation has to accelerate if the lower level of unemployment is to be maintained. To repeat, for high rates of inflation this will be widely accepted and is undoubtedly true.

The "equilibrium" theory generalizes this analysis also for mild cases of inflation. It assumes that at any time there exists a "natural" level of employment and unemployment which is compatible with stable noninflationary equilibrium. This natural or equilibrium rate of unemployment is determined by the basic (nonmonetary) facts of the economy, such as the existing structure of the labor market, composition of the labor force, mobility of labor, the market power of unions, degree of competition and other institutional arrangements, including governmental restrictions and regulations such as minimum wages which tend to raise the level of equilibrium unemployment. Now whenever a conscious attempt is made to increase employment above its "natural" or "equilibrium" level or, expressed differently, to reduce unemployment below its equilibrium level by means of inflationary policies, the train of effects described above is set in motion which tends to restore the equilibrium position.[10]

The equilibrium theorist realizes, of course, that such a process takes time and that the reaction time will vary with circumstances; for example, the higher the rate of inflation the swifter will people adjust to it. Interest rates will probably react more quickly than wage rates.[11] All this to my mind is quite true and should dispose once for all of the notion of a stable long-run trade-off function between inflation and unemployment.

But the equilibrium theorists sometimes give the impression that the process of adjustment can be telescoped and the long-run equilibrium point reached almost instantaneously. This is, indeed, not entirely impossible. Expectations are capable of changing and adjusting rapidly.[12] Such a state of affairs of instantaneous adjustment may be actually approached under the type of high inflation that is prevalent in many less-developed countries. When prices rise 30 percent or more a year, as they do in some Latin American countries, wages, interest rates and other monetary magnitudes are quickly adjusted. But it would be unfair to interpret the equilibrium theory literally as saying that under highly inflationary conditions *real* equilibrium will be closely approximated and continuously maintained. In practice the adjustment is certain to be very inaccurate because future inflation cannot be accurately foreseen. Expectation of future price rises entertained by different individuals and groups will usually not be the same, but will as a rule be contradictory. Moreover, since rapid inflation is bound to disturb vital economic processes, for example the rate of saving, investment and international capital flows, we must assume that the equilibrium rate of unemployment itself will be affected and cannot be closely approximated merely by adjusting money wages and interest rates to the expected rate of inflation.

However, with low rates of inflation as we usually find them in the United States and other mature countries, the equilibrium theory if strictly interpreted runs into other difficulties. It assumes that money illusion disappears when prices rise and that the vanishing purchasing power of money is a fairly clear-cut phenomenon, unique and visible to all or most people. Actually, with prices rising at, say, 3 or 4 percent a year on the average, money illusion seems to persist for a fairly long time and it seems to be possible to revive it quickly, after it has been eroded, by means of comparatively short spells of uneasy price stability. In the United States it took almost thirty years of intermittent inflation and four or five years of continuously accelerating price rises (since 1965) to create the inflationary psychology (erosion of money illusion) from which the United States' economy has been suffering since the late sixties.

Variable, intermittent inflation is clearly much less destructive of money illusion than continuous, uninterrupted inflation with the same average annual rise in prices. Moreover, there seems to be a threshhold of variable magnitude; that is to say, only if prices rise more than say, 1½ or 2 percent a year the money illusion gets eroded. The concept and actual measure of price levels and purchasing power of money is necessarily vague and means different things to different people. What matters are the expectations for the future, and it would be a strange coincidence if expectations of different people did not diverge even if the historical record were clear and unambiguously the same for everybody.

Now, all these refinements can perhaps be ignored for sharp price rises, but they blur the picture for periods of moderate inflation.

The upshot of these critical remarks is not to reinstate a stable Phillips curve over long periods, but rather to suggest that under conditions of mild or moderate inflation a slowly changing trade-off between inflation and unemployment may exist for extended periods; for the long run consists of successive short periods, each with a fresh start, separated by spells of uneasy price stability which serve to restore confidence in money and revive "money illusion."

Notes

NOTES TO CHAPTER 1

1. "Informal rationing" means that it depends on the whims and favors of the seller (shopkeeper, producer) who gets the scarce commodities and who has to do without. Or those who get to the shop first or "queue" the longest will be served. In the Communist countries "queuing," which makes shopping an ordeal, is a universal feature of daily life. In the West, it is usually a wartime phenomenon.

2. But it is no value judgment to point out that there are many ways to evade price and wage controls and that these evasions as well as the effort by the authorities to prevent them and to close loopholes are costly, that they progressively impair the efficiency of the economy, reduce output and consumer satisfaction, and undermine the public's respect for law.

Examples of such evasive actions are deteriorating quality of products, sloppy workmanship entailing more frequent and costly repairs, and frequent absence from the shelves of lower price products. In the labor market wage controls can be evaded by upgrading, substitution of fringe benefits for wage increases and similar measures.

3. As any aphorism, Churchill's dictum exaggerates, but not in the sense that many readers may think. "Misery" must, of course, be interpreted in the comparative sense. For example, what accounts for the very large difference in the standard of living between, say, East and West Germany, Austria and Czechoslovakia, Yugoslavia and Greece? In the pre-Communist past these pairs of countries enjoyed approximately the same standard of living; climate, human and natural resources are about the same. It is difficult to think of any other factor but the comparative efficiency of the individualistic and collectivistic (centrally planned) economics that accounts for the present very large differences in output and standard of living. There is furthermore the sharp decline in output and living standards in Cuba when Castro nationalized industries and introduced central planning. The Communist regime in Cuba has lasted too long to make it possible to attribute the economic decline to transitional difficulties. The catastrophic descent of the Chilean economy, on the other hand, was much aggravated by the anarchy and near-civil war atmosphere created by the policy of nationalization of major industries and central planning that a minority president, the late Salvador Allende has forced on an unwilling majority.

Churchill's aphorism exaggerates, however in the following respect: Misery is not shared equally by all under communism. Actually as the Communist regimes have been solidified and their economies have settled down into some routine, the income distribution has become very unequal indeed. Not only is the standard of life of the ruling class enormously higher than that of the ruled masses, but it has become necessary, in the interest of efficiency and growth, to provide incentives which in turn make it necessary to create wage and salary differentials throughout the system of about the same order of magnitude as in the West.

4. As with all economic concepts, there are innumerable finer points of definition and delineation. An important one is whether time deposits or savings deposits should be regarded as part of the money stock. This question as well as many similar ones have been lucidly discussed by Milton Friedman. See especially his authoritative book written jointly with Anna Jacobson Schwartz, *A Monetary History of the United States 1867-1960* (New York, 1963).

5. This is now often referred to as "the crowding-out effect" of deficit spending, government expenditures crowding out private expenditures. See for example numerous publications of the Federal Reserve Bank of St. Louis which has done a superb job of explaining complicated economic problems to the general public.

NOTES TO CHAPTER 2

1. Strictly speaking, this statement presupposes that the resulting budget deficit is financed in such a way that it does not reduce automatically private expenditures. But that is usually taken for granted—at least in the predominantly Keynesian literature. The problem will be discussed further in the next chapter.

2. The terminology is not entirely uniform and consistent. The words "growth" and "development" are usually used interchangeably. But sometimes a more or less subtle distinction is made: growth refers then to measurable output—GNP in the aggregate or per head—while development, the broader term, makes allowance for imponderables (improvement in the "quality of life" or similar things). Some writers speak of "economic welfare" as the broader phenomenon, which is determined (or measured) by growth in GNP as well as by improvements in the "quality of life."

3. Cyclical peaks do not, of course, always represent literally full employment, and the distance from full employment is not the same at each peak. This creates statistical difficulties which cannot be further discussed here. Over longer periods spanning several cycles, the inaccuracies caused by this circumstance are negligible.

4. Sometimes the increase in output per unit of invested capital is computed and then an average of productivity of labor and capital calculated. This refinement presents serious conceptual and statistical difficulties and is of questionable value. Fortunately, the results do not diverge much from the simple labor productivity figures. It should be observed, however, that the term "labor productivity" can be misleading if one does not keep in mind that output per man (or man-hour) largely depends on the amount of capital cooperating with labor in a firm, an industry and in the economy as a whole. Thus an increase in "labor" productivity reflects not only the contribution of more efficient labor (e.g., better-educated labor) but also that of a larger capital stock. Increases in labor efficiency can partly be attributed to capital expenditure in education, often called "human capital."

5. The statement that when people get richer they "consume" an increasing part of their larger income in the form of leisure is not invalidated by the fact that compulsory government regulations concerning maximum workweek and double pay for overtime usually go far beyond the real wishes of the workers. These regulations are largely a device to push up money wages; they cause inefficient distortions in cost and prices, because different sectors of the economy are affected differently (some can adjust more easily to arbitrary restrictions than others),

and lead to wasteful and inefficient moonlighting and other types of costly evasions. Hence, although the introduction and intensification of such measures give a boost to *money* wages, they reduce the efficiency of the economy and have thus an adverse effect on the trend of *real* wages.

5a. On this point see Gottfried Haberler "Monetary and Fiscal Policy for Economic Stability and Growth" in *Il Politico* Pavia, Italy 1967, vol. 37, p. 33.

6. Present-day criticism of *neoclassical* economics could be closely paralleled by quotations from Friedrich List's (*The National System of Political Economy*, 1841) criticism of the English *classical* writers. List charged that the classical economists were interested in "value problems" and not in "the development of productive capabilities."

7. The assumption of a constant income-saving ratio is even more restrictive than the Keynesian assumption of a fixed propensity to save. Keynes himself was careful to say that he regarded the propensity to consume (as well as the other determinants of his system) as fixed and unadjustable only under certain circumstances ("sometimes" was the word he used, *General Theory*, p. 65).
He surely would have strongly disapproved of the transposition of his theory from the short run (the business cycle and employment context) to the area of long-run growth.

8. A consequence of this extreme assumption is that the theories in question picture a private enterprise economy as extremely unstable. A slight deviation from the equilibrium path in either direction sends the economy into cumulative spirals of expansion and contraction, of inflation or deflation. This feature is in the literature referred to as the Harrod-Domar "knife-edge." It surely is a gross misrepresentation of reality.

9. I put *Keynesian* in quotes, because Keynes himself is not responsible for "Keynesian" growth theories which imply an illegitimate transfer of short-run monetary connections to long-run phenomena. There are good reasons to believe that Keynes himself would have rejected the use of his short-run theory for problems of long-run growth.
Actually, modern growth theory has gradually worked its way back from the blind alley into which it was led by uncritical application of Keynesian theory to its classical and neoclassical foundations. The way goes from Harrod-Domar-Kaldor to J. E. Meade's *A Neoclassical Theory of Economic Growth* (see especially 2nd rev. ed., 1962. See also Meade's *Principles of Political Economy*, vol. 2, *The Growing Economy*, London 1968).

10. The short-run stimulating multiplier effect of such expenditures on the level of employment in a period of depression and unemployment does

not, of course, depend on the classification. It is only the growth-promoting, efficiency-raising consequences that are here at issue.

11. By "nonexistent" I mean that the same expenditure may at the same time give pleasure to the spender and improve his future earning power; that is to say, it may be consumption and investment at the same time. For example, expenditures on education, study, travel, and recreation often belong to that category of "productive consumption" as it might be called. Not enough attention has been paid in economic literature to that possiblity.

12. Absence of investment opportunities would lead to low interest rates which would eventually check saving and encourage dissaving. It would also mean that output (GNP) could not rise except through improvements in the methods of production.

13. Technological inventions can, however, be "capital saving"; in other words they can reduce the need for capital instead of increasing it.

14. Even France has been said to have been held back in its economic development by a dearth of entrepreneurial talents!

15. This statement needs qualification from the social and political standpoint. There obviously are limits to the absorptive capacity for immigration. The influx of large numbers of immigrants, especially when they differ from the natives in race, color, religion and general cultural background, can easily lead to serious tensions or worse. The problems involved have been well analyzed by John V. Van Sickle in his important book *Freedom in Jeopardy: The Tyranny of Idealism* (Principles of Freedom Series, New York, 1969). Louis Rougier in his fine study *The Genius of the West* (Principles of Freedom Series, Los Angeles, 1971) describes the great contribution to Western progress and development which has been made by migration. He also gives counter examples from the closed societies in Eastern countries (see especially ch. XVI, pp. 176-77). Currently the newspapers in Western Europe carry frequent reports about social and racial frictions caused by immigrant labor and the resulting tendencies to restrict the inflow of foreign workers.

16. First ed., London, 1940; second ed., London, 1951.

17. On the spectacular economic development of Brazil after the overthrow of the extreme leftist regime of President J. Goulart in 1956 see Donald Syvrud: *The Foundations of Brazilian Economic Growth* (Washington, D.C., American Enterprise Institute, 1974).
On the equally impressive case of Malaysia see Wolfgang Kasper: *Malaysia: A Case Study in Successful Development* (Washington, D.C., American Enterprise Institute, 1974).

The international trade and trade policy aspects of the matter will be taken up at greater length in ch. 8, sect. A.

18. Many other measures and policies, both of commission and omission, could be mentioned. Streamlining and cheapening the administrative apparatus of the government, refraining from adding to the innumerable functions of government, would liberate resources for productive uses.

Let me cite one more category of measures which plays a great role in modern development literature: If there exist "external" economies or diseconomies, measures to activate the former or eliminate the latter by "internalizing" existing positive or negative "externalities" would bring about a once-for-all increase in GNP. An example of external diseconomies is air and water pollution. Thus, pollution control belongs to the category of measures here under discussion.

19. This was already known to Adam Smith (see his *Inquiry into the Nature and Causes of the Wealth of Nations,* vol. 1, bk. IV, ch. II, Cannen ed., p. 425). Let me mention that there exists a theorem, very popular in modern abstract-mathematical growth literature, which says that no *permanent* increase in the growth rate can be achieved by merely saving and investing, without additions to technological knowledge. It would lead too far to discuss this theorem in detail. Suffice it to say that it rests on the unproven assumption that investment opportunities are limited. This may be true in the sense that the rate of return on capital would asymptotically approach zero in practically infinite time (without improvements in technology). In that case saving and investing will boost the rate of growth, though at a diminishing rate, for the practically infinite future.

20. It is, of course, a simplification to speak of *the* capital market and *the* rate of interest. Actually there is a system of numerous interrelated capital markets and interest rates. But for our purposes we need not go into details.

That capital cost as expressed by the interest rate cannot be ignored in any economy without courting disastrous inefficiencies is highlighted by the fact that even the economic planners of the Communist countries, steeped though they are in Marxist dogmas and prejudiced against interest, find it necessary to reintroduce the interest rate through the back door. But failure to allow for it explicitly and systematically has caused great inefficiencies. See Abram Bergson, *The Economics of Socialist Planning* (New Haven, Conn., 1964), and G. Haberler, "Theoretical Reflections on the Trade of Socialist Economics," in *International Trade and Central Planning* ed. Alan A. Brown and Egon Neuberger (Berkeley, Cal., 1968).

21. See, for example, Paul Sweezy's contribution to the "Symposium: Economics of the New Left," *The Quarterly Journal of Economics,* Nov.

1972. "It is . . . naiveté or deception to cite the Soviet Union to prove anything about socialisms: it is not a socialist society and . . . it is not moving towards but away from it" [p. 660].

22. To the extent that destruction of wildlife results in damage to the physical environment of man, for example through the disappearance of natural enemies of dangerous or damaging animals, it is an economic problem. If it is just disappearance of a rare species which has no use by itself, the situation is different.

Some may object to this kind of distinction. The demarcation line between economic and noneconomic changes of the environment is unavoidably somewhat vague. I would only plead that we have to draw a line somewhere.

23. These problems have also been discussed under the heading of a discrepancy between the "private" and "social" utility, product, "marginal net product," productivity of certain firms, industries or investment projects. External economies imply a shortfall of the private below the "true" social utility, and an external diseconomy implies an excess of private utility. In either case there is a deviation of the actual allocation of productive resources from the optimum. The latter is called the "Pareto-optimum"; it can be defined as a situation in which it is impossible to increase the output of any commodity without reducing that of any other or to raise the income of any individual without reducing that of any other. Pareto-optimality is a conditional and not an absolute optimum, because it accepts the income distribution which market forces throw up. Measures to change the income distribution, e.g., to make it more equal in some sense, are not excluded. But care must be taken that the measures taken to change the income distribution—e.g., a highly progressive income tax—do not introduce new distortions. These are very complicated problems which have been extensively discussed by economists.

24. *Positive* external economies—that is, favorable, nonmarket influences—emanating from the growth of output of some firms or industries and benefiting other firms and industry, have always been more problematic and difficult to evaluate. Note that the *internal* economies, by reducing cost and prices of the product concerned, are automatically transmitted through the market.

25. Therefore the older economists recommended special taxes to "internalize" external diseconomies, and subsidies to internalize external economies. Governments have, of course, in many cases imposed special regulations to prevent damage to others.

26. This passage comes from an article by two biologists, William Murdoch and Joseph Connell ("All about Ecology," *The Center Magazine*,

vol. III, no. 1, Jan./Feb. 1970, p. 63). The qualification about under-developed countries gives away much of the case. At what level of income does underdevelopment end and disastrous affluence begin?

27. Universe Books (New York, 1972). The authors are D. H. Meadows, D. L. Meadoros, Y. Randers and W. W. Behrens, all scientists from M.I.T. The models of world development which the book presents are based on Jay W. Forrester's book *World Dynamics* (Cambridge, Mass., 1971).

28. The quotations come from the "Commentary" of the executive directors of the Club of Rome on the M.I.T. team's report *The Limits of Growth*, pp. 185-97.

29. On all three see *Newsweek*, March 13, 1972. See also the criticism by Carl Kaysen, "The Computer that Printed out W*O*L*F*" *Foreign Affairs*, July 1972, pp. 660-68.

30. "Economists, Scientists and Environmental Catastrophe" in *Oxford Economic Papers*, Nov. 1972. See also the criticism of Jay W. Forrester's *World Dynamics* by Harold Barnett in *The Journal of Economic Literature*, American Economic Association, Sept. 1972, p. 851.

31. It would take too much space to give concrete examples. I must refer to Professor Beckerman's article. See also John Maddox, *The Doomsday Syndrome* (New York, 1972).

32. The potency of the price mechanism and private initiative if they are allowed to function and are fortified, when necessary by tax measures, is completely ignored in *The Limits to Growth*.

33. For details see the paper by Murdoch and Connell cited above (note no. 26).

34. It is not claimed that a policy of complete laissez-faire would always produce an optimum speed and optimum pattern of industrialization. But in many cases private enterprise, if left alone, would have done much better than government planners.

35. On some of these problems see the impressive paper by William Nordhaus and James Tobin "Is Growth Obsolete" in *Economic Growth* (50th Anniversary Colloquium V, National Bureau of Economic Research, New York, 1972). See also the discussion of this paper by Moses Abramovitz and R. C. O. Matthews (ibid., pp. 81-92).

36. Nordhaus and Tobin in the paper just cited (note no. 35) grapple with some of the statistical problems and present figures. One occasionally

hears of estimates running into the hundreds of billions of dollars of what it would cost to clean up all polluted American rivers and to restore the air over major cities to their pristine purity. This may be so, but one should, of course, not charge the ecological backlog of hundreds of years to the current period output. Only the cost of preventing any further deterioration should be deducted from current GNP.

NOTES TO CHAPTER 3

1. Employers often do not find immediately suitable replacements of open jobs. Thus some vacancies and some unemployment always exist side by side. Their numerical relationship is often regarded as an index for the state of the labor market. If the number of unemployed exceeds the number of vacancies, the labor force is said to be underemployed. If the number of vacancies is equal to that of the unemployed, there is full employment. If vacancies exceed unemployment there is "overfull" employment. But the matching, or mismatching, of vacant jobs and applicants for jobs must be assumed to present a complex and constantly changing pattern. Hence, the numerical relationship of vacancies and unemployeds cannot be more than a very rough and unreliable index of underemployment or overemployment.

2. It is true, economists often speak of "overfull employment" which suggests that output can exceed, as well as fall short of, the full employment level. We shall return to that problem later on. It is enough to say at this point that there is an essential asymmetry: While GNP can and occasionally does fall substantially below the full employment level, it can, practically speaking, not rise much above the full employment mark. (This does not necessarily mean that comparatively small deviation in the upward direction—say, 2 or 3 percent—may not have serious inflationary consequences.)

3. The descriptive characteristics of business cycles have been definitively established in numerous publications of the National Bureau of Economic Research (New York). See especially A. F. Burns and W. C. Mitchell, *Measuring Business Cycles* (1946); W. C. Mitchell, *What Happens During Business Cycles* (1951); and Geoffrey Moore, *Business Cycle Indicators,* 2 vols. (1961).

4. The cyclical calendar is kept up to date in a monthly publication *Business Cycle Developments,* later rechristened *Business Conditions Digest* published by the U.S. Department of Commerce. This remarkable publication, which has become the model for many similar endeavors in

foreign countries, grew out of the pioneering work of the National Bureau of Economic Research under the leadership of Arthur F. Burns and Geoffrey Moore. There are occasionally changes of the cyclical calendar. Statistical data are revised which may result in shifting the turning point by one or two months. Other investigators, using different methods of analysis and description, have confirmed the National Bureau calendar of cycles. See, e.g., J. A. Schumpeter, *Business Cycles* (New York, 1939); Edwin Frickey, *Economic Fluctuations in the U.S.* (1942).

5. Such a mini-recession occurred in 1962, and again in 1967 as a reaction to the "credit-crunch" of 1966.

6. In the postwar period there have been many "foreign exchange crises" and some pretty sharp declines on the stock exchange, but no waves of concentrated bankruptcies or runs on the banks. In the summer of 1966 and in the spring of 1970 there were "credit squeezes" or "crunches," but they did not snowball into full-blown financial crises. Financial crises, as a fairly regular feature of the business cycle, are probably a thing of the past.

7. Changes in the rate of growth of GNP and industrial production may or may not be accompanied by changes in employment and unemployment. Consider an economy that experiences a rapid long-run rise in productivity (output per man or man-hour) resulting from technological progress and a large volume of saving and investment. In such an economy, for example Germany or Japan in the postwar period, a decline in the rate of growth of output (GNP), without an absolute drop, can result in fairly large unemployment. In an economy with a lower long-run growth rate of productivity changes in the level of unemployment will tend to be correlated with an absolute rise and fall in GNP. In recent years economists have come to pay more attention to what they call "growth cycles." See the authoritative study by Ilse Mintz "Dating American Growth Cycles" in *The Business Cycle Today,* 50th Anniversary Colloquium ed. by Victor Zarnowitz National (New York, 1972) p. 39

8. This is usually true also of milder fluctuations, mini-recessions, which do not qualify as cyclical recessions.

9. It may be impossible and is, fortunately, not necessary to disentangle in a general fashion their respective contribution, although in many cases the influence of overriding exogenous forces is clearly visible. There are finer questions which have been much debated but need not be taken up here, such as this: Is the nature of the endogenous mechanism such that cyclical movements would continue even in the absence of exogenous shocks, or would the cyclical fluctuations gradually become milder and eventually abate altogether if external shocks were absent? It is easy to construct different models of cyclical behavior based on broadly plausible

assumptions that display qualitatively different behavior—"regular oscillations," "damped oscillations," "explosive oscillations," etc., with or without exogenous shocks. There exists an *embarras de richesse* of such models, both theoretical and econometric ones, the latter based on actual statistics. This kind of approach to the problem of cycle, which ten years ago enjoyed great popularity, especially among Keynesian economists, has turned out to be an ephemeral fad, devoid of any real usefulness.

10. For small countries that are tightly knit into the world economy or into a regional bloc such as the European Community (EC, the official title of the European Common Market), what is exogenous from the point of view of the national economy may be better regarded as an endogenous movement of the group as a whole. But even in the EC, the most tightly knit regional bloc in existence, the business cycle is not yet fully synchronized and each member has still some, though not much, "cyclical autonomy," i.e., scope for independent business cycle policy. The latter is, in contrast, almost entirely lacking in individual regions of even the largest national economies.

11. In modern times, the main source of these deficits in less-developed countries is almost always grossly inefficient and grotesquely overstaffed public enterprises—railroads, telephone, telegraph, shipping, oil refining, steel mills, etc., which have been taken over by the state from foreign and domestic private owners.

12. It is sometimes said that the United States has been living under conditions of secular inflation during some 150 years before the Great Depression of the 1930s. Since this period was one of rapid growth and development of the American economy, the conclusion is sometimes explicitly drawn or subtly suggested that there is no reason to worry about secular inflation.

This is an extremely misleading argument. True, the wholesale price index, when plotted over the period of 1800 to 1920—or 1945—gives, superficially viewed, the impression of having a rising trend. But what really happened was that in each major war inflation—1812, Civil War, World War I, World War II—the price curve was raised to a new high; after the war prices fell sharply but failed to return to the prewar level. Between the war peaks there is no clear-cut inflationary trend visible. Since World War II the picture has been different. No decline in the price level has occurred, and none is in prospect in the United States or anywhere else in the world.

13. In 1966-67, for the first time in the postwar period, Germany had a recession with an absolute though slight decline in GNP, industrial production and so on.

14. If the labor force grows rapidly the volume of *employment* need not exhibit any absolute drop, but only a reduction in the rate of growth.

15. Statistically, unemployment may be masked by cyclical changes in the rate of labor-force participation.

NOTES TO CHAPTER 4

1. In theories of that sort, a distinction between two phases of the upswing is usually made or implied: A "healthy" phase "recovery" or "expansion" and then an "unsustainable" extension, often called "boom."

2. It would be wrong to say that it was universally accepted by conservative or laissez-faire liberal economists. For example, the National Bureau of Economic Research and Chicago groups of economists never adhered to it. Nor did A. C. Pigou, whom Keynes treated as the arch-classicist. On Pigou's views on the question how to deal with the depression in the 1930s, see T. W. Hutchison, *British Economics and Economic Policies 1946-1966* (London, 1968). The author demonstrates that Pigou's position has been completely misrepresented by some of the Keynesians. See especially Herbert Stein, *The Fiscal Revolution in America* (Chicago: 1969). On the views of "the Chicago School," see Don Patines in "Friedman on the Quantity Theory and Keynesian Economics," and Milton Friedman's reply in "Comments on the Critics," both in *Journal of Political Economy*, vol. 8, no. 5, Sept./Oct. 1972, pp. 883-953. Also J. Ronnie Davis, *The New Economics and the Old Economists* (Ames, Ia., 1971).

3. M. Friedman and A. J. Schwartz, *Monetary History of the U.S.* (Princeton, 1963), p. 691.

4. The free enterprise economy, hobbled though it is by government interventions, union restrictions and so on, has shown a remarkable capacity to adjust even to large shifts in demand. This has been dramatically demonstrated by the comparative ease with which the transition from a war economy to peace production was accomplished after the first as well as after the second world war. The so-called postwar depressions after World War I (1920-21, 1929-33) were caused by deflationary developments and had nothing to do with the physical difficulties of relocating real resources (including labor) from war to peace production. After World War II the deflationary developments were avoided and there were no postwar depressions comparable to those after World War I. (There were five mild recessions since World War II, but they had nothing to do with the war.)

It has never been explained satisfactorily why the alleged real distortions in a peacetime boom should be so much more destructive and difficult to correct than the infinitely larger distortions caused by a major war.

5. The fact that the prolonged inflation since 1965 has proved to be more resistent to mild disinflationary measures than optimistic policy makers had assumed will hardly prove to be an exception. On the other hand, there is a clear tendency of severe depressions being followed by long periods of expansion. This is easy to explain: Naturally it takes longer to get back to a full employment level if the expansion starts from a position with much unemployment and slack than if it starts from a position with little unemployment and slack.

6. Schumpeter and others flirted with the idea that the coincidence in the early 1930s, accidental or otherwise, of the contraction phases of several superimposed types of concurrent fluctuations accounted for the exceptional severity of the slump. But Schumpeter himself did not take very seriously his own suggestion that the convergence of the downturn of what he called the Kondratieff, Juglar and Kitchin cycles in the early 1930s explained the sharp decline in economic activity. His fully considered opinion is reflected in the remark that "the darkest hues of cyclical depressions ... are due to adventitious circumstances." "Historical Approach to the Analysis of Business Cycles," in *Conference on Business Cycles* (New York: National Bureau of Economic Research, 1951), p. 150.

7. Technically, according to the authoritative National Bureau of Economic Research cycle calendar, the depression which started with the crash on the New York Stock Exchange in 1929 came to an end in March 1933. The next very sharp decline was from May 1937 to June 1938. Between March 1933 and May 1937 GNP rose fairly fast from the extremely low level it had reached. But the recovery was far from complete. In 1937 unemployment was still 14.3 percent and the economy did not get back to its 1929 level until after the outbreak of the second world war. In 1939 unemployment still was 17 percent of the labor force. Hence, when referring to the Great Depression we mean the whole depressed decade of the 1930s.

8. The best description and analysis, especially of the monetary side of the Great Depression one finds in the "truly great" book (Sir Roy Harrod's words) by Milton Friedman and Anna J. Schwartz, *Monetary History of the U.S.* National Bureau of Economic Research (Princeton, 1963). See especially the "magnificent" Chapter VII (Harry Johnson's words) on "The Great Contraction, 1929-1933." Chapter VII appeared also in a separate paperback edition (Princeton, 1965).

If anyone finds the statement concerning the weaknesses of the unit banking system (without deposit insurance) and its consequences exaggerated, let him read Jacob Viner's blunt, convincing and well-balanced analysis, "Recent Legislation and the Banking Situation," *American Economic Review* (Mar. 1936, Supplement 26), pp. 106-19. Here are some of Viner's conclusions:

> An outstanding aspect of the depression in the United States was the extraordinary weakness which the American banking system revealed under pressure. The mass withdrawals of cash from the banks, the forced liquidation of their assets by the banks in their desperate attempts to remain open, the repeated waves of banking failures . . . the final closing of the system as a whole, these phenomena were without a near parallel in any other country, although this was a depression which no Western country escaped. The depression, it is true, was more severe in the United States than in most other countries, but the weakness of the banks must be held largely responsible for this . . . The deflation of bank credit was carried much further in the United States than in almost any other country for which comparable data are available. . . .
>
> What are the causes of this peculiar weakness of the American banking system? The explanation, I am convinced, lies in the fact that of all the modern national banking systems [the United States] alone has adhered predominantly to the eighteenth-century model of individual small-scale units, as distinguished from large-scale banking institutions with many branches. The American bank-closings of 1931 to 1933 were but a typical reproduction of the normal events of an English business depression before the development in England of branch banking on a large scale. [pp. 106-07]

9. On Keynes' criticism of the New Deal policies, see R. F. Harrod, *The Life of John Maynard Keynes* (New York, 1951), p. 447. Gunnar Myrdal told the author of the present book that Leon Blum, too, spurned the advice of British and Scandinavian socialist friends who urged him to concentrate on recovery and put off reforms.

10. Nazi-Germany's antidepression policies were better conceived and more efficiently executed than the New Deal policies. Needless to add that a large and increasing part of the additional output was channeled into nefarious uses (party purposes and preparation for war). But it would be quite wrong to say that the "poorer classes" did not participate in the recovery. Wage *rates* did not rise much but real labor *income* rose sharply because unemployment and short-time were quickly eliminated.

11. Further elaboration will be found in my contribution to the volume, *Keynes' General Theory: Reports of Three Decades,* ed. R. Lekachman (New York, 1964), pp. 294-96.

12. Thus international liquidity, measured by the ratio of gold stock to the volume of world trade, was gradually increased and reached record

heights when the Second World War broke out providing the monetary basis for the post-war inflation.

13. The comparison between the New Deal and the Nazi policy executed by Hjalmar Schacht is very instructive. Both regimes came to power at the same time under similar circumstances of deep depression. It would be wrong to brush the comparison aside on the ground that a totalitarian regime could do things which a democracy could not do. The cardinal mistake committed by the New Deal (which Schacht avoided) was to push up costs by fostering labor and business monopolies. As a consequence an unusually large part of the rise in money GNP (effective demand) went into prices and only an unusually small part into larger real output and employment. It was a case of a government-produced cost-push inflation which took a lot of doing and could have been easily avoided. We shall come back to the cost-push aspect of the episode in Chapter 6.

14. One of the first places where this was clearly stated is not in any of Keynes' writings or that of any Keynesian, but in *Economic Stability in the Postwar World* (Report of the Delegation on Economic Depressions, pt. II, League of Nations, Geneva, 1965). The leading spirit of the Committee was the late Alexander Loveday, who was a member of the Mont Pelerin Society. Other members were: W. W. Riefler (chairman), R. H. Brand, Robert Marjolin, Louis Rasminsky and Oskar Morgenstern. The present writer helped to formulate the passage under consideration.

15. A tax reduction that is limited to a certain period will be less effective than a permanent one, because people will regard a temporary tax reduction as a windfall or capital gain rather than an increase in their disposable income, and therefore they will not increase their expenditures correspondingly.

16. Actually, fiscal policies cannot be tuned sufficiently fine precisely to offset such problematic differences in the effectiveness of different policy tools.

17. There are two finer points here which I shall not discuss in detail. At a higher interest rate private individuals may use their cash balances more effectively so that even with a constant quantity of money an increase in aggregate expenditure would result from a higher velocity of circulation of money. To the extent that this is the case, it would not be difficult to allow for the change in velocity; but it would seem to be only a minor qualification.

The other point is the theory that larger government *expenditures*, even if financed by higher taxes and not by borrowing, has an *overall* stimulating effect. (That tax-financed expenditure increases can stimulate particular industries is not questioned.) This theory, which at one time had a certain popularity in Keynesian circles—it was called the theory of "the balanced-budget multiplier"—is in reality a perversion of the Keynesian doctrine and is totally unacceptable from the liberal standpoint, even if it contained a tiny grain of truth. The "balanced-budget multiplier" is a wholly different animal than the ordinary "deficit multiplier."

18. This quote comes from *Money, Interest Rates and Economic Stability* (proceedings of a symposium sponsored by the American Bankers Association, New York, 1967), pp. 110-11.

Friedman has developed his theory in many important writings. The basic papers are "The Effects of a Full-Employment Policy on Economic Stability: A Formal Analysis" and "A Monetary and Fiscal Framework for Economic Stability," in *Essays in Positive Economics* (Chicago, 1953).

See also the two collections of popular writings *Dollars and Deficits* (Englewood, N.J., 1968) and *An Economist's Protest: Columns in Political Economy* (Glen Ridge, N.J., 1972), and the collection of more advanced papers, *The Optimum Quantity of Money and Other Essays* (Chicago, 1969).

19. Friedman emphasizes that "automatic movements in government expenditures and receipts ... are stabilizing. These are the stabilizers." Clearly, it cannot make much difference whether a *given* change in government receipts or expenditures has come about automatically or was contrived ad hoc.

A minor qualification of this statement might be that an ad hoc change may have an "announcement effect" which would presumably be absent in the case of an automatic unannounced change. This could possibly make the discretionary measures a little more effective, dollar for dollar, than the automatic changes.

20. An NBER monograph by Victor Zarnowitz, *An Appraisal of Short-Term Economic Forecasts* (New York, 1967), executed with the meticulous care and scrupulous objectivity one expects from an NBER publication, has shown how poor the record of forecasting endeavors has been and still is.

21. There are also cases on record where the right measures were taken demonstrably by chance for the wrong reasons. For example, in 1948 Congress passed a tax reduction bill over the veto of the president who had been advised by his economic experts, whose view, shared by many well-known economists, was that a tax cut was not warranted by the cyclical situation. Later, the tax cut turned out to be almost perfectly timed. It went into effect several months before the onset of the first postwar recession which started in November 1948. It would be overgenerous to assume that Congress had planned it that way.

21a. The literature on the subject is immense. The "monetarist" position has been repeatedly stated by Milton Friedman. See his works previously cited. An excellent statement, precise but in plain language, will be found in the article "The State of the Monetarist Debate" by Leonall C. Anderson with two commentaries by Lawrence R. Klein (a non-monetarist) and Karl Brunner (a monetarist) Federal Reserve Bank of St. Louis. Review vol. 55, No. 9, September 1973.

22. Critics have objected that the monetarist rule is not sufficiently precise because the concept of money can be defined in different ways, e.g., including or excluding time deposits. This criticism is, however, not convincing for two reasons. First, what matters is steadiness of monetary growth and not its absolute magnitude. Second, although there may be institutional changes calling for a change in the definition of money, these changes are likely to be infrequent and slow; there is then no objection to change the concept of money from time to time. It therefore does not matter much that by using different monetary aggregates the rate of monetary growth varies somewhat.

23. The difference between majority and minority was that they recommended different target figures for the annual growth of money supply. The majority says that money supply should rise by 3 to 5 percent a year; the Republican minority, more conservative, proposed 2 to 4 percent.

24. From October 1966 to June 1967 industrial production declined slightly, interrupting temporarily the steep upward trend which spans the whole period from 1966 until 1969. GNP figures, too, show a marked decline in the rate of growth, though not an absolute decrease, from the 4th quarter of 1966 to the 2nd quarter of 1967.

25. A frank admission of past mistakes and a firm promise to change course was made by George Mitchell, member of the Board of Governors of the Federal Reserve System. See *U.S. News and World Report,* Jan. 20, 1969. Governor Mitchell said: "The Federal Reserve Board . . . thought the tax increase in 1968 would quickly exert a dampening influence on the rate of business expansion. It turns out that we were wrong." To the question whether the board was determined to get inflation under control, Mitchell answered: "Yes indeed. We mean business in braking the inflation psychology that has developed." He promised to "proceed in an orderly fashion," but admitted that there was the risk of a recession which, he said, cannot be avoided.

26. The Federal Reserve Bank of St. Louis has put all economists in their debt by computing and publishing all these figures continuously in very handy form.
It should be observed that the figures quoted in the text are the average rate of growth. Both price and money growth accelerated somewhat during the period.

27. "Milton Friedman's *A Program for Monetary Stability: A Review,*" in the *Journal of the American Statistical Association,* vol. 57, Mar. 1962, pp. 211-20.

28. *The Intellectual Revolution in U.S. Economic Policy Making* (The Second Noel Buxton Lecture of the University of Essex, London, 1966), pp. 4 and 6.

29. Schumpeter is the only theorist who toyed with the idea that "inflection points mark equilibrium positions." But he did not really take his idea seriously.

30. This is now generally admitted even by Keynesians. Keynes himself denied it in the first part of his book where he presented an overly simplified version of his "General Theory," but in fact abandoned the idea in a later chapter where he offered a fuller picture of his theory. The lengthy discussions of the so-called "Pigou effect," "Keynes effect" and "Lerner effect" have clarified the various routes through which full employment is established. It should also be observed that in a progressive economy where output per man-hour (productivity) increases steadily no *absolute* decline in wages would be necessary but only a decline relatively to the upward trend. I am speaking here of the wage *level,* not of wages of any particular group ("relative wages").
The proposition that Keynesian unemployment is incompatible with perfect competition in the labor market (flexible wages) has been challenged by Axel Leijonhufvud in his brilliant book *On Keynesian Economics and the Economics of Keynes* (New York, 1968). But his attempt amounts to downgrading and interpreting Keynesian unemployment as frictional unemployment. This surely was not Keynes' intention. It is true, however, that *The General Theory* is such an untidy and loosely written book that it is possible to find passages which seemingly support the weirdest interpretations.
We briefly return to Leijonhufvud's theory in Chapter 5 in connection with a discussion of different types of unemployment.

31. It should be observed that the word "marginal" is here used in its common sense meaning of "least skilled," "on the margin of employability" and not in the technical sense of marginal productivity theory. We return to the impact of minimum wages in the following chapters.

32. This was stressed by Keynes himself, and he surely would have taken the same position with respect to minimum wages.

33. The doctrinal roots of the two schools cannot be traced in greater detail here. Nor will all the theoretical issues involved be taken up. I confine myself to exploring the comparative effectiveness of monetary and fiscal policy as stabilization devices.

An exhaustive review and penetrating analysis of all issues involved can be found in various writings of David Fand. See especially his articles: "A Monetary Interpretation of the Post-1965 Inflation in the U.S.," "Some Current Issues in Monetary Economics," and "Monetarism and Fiscalism" (*Banca Nazionale del Lavoro Quarterly Review,* Rome, June 1969, Sept. 1969, and Sept. 1970). "Keynesian Monetary Theories, Stabilization Policies, and the Recent Inflation," *Journal of Money, Credit, and Banking* (Aug. 1969). See also the "Symposium on Friedman's Theoretical Framework" *Journal of Political Economy* (vol. 80, Sept./Oct. 1972), with contributions by James Tobin, Karl Brunner and Allen H. Meltzer, Patinkin and Friedman himself.

34. It is significant that the most energetic and influential sponsor in the U.S. Congress of this basic change in policy was Senator Paul H. Douglas, formerly a professor at the University of Chicago, who in the matter of monetary policy was under the strong influence of his former colleagues at the university.

35. In *The General Theory* Keynes never categorically asserted the actual existence of a liquidity trap; in other words, of an insatiable propensity to hoard additional sums of money which the monetary authorities are willing to create. (The unKeynesian hoarding terminology has the advantage of highlighting the utter implausibility, if not absurdity, of the idea of an absolute liquidity trap.) Liquidity traps and complete inelasticity of investment with respect to the rate of interest are usually referred to in *The General Theory* as situations that may be approximated or might arise in the future, not as an actually existing condition.

36. Professor Samuelson put it this way: A pure fiscalist says "Money does not matter"; a pure monetarist says "Money alone matters." "There is nobody" he said "worth our notice at the American scene" who takes the extreme fiscalist position "although there still do exist in England men whose minds were formed in 1939, and who haven't changed a thought since that time, and who say . . . money doesn't matter." P. A. Samuelson, "The Role of Money in the National Economy," in *Controlling Monetary Aggregates* (monetary conference sponsored by *The Federal Reserve Bank of Boston,* Boston 1969), p. 7.

37. To express it differently, the sums saved by the government must be somehow "sterilized" and not put into circulation by placing them in the capital market.

38. The assumption often made is a perfectly elastic liquidity schedule (liquidity trap) implying perfectly elastic money supply without the help of the Central Bank. True, Keynes' theory does not require this unrealistic simplification. But it is also true that it does not provide the tools for the required monetary analysis.

39. Aggressive sales of government securities and imposition of higher reserve requirements for banks will raise interest rates and reduce private expenditures, mainly on investment. Government deficit spending, if financed in such a noninflationary way, will "crowd out" private spending.

40. Thus, during the early New Deal, as was mentioned earlier, anti-business policies and talk undoubtedly frightened investors and deprived the easy money policy of much of its effects.

41. Only in a severe depression when prices are falling and further price declines are expected, as was the case in the early 1930s, is it at all possible to doubt the effectiveness of monetary policy. This is the position taken by J. R. Hicks. In a review of Milton Friedman's book *The Optimum Quantity of Money*, he writes:

> When he [Friedman] maintains that a better monetary policy in the United States, in the winter of 1929-30, or in early 1930, would have averted the subsequent depression he raises a question on which a moderate Keynesian, like myself, can have an open mind. But that is not really the issue. At the time when Keynes was writing his book (I suppose between 1931 and 1934) that phase was long past. Is Friedman really maintaining that *after* the crash—when the world economy had already departed a very long way from its equilibrium path—there is any purely monetary policy which could have been a sufficient restorative? That is where one must beg leave to differ. And to differ also, for essentially the same reason, in the modern application—when there has again been a major departure from monetary stability, though in the opposite direction. *[The Economic Journal,* vol. 80, Sept. 1970, p. 672]

Let us recall that in 1931-1933 in the United States thousands of banks collapsed and the money stock shrank precipitously. Is it possible to doubt that energetic monetary policy could have prevented these things from happening? Furthermore, suppose the contraction of the money stock and the wave of bank failures had been prevented, is it possible to doubt that this monetary action would have been effective in the sense that the decline in money GNP and real GNP would have been at least sharply alleviated? I find it impossible to believe that maintenance of the stock of money, let alone in increase, would not have induced people to increase their expenditures. But I certainly would not object to the use of both fiscal and monetary policy to stop the spiral of inflation in such a situation. In fact, I would strongly recommend it. One need not be a Keynesian to accept this, and a Friedmanite need not deny it.

When Hicks hints at the ineffectiveness of monetary policy to bring an entrenched inflation to a halt, the problem is a little different. Surely an inflation, however rapid and prolonged, can always be stopped by sufficiently tight money. What could be questioned is whether a monetary cure could be effective without creating intolerable unemployment. But here the alternative would have to be incomes policy, not fiscal policy. (Incomes policy will be discussed in Chapter 7.)

42. *General* fiscal policy, that is to say. It could be argued that government expenditures can be directed toward depressed areas with much unemployment or reduced in areas that experience special demand pressure (e.g., construction). But *selective* fiscal policy of that type faces enormous administrative difficulties.

NOTES TO CHAPTER 5

1. The provision in the definition "would work at a wage higher than the wage ruling for the type of work they can do" is essential. Many people who are not in the labor force at the ruling wage for the type of work they can do would be happy to work at a much higher wage if it were offered, and most of us would be willing to work much longer hours if the rate for overtime work were much higher than it is. In that sense, there would always be a lot of unemployment, even in periods of full employment.

2. The terms voluntary and involuntary unemployment were introduced by Keynes. He accused the so-called "classical" economists of recognizing only "voluntary" unemployment and denying the possibility of "involuntary" unemployment. Keynes' discussion of the problem is, however, very confused and confusing. The classical economists he referred to denied the possibility of nonfrictional unemployment in *equilibrium* in a *competitive* economy where wages are flexible. This is an entirely different thing than recognizing only voluntary unemployment. Unemployment resulting from an excessively high wage level, imposed by powerful labor unions, could be called "voluntary" from the point of view of the union. For the individual worker it is, however, "involuntary" provided the individual would work at the prevailing wage. But what if a worker as a good union member refuses a job offer at a rate slightly below the union wage? I think in the spirit of the classical theory we still have to classify him as involuntarily unemployed, although it may sound a little artificial to distinguish between his preference as an individual and his action as a faithful union member.

Suppose a minimum wage law keeps workers out of work. They surely are involuntarily unemployed, even if they refuse a job at a wage slightly below the minimum which they would take if there were no legal minimum.

3. If there is unemployment relief and if it is liberally administered, the unemployment figure will contain a certain number of people who are voluntarily unemployed because there are always on the welfare roll many "unemployables" or people who do not care for work at the prevailing wage. This is in addition to the increase in real, involuntary unemployment which a liberal policy of unemployment benefits is likely to create by making wages rigid downward, thus raising the level below which wages of even the least skilled workers cannot fall.

4. The word "structural" is often used as the opposite of general or "Keynesian" unemployment. The latter is due to a fall or inadequacy of aggregate effective demand (deflation). "Structural" unemployment in that sense is thus a *portemanteau* expression designating all unemployment that is caused by other factors than insufficiency of aggregate effective demand.

5. Liberal unemployment relief and welfare payments have the same effect on employment as minimum wages. These measures create, as was pointed out above, spurious (voluntary) unemployment as well as real (involuntary) unemployment.

6. Thus unemployment among teenagers, especially nonwhite teenagers, has been shockingly high even in times of prosperity and "full employment." In August 1967 when the overall percentage of unemployment was down to 3.7 percent, well over 20 percent of nonwhite teenagers were unemployed.

By periodically raising the minimum wage and extending the scope of minimum wage legislation to groups of workers to which it did not apply in the past (e.g., recently to agricultural workers), the administration and Congress make sure that this kind of "structural" unemployment is maintained or increased.

Unemployment caused in the U.S. by the existing system of minimum wages has been exhaustively analyzed by Martin Feldstein in two important papers: *Lowering the Permanent Rate of Unemployment,* Study Prepared for the Use of the Joint Economic Committee, U.S. Congress, 93rd Congress, 1st session, Joint Committee Print (Washington, D.C.: Government Printing Office, 1973), 55 pages; and "The Economics of the New Unemployment" in *The Public Interest,* no. 33 (Fall 1973), pp. 3-42. Feldstein shows that the persistent "new" unemployment in the post-war period is *not* due primarily to a Keynesian deficiency of aggregate demand and hence is not curable by monetary-fiscal expansion. It is primarily what is called in the text "frictional," "structural" and "institutional" unemployment. The author points out that "the current minimum wage law prevents many young people from accepting jobs with low pay but valuable experience." Thus "for the disadvantaged, the minimum wage may have the ironic effect of lowering lifetime incomes by a very large amount." "We encourage and subsidize expenditure on formal education while blocking [through the minimum wage] the opportunity for . . . on-the-job training." This is most unfortunate because on-the-job training is a major factor promoting growth and development.

Feldstein also deals with the unemployment created by the current system of unemployment benefits both in the U.S. and the U.K. The disincentive to look for and accept a suitable job provided by liberal unemployment benefits is often very strong. He shows that, in some cases persons who give up the dole and go back to work suffer an absolute loss of income because income from regular work is taxable while unemployment benefits are not.

The author makes numerous constructive suggestions for changes in policy (other than monetary expansion) designed to reduce unemployment, to eliminate existing inducement for idleness and to remove obstacles to the employment of young, inexperienced workers.

6a. The nature and magnitude of the "irreducible" unemployment, due to the frictional, structural and institutional factors mentioned, have been thoroughly analyzed by William Fellner, Martin Feldstein and Geoffrey H. Moore. "Irreducible" means that it cannot be reduced (except temporarily at the cost of excessive inflation) by monetary-fiscal expansion. See W. Fellner, *Case for Moderation in the Economic Recovery of 1971* (Washington, D.C., American Enterprise Institute, 1971); idem, *Employment Policy at the Crossroads: An Interim Look at Pressures to be Resisted* (Washington, D.C., American Enterprise Institute, 1972); idem, "Aiming at a Sustainable Second Best During the Recovery from the 1970 Recession," in *Economic Policy and Inflation in the Sixties* (Washington, D.C., American Enterprise Institute, 1972) idem, "Employment Goals and Monetary-Fiscal Overexpansion," in *A New Look at Inflation: Economic Policy in the Early 1970s* (Washington, D.C., American Enterprise Institute, 1973); G. H. Moore, *How Full is Full Employment? And Other Essays on Interpreting the Unemployment Statistics* (Washington, D.C., American Enterprise Institute, 1973); Martin Feldstein, see works cited in preceding footnote.

7. This does not, of course, exclude specific measures such as training, retraining, spreading information about job opportunities, and providing subsidies for the transfer to other geographic areas of unemployeds.

8. The chances are that, in this event, the minimum wage will be raised. In fact this policy response makes institutional unemployment totally incurable by global measures of expansion.

9. As the late Professor W. Roepke pointed out, "repressed" is a better word than "suppressed," because what is suppressed is not inflation itself but some of its symptoms, and what is stabilized by these policies of

forced draft is not the price level but the price index. As with most economic statements, these require some minor qualifications. They will be provided later.

10. Inefficient plant and equipment is not always scrapped but often kept as a standby for unforeseen emergencies and unexpected spurts of demand. It thus does not constitute overcapacity and slack although, undoubtedly, it often gets into capacity figures. This is the main reason why global capacity figures must be regarded with some suspicion. Thus, full employment fanatics have claimed that the British economy a few years ago, when unemployment stood at 1.5 percent and prices were rising, was operating at no more than 85 percent of capacity and that, therefore, expansionary measures were indicated!

11. See Dudley Seers, "Theory of Inflation and Growth in Under-developed Economies Based on the Experience of Latin America," *Oxford Economic Papers,* June 1963. The opposing views on inflation were threshed out at a conference in Rio de Janeiro, 1963. Papers and proceedings were published in the volume *Inflation and Growth in Latin America* (ed. Werner Baer and Isaac Kerstenezky, Homewood, Ill., 1964). R. Ruggles and G. S. Dorrance present the monetarist school and Dudley Seers presents the structural position. In *Latin American Issues* (ed. Albert O. Hirschman, New York, 1961) the monetarist view is ably presented by Roberto Oliveira Campos and the structuralist position by David Felix and Joseph Grunwald.

12. "On Structural Inflation and Latin American 'structuralism'," *Oxford Economic Papers* (N.S.), vol. VII, Nov. 1964, pp. 333-54.

13. On the Brazilian system, see J. B. Donges, *Brazil's Trotting Peg, A New Approach to Greater Exchange Feasibility in Less Developed Countries,* with a foreword by Gottfried Haberler (Washington, D.C., American Enterprise Institute, 1971), and Donald E. Syvrud, *Foundations of Brazilian Economic Growth* (Washington, D.C., 1974).

14. Zero inflation does, of course, not mean literally constant price level all the time. Prices rising 1½ or 2 percent can probably be tolerated if the rise is not continuous, but with intermittent periods of rising prices alternating with spells of stable and possibly slightly declining prices.

15. The intensity of a repressed inflation is, however, not easy to define or to measure. If we take the rate of change in the quantity of money or the rise in prices as an index, the repressed inflation after World War II was much less severe than the open inflation after World War I.

16. Quite a few less developed countries have managed to keep inflation at the creeping pace. Mexico, Peru, Malaysia, Taiwan and Jamaica are

NOTES

examples. It is gratifying to see that they have done quite well as far as growth is concerned compared with those that have rapid inflation.

17. If wholesale prices are stable and consumer prices rise by, say, 1.3 percent per year, as was the case in the United States from 1958 to 1965, we may say that there is no inflation, because such a small price rise would hardly be noticeable and can perhaps be explained by statistical inaccuracies, such as failure to allow sufficiently in the cost of living index for quality improvements, for the appearance of new products and the like. There seems to be a systematic discrepancy between the wholesale price index and the consumer price index. Because the latter is heavily weighted with services where productivity growth is slower, the consumer price index usually rises faster than the wholesale price index.

18. Even Keynes, who is often regarded as an out-and-out inflationist, summed up his position this way: "I am not yet converted, taking everything into account, from a preference for a policy today which, whilst avoiding deflation at all costs, aims at the stability of purchasing power as its ideal objective." This quotation comes from his earlier book, *A Treatise on Money* (London, 1930), vol. II, p. 163. There is, however, good reason to believe that in *The General Theory* he did not change his view as expressed in the *Treatise* or at least reverted to it later. On this see my pamphlet, *Inflation: Its Causes and Cures,* rev. ed. (Washington, D.C., American Enterprise Institute, 1966), p. 97 et seq.

19. I shall not try to identify in detail the views of different writers. Milton Friedman's relaxed attitude applies to open, uncontrolled inflation only. He is very much concerned, rightly in my opinion, about repressed inflation. The adherents of the New Economics, on the other hand, are prepared to accept a good deal of controls. See M. Friedman, "What Price Guideposts?" in *Guidelines, Informal Controls, and the Market Place,* ed. G. P. Schultz and R. Z. Aliber (Chicago, 1966); reprinted in M. Friedman, *Dollars and Deficits,* 1968; P. A. Samuelson and R. M. Solow, "Analytical Aspects of Anti-Inflation Policy," *American Economic Review,* 1960.

20. This statement is not contradicted by the general concern about the unemployment and slack caused in 1970 by the attempt to slow down inflation. Unemployment of 5 to 6 percent does not constitute a severe depression, especially in view of the strong probability that, for reasons mentioned earlier, the level of irreducible unemployment is higher now than it used to be. It is true, however, that the standard of judging the severity of recessions has changed. We have raised our sights and are less patient than we were with unemployment rates of 5 percent or more.

21. See my study, *Inflation, Its Causes and Cures,* enlarged ed. (Washington, D.C., American Enterprise Institute, 1966), p. 95.

22. The principal new inflationist is Robert J. Gordon. See his "Steady Anticipated Inflation: Mirage or Oasis" in *Brookings Papers on Economic Activity 2-1971*, as well as earlier papers quoted there and Gordon's statement before the Joint Economic Committee, *Hearings,* July 21, 1971. James Tobin gave his approval to Gordon's "able testimony" (see *Hearings,* Joint Economic Committee, Sept. 9, 1971, p. 377) and expressed similar sentiments in James Tobin and Leonard Ross, "Living with Inflation," in *New York Review of Books,* May 6, 1971. Gordon's theory was criticized by William E. Fellner, "Phillips-Type Approach or Acceleration?" and Arthur M. Okun, "The Mirage of Steady Inflation," in *Brookings Papers* cited above.

23. Tobin and Ross, *New York Review of Books,* p. 24. It should be added, however, that in a full-dress scholarly presentation of his views, Tobin has considerably modified his position. See his masterly presidential address "Inflation and Unemployment" *(American Economic Review,* Mar. 1972). He there tries to make a case for permanent, nonaccelerating—not only harmless but positively beneficial—inflation, without recourse to money illusion. The sophistication of the argument and the command over theories and facts are of the highest order, and the analysis in many ways extremely suggestive and illuminating. But the conclusion concerning permanent harmless inflation is still quite unconvincing.

24. These reforms would be quite sensible on general grounds. They have been demanded for a long time by the monetarist school and it is interesting to observe that on this point, as well as on the rejection of the wage-push theory, neoinflationists and monetarists are in broad agreement.

25. Gordon, *Hearings,* p. 140.

26. Okun, too, reaches the conclusion that "after three years of fairly steady inflation at a rate close to 5 percent, the U.S. economy is nowhere in sight of fully anticipated inflation." [op. cit., p. 491] (It should be kept in mind that the question is whether the rate of inflation should be reduced, hopefully to zero in the end, and not whether a compensating *deflation* should be attempted.)

27. If it were a case of a pure "demand" inflation or what Keynes (in *The Treatise on Money)* called a "profit" inflation, and not a "cost-push" inflation (what Keynes called an "income" inflation), it would be comparatively easy to call a halt to rising prices by monetary measures. The reason is that in a demand inflation profits run ahead of wages (and other contractual incomes) and profits are easier to squeeze than wages, which are rigid downward and are pushed upward by powerful unions.

28. This analysis implies a shift in the Phillips curve or, in other words, a change in the inflation-unemployment trade-off. Gordon and Perry have

tried to show with the help of econometric analyses that the Phillips curve has *not* shifted in recent years. (See *Brookings Papers,* note 22). Strictly speaking what these studies claim is not an unchanged (two-dimensional) Phillips *curve,* but what might be called an unchanged more-than-two-dimensional Phillips *structure.* For they introduce labor market factors other than wages into the picture. At this point I confine myself to saying that I find these studies unconvincing (see Fellner's detailed criticism, op. cit., note 22). The Phillips curve is discussed in greater detail in Appendix C.

29. Added in the proofs, December 1973.

30. The figures represent the rise in consumer prices (seasonably adjusted annual rates) over three months ending October 1973. (OECD, *Economic Outlook,* no. 14 [Paris, December 1973], p. 35).

NOTES TO CHAPTER 6

1. People got rid of their money as fast as they could. For a while wages and salaries were paid twice or even three times a day, and people rushed to the shops to buy what they could before prices were again marked up. Thus, velocity of circulation rose to many times its usual level. As a corollary the "nominal" quantity of money (in terms of depreciating marks), although it multiplied fast, rose much less sharply than prices, and the "real" quantity of money (nominal quantity corrected for the loss of purchasing power of money) fell sharply. It is amusing that some well-known German economists argued at that time that the increase in the (nominal) quantity of money had nothing to do with the rise in prices, because the *real* quantity of money (money stock expressed in constant purchasing power or gold) declined!

It is a fairly general rule that an increase in the *nominal* quantity of money at a rate which causes rapid inflation will cause a decrease in stock of *real* money. The reason is that people will economize on the use of money if its purchasing power is expected to decline. This implies an increase in the velocity of circulation of money. Therefore, prices rise faster than the quantity of money, and this implies a decrease in the real value of the money stock.

2. However, the drop during the Great Depression was of an entirely different order of magnitude than the rise during hyperinflation. There is a striking asymmetry between inflation and deflation. It has often happened that prices have risen to many times their former level. But even in the worst deflation of the 1930s, the price level fell "only" by 50 percent. A

10 percent general price decline due to monetary contraction is already a calamity. This asymmetry has its roots in the downward rigidity of prices, especially of wages, and in the existence of fixed money contracts and debts.

3. The theory of the "Phillips Curve" is discussed in some detail in Appendix C.

4. Incomes policy is usually defined as the broader term, relating to other incomes than labor as well. By 1970 the term had become popular in the United States, but with some change in meaning.

5. See, for example, M. Friedman in *Guidelines,* etc., as quoted previously and Allan Meltzer, "Is Secular Inflation Likely in the United States?" in *Monetary Problems of the Early 1960s,* (Atlanta, Ga., Georgia State College, 1967).

6. What is rigid is money wages. "Efficiency wages" are not quite so rigid. We have seen that labor efficiency declines when the labor market is tight and employment becomes full or overfull. Efficiency increases when the labor market is slack and unemployment increases. That means that even when money wages remain constant, efficiency wages fall somewhat in depressions and rise faster than money wages when unemployment declines.

Real wages, too, are less rigid than money wages, because as a rule money wages are not promptly corrected for changes in the cost of living. But this tends to change in a long drawn-out inflation because more and more cost-of-living clauses are put into wage contracts and such "escalators" usually work only in the upward direction.

7. Suppose overall demand rises in proportion to the gradual growth of output. There is, thus, no inflationary demand pull. Now assume that there are, from time to time, shifts of demand from one group of commodities to others. Then wages will rise where demand increases, but will not fall where demand declines. Thus, in the long run, it is possible that through this ratchet mechanism the price level will be jacked up. A theory of inflation along these lines was put forward by Charles L. Schultze. See his study, *Recent Inflation in the U.S.* (Study Paper No. 1, Joint Economic Committee, 86th Congress, 1st Session, Sept. 1958), and my criticism in *Inflation: Its Causes and Cures* (American Enterprise Institute, 1966 ed., p. 86).

8. It should be pointed out, however, that *indirectly* the cost-push has greatly contributed to the rapid expansion of nominal income. For there can hardly be any doubt that the authorities would not have let the quantity of money increase so fast, if not "so large a part of the growth of

nominal income [had been] absorbed by rising prices" and if consequently unemployment had fallen more rapidly and output had approached the full employment level more quickly. The cost-push and monopolistic price increases were largely due to the ill-advised policies of the New Deal. This analysis is fully acceptable, in principle at least, for Keynesians. Thus, Alvin Hansen in his *A Guide to Keynes* (New York, 1953) points out that "to the extent that this occurs [viz., that money wage rates rise before full employment is reached] the increase in aggregate demand is unnecessarily dissipated in higher prices with correspondingly less effect on output and employment." [p. 193] It is true, however, that few other Keynesians have stressed this point as much as Hansen has.

9. Friedman, op. cit., p. 22. Let us recall that in 1940, after seven years of the New Deal, 14.6 percent of the labor force was still unemployed—a colossal failure of policy unparalleled in other countries.

10. For example, during the recession from July 1957 to April 1958 wages continued to go up in the face of substantial unemployment. This clearly suggests union pressure; and since unemployment, though substantial, was much smaller than in 1933-1937 less "market power" was required than in the earlier period.

It would not be difficult, furthermore, to find cases where unions were able to secure wage increases through strikes in particular industries (e.g., the steel industry) despite the fact that there was a good deal of unemployment in that industry at that time. Another glaring case is that of the construction workers. Their wages have risen sharply despite much unemployment and slack in the industry.

If unions are able to push up wages in slack periods and in depressed industries, they are *a fortiori* able to do it in boom periods and in industries that operate at or near full capacity. That is to say, wage-push reinforces demand-pull.

11. It could be argued that the mere fact that the economy operates at a higher level of capacity makes the demand for labor less elastic and this in itself implies greater monopoly power for the suppliers of labor (unions). But this line of argument would support the wage-push theory.

12. Harry G. Johnson in *Proceedings of the 24th Annual Winter Meeting*, New Orleans, Dec. 1971, ed. Gerald G. Somers (Madison, Wis.: Industrial Relations Research Association, 1972), pp. 168-69. See also my reply to Johnson, ibid., pp. 172-73.

13. Johnson considers "the central issue [to be] political and not economic" (ibid. p. 169). What he seems to refer to is the necessary monetary policy reaction to the unemployment, created or threatened by monopolitic price and wage increases. But wage-push and intolerance to

unemployment are a fact of life in the present world and to call this fact "political" rather than "economic" does not change its nature and relevance in the slightest.

Since, as Max Weber pointed out, most scholars are reluctant to use somebody else's terminology as if it were his toothbrush, it may be useful to restate our theory of the inflationary impact of union monopoly in monetarist language: At any moment of time there exists a "natural rate of unemployment" which "would be ground out by the Walrasian system of general equilibrium equations, provided there is embedded in them the actual characteristics of the labor and commodity markets." (See Milton Friedman's magistral presidential address, "The Role of Monetary Policy," *American Economic Review*, vol. 58, March 1968. Reprinted in *The Optimum Quantity of Money and Other Essays*, Chicago, 1969, p. 102.) Among these characteristics is "the strength of labor unions" which "makes the natural rate of unemployment higher than it would otherwise be." It surely is not farfetched to assume that unions make unemployment higher than modern society is willing to tolerate. The natural reaction is monetary expansion and inflation, to which unions will react with a lag by making larger wage demands which, in turn, threaten to produce unemployment and put pressure on the monetary authorities to maintain or restore full employment and growth by further monetary expansion.

Monetarists who absolve unions and other monopolies from any responsibility for inflation seem to assume that in the final equilibrium the impact of unions is small compared with that of other factors and that the dynamic process runs its course so fast, i.e., that inflation accelerates so quickly, that the monetary authorities will soon desist from trying to maintain employment above its "natural" level.

The first assumption is debatable. The second is clearly and unambiguously contradicted by the long spell of inflation in many parts of the world.

There exist, of course, other powerful motives and reasons for inflationary policies, but wage push by threat of strike is surely the most intractable force making for inflation in modern industrial countries.

Two important recent books which appeared after the present manuscript was completed have come to the same conclusion: Emerson P. Schmidt, *Union Power and the Public Interest* (Los Angeles, 1973), and W. H. Hutt, *The Strike-Threat System: The Economic Consequences of Collective Bargaining* (New Rochelle, New York, 1973).

14. Another argument against the wage-push thesis is that in periods of rapidly rising employment wages of nonunionized workers often rise faster than union wages. This is, however, in most cases a frictional phenomenon of strictly temporary importance. It arises from the fact that union contracts usually run for a year or two, occasionally for longer. Thus it may happen that wage-push is overtaken, so to speak, by demand-pull. But where unions find themselves caught napping they quickly make up for lost time. Wage contracts are broken by wildcat strikes with or without the

tacit consent of the union leaders, and during inflation the wage-contract period is shortened and cost-of-living clauses put into wage contracts.

15. There are exceptions to this rule. Thus, John L. Lewis, president of the United Mine Workers was supposed to have consciously traded dwindling employment in the mines for rapidly rising wages. Another case where the connection between rising wages and employment is immediate, and for all to see, is that of export industries in small countries where exports are a large proportion of output and a small fraction of the world market. Since world demand for the product is very elastic, workers know that exports would fall sharply and they would lose their jobs if wage costs rose faster than abroad.

16. See especially Milton Friedman's masterly presidential address, "The Role of Monetary Policy," *American Economic Review,* Mar. 1963, p. 8.

17. This is one of the cases where what James Tobin aptly calls "the myth of macroeconomics" leads astray. The myth is "that the equilibrium relations among aggregates [wage level, price level, employment in our case] are analogous to relations among corresponding variables for individual households, firms, markets." (See Tobin, "Inflation and Unemployment," *American Economic Review,* Mar. 1972, p. 9.) "The myth is a harmless and useful simplification in many contexts," but it can lead to wrong conclusions in some cases. This would seem especially to be the case when monopolies and oligopolies are involved.

18. We shall discuss in the next chapter whether incomes policy can help to get over this phase of disinflation.

19. He argued his case in numerous writings. The latest where he took that position was his study *Rise and Fall of Incomes Policy, Institute of Economic Affairs* (London, 1969). A second edition appeared in 1971.

20. This could be described as an upward shift or jump of the Phillips curve. But neither Paish nor Meade (see note 21) use that expression.

21. James E. Meade, *Wages and Prices in a Mixed Economy* (Wincott Memorial Lecture, Institute of Economic Affairs, London, 1971).

22. Another prominent British economist who has changed his position on inflation is Lord Lionel Robbins. See his article "Inflation: The Position Now," *The Financial Times* (London), June 25, 1971. Meade's and Paish's findings are supported and confirmed by Martin Feldstein's important research which was quoted earlier: "The Economics of the New Unemployment," in *The Public Interest,* no. 33 (Fall 1973), and *Lowering the Permanent Rate of Unemployment,* Study Prepared for the Joint

Economic Committee, U.S. Congress, Joint Committee Print (Washington, D.C.: Government Printing Office, 1973).

23. Meade points out that in Great Britain during the critical period direct and indirect taxes were sharply raised to make room for larger exports in order to eliminate a balance of payments deficit. In other words some tightening of belts was necessary, because the country had been overspending its income. Such a balance of payments effect would be negligible in the United States.

24. Monetarists, too, have noted that higher taxes may induce labor to increase its wage demands. With the British experience in mind, Harry Johnson says that "workers whose incomes have been allowed to rise faster than productivity by a governmentally allowed balance of payments deficit . . . try to rectify the situation by increasing their wage demands." (See his remarks in *Industrial Relations Research Association* series, ed. Gerald Somers, Madison, Wis., 1972, p. 169.) This is exactly what Meade says. But unlike Meade, whom he sharply criticizes, Johnson seems not to recognize that this reaction of workers implies wage-push by monopolistic unions. In a competitive labor market higher taxes could not simply be passed on by raising wages and prices. What could happen under competition is a reduction in the labor supply. But that would be voluntary unemployment. Moreover, depending on the shape of the supply curve, the actual supply of labor (employment) could either increase or remain constant.

25. Monetarists do not accept this analysis. Thus, David Laidler puts forward a theory which explains the recent British inflation entirely in terms of the rising money supply, inflationary expectations and devaluation of the pound. (D. Laidler, "The Current Inflation—Explanations and Policies," in *National Westminster Bank, Quarterly Review,* Nov. 1972.) I fully agree that inflation cannot be stopped unless the supply of money is brought under control and that with fixed exchange rates Britain has to follow American inflation. It is also true, as I stressed myself, that inflation strengthens union power. But has Meade not a point when he says that inflation and other developments have given the unions an unexpected glimpse of their monopoly power which has permanently changed their attitudes? All this Laidler brushes aside with the remark, "I know of no evidence that would compel disbelief in the assertion of union leaders that their 'militancy' in recent years has been the result of their desire to protect their members' living standards against erosion by inflation." If this were the whole trouble, the cure would be very simple: Insert cost-of-living clauses into wage contracts. Does Laidler really believe that unions would be satisfied with this concession? Can anyone believe that the new developments mentioned by Meade and Paish had no influence at all on union attitudes and on the level of equilibrium unemployment?

26. "Excessive" in the sense of exceeding the real preferences of the workers as revealed by moonlighting and similar practices.

27. See the thorough theoretical and statistical study *Unionism and Relative Wages in the United States: An Empirical Inquiry*, H. G. Lewis, (Chicago, 1963).

28. This is particularly true of unions of specialized, skilled workers (craft unions), but is by no means confined to these as is clearly shown by the success of the United Mine Workers' Union.

29. Some abuses were stopped later by the famous Taft-Hartley Act, but the power of unions was never seriously challenged. On the contrary, in the post-World War II period, extended welfare measures have further enhanced union power by sharply reducing the "terror of unemployment" (Meade).

30. I reached this same result in earlier publications (see, for example, my *Inflation Its Causes and Cures*, 3rd ed., 1966; and *Incomes Policy and Inflation*, Washington, D.C., American Enterprise Institute, 1971. But in one important respect, I have changed the analysis. I used to argue that business monopolies and labor unions were different in that the influence of the former on inflation was a one-shot affair when monopolies are first introduced or when the underlying situation changes in such a way that the market power of existing monopolies is enhanced; whereas labor unions exert a continuing inflationary pressure on wages and prices by pressing every year for wage increases higher than compatible with stable prices at full employment. My monetarist friends have convinced me that the theory of this difference in the modus operandi of business and labor monopolies is invalid. But this change in analysis in no way changes the proposition that unions pose a threat to price stability—the essential role of monetary expansion I have always stressed—nor does it affect the judgment that business monopolies have much less influence on inflation than unions. The analysis in the text tries to demonstrate that, although qualitatively the same, quantitatively the impact of business monopolies on inflation is much smaller than that of labor unions.

31. Thus the activities of the Civil Aeronautics Board (CAB) which regulates air fares results in fares perhaps 40 percent higher than necessary. This is demonstrated by the fact that fares of intrastate lines (in Texas and California) which are not controlled by CAB are much lower. (See Milton Friedman, *An Economist's Protest* [Glen Ridge, N.J., Thomas Horton and Co., 1972], p. 167). Another glaring example is the regulation of freight transportation by the Interstate Commerce Commission. Since the transportation industry has become highly competitive when the railroads lost their monopoly through the rise of road and air transport, no regu-

lations are necessary anymore. Actually the regulations stifle competition and contribute to poor service. The cost to the economy has been estimated at about $10 billion a year. See Thomas G. Moore, *Freight Transportation Regulation Surface Freight and the Interstate Commerce Commission* (Washington, D.C., American Enterprise Institute, 1972).

32. The great bulk of what is statistically reported as "corporate profits" is what economists call "normal profits" and not monopoly profits. Normal profits comprise the yield of capital invested in the enterprise, risk premium and possibly also wages of management. There is furthermore what might be called "Schumpeterian profits," that is to say, profits resulting from *temporary* monopoly positions which innovating entrepreneurs temporarily enjoy who introduce some new products or new process—profits without which innovational activity would slacken and economic growth be slowed down. Obviously these temporary monopoly positions are *not* what we have in mind when we contrast business monopolies to labor monopolies in the context of inflation.

These distinctions are very important and must be made even though it is extremely difficult to quantify them. The cartel of oil-producing countries is no exception because it is not a private but a governmental organization.

33. The situation was, of course, different in the nineteenth century. But times have changed, while liberal clichés have not.

34. On the numerous legal immunities and privileges of labor unions, see the authoritative study of Roscoe Pound, *Legal Immunities of Labor Unions* (Washington, D.C., American Enterprise Institute, 1957).

35. Harry Johnson has completely misunderstood the theory of the wage-push element in inflation when he says that it relies on "unaccountable wickedness and irresponsibility" rather than on monetary factors, time lags and inflationary expectations (op. cit., p. 167).

Labor unions are traditionally regarded as representatives of the poorer classes. This view is completely out of date. With some exceptions labor unions rather represent the middle and upper ranges of the working population. Some of the most effective unions can be found in strata of the population which usually are not regarded as workers such as aircraft pilots, professional people, public servants, teachers and the like. Then there are the other pressure groups which, in one way or the other, either restrict entry into their professions or boost prices of their products, as in the case of the medical profession and farmers.

36. Drastic liberalization of imports could have a sharp antiinflationary effect if it were used as a vehicle for monetary deflation by not recycling the domestic money that importers hand over to the Central Bank for the foreign exchange which they need to pay for the additional imports. This antiinflationary use of import liberalization requires, of course, the pos-

session of large international reserves or credit lines—unless the country started from a surplus position. In the latter case, import liberalization does not reduce the money supply but stops ongoing inflation which resulted from the export surplus.

36a. This way of looking at the problem is, however, not new. For example, it can be found in the important paper by E. B. Bernstein and I. G. Patel, "Inflation in Relation to Economic Development" in *Staff Papers,* International Monetary Fund, November 1952, p. 371 et seq. The authors stress the paramount importance of the wage push by organized labor. Their analysis of inflation is quite general, although they apply it to the problems of less developed countries.

37. James Tobin, "Inflation and Unemployment," op. cit., p. 13. Tobin develops his highly ingenious theory "of a disaggregated wage pattern system" to deal with frictional unemployment caused by insufficient information, stickiness of wages, factor immobility and the like, in the absence of powerful unions and other monopolies. After the long section on frictional unemployment containing the quoted passages follows a short and rather perfunctory section on "the role of monopoly power." To describe a dynamic, disaggregated inflation process of this kind, without reference to monopolies and pressure groups, is like playing Hamlet without the Prince of Denmark!

38. Johnson, op. cit., p. 169. However, speaking of the U.K. and U.S. he attributes the stop-go pattern to periodic "policy-induced bursts in demand" to speed up lagging growth; these efforts run into balance-of-payments difficulties which in turn force a switch in policy. For the U.K. the balance-of-payments has been a real constraint on many occasions. In the United States, the balance-of-payments constraint on the great sweep of internal monetary and fiscal policy had practically disappeared early in the Johnson administration. What constrains macropolicies is fear of inflation. At any rate, to leave out from the cyclical mechanism wage and price boosts by labor unions and other pressure groups means again playing Hamlet without the prince.

39. Friedrich Lutz, "Dilemmasituationen Nationaler Antiinflationspolitik," in *25 Jahre Marktwirtschaft in der Bundesrepublik Deutschland* (Stuttgart, 1972).

NOTES TO CHAPTER 7

1. The Keynesian expression "profit-inflation" would be more descriptive than demand inflation. For aggregate demand in the sense of money GNP (MV, aggregate expenditure) has *not* stopped rising. Only its

rate of increase has been slowed. Thus, from the 2nd quarter 1968 to the 3rd quarter 1969 "total spending" (GNP in current dollars) rose at an annual rate of 7.8 percent. From the 3rd quarter 1969 to the 4th quarter 1970, it rose by 4 percent while "real" GNP (in 1958 dollars) declined slightly by 1½ percent. What had been squeezed was profits. Increases in monetary demand had not been "eliminated."

2. "Wages and Prices by Formula," *Harvard Business Review*, March-April 1965. Reprinted in A. F. Burns, *The Business Cycle in a Changing World* (New York, 1969, pp. 232-53). He has spelled out his ideas on the new incomes policy in numerous speeches and testimonies before Congressional committees. See especially his speech "The Basis for Lasting Prosperity" at Pepperdine College, Los Angeles, Dec. 1970 (mimeographed).

3. Other measures included in the new incomes policy are "expansion of Federal training programs to increase the supply of skilled workers," establishment of national building codes to break down barriers to the adoption of modern production techniques," "liberalization of depreciation allowances to stimulate plant modernization." General wage guidelines, wage or price freezes are not part of Burns' incomes policy. He has, however, edged toward acceptance of at least partial readmittance of guidelines by suggesting that a wage and price review board be set up to evolve principles of wage and price setting in certain areas. Similar proposals have been made by CED, "Further Weapons against Inflation—Measures to Supplement General Fiscal and Monetary Policies," *Committee for Economic Development* (New York, 1970).

4. This difference has been forcefully stated by James Meade, an economist of strong egalitarian conviction (op. cit., pp. 30-32). He argues that the proper instrument for any redistribution of income that may be desired is taxation and social security measures and not price controls which disrupt the market mechanism and thereby reduce output.

Needless to add that tax measures, too, if pushed too far and improperly managed can impair the economy's efficiency. But this is not the subject of the present volume.

5. This does not mean that perfect or pure competition in the strict theoretical sense is the rule. Far from it. I have discussed elsewhere why I think that "monopolistic competition" is essentially competition rather than monopoly. See "Wage Policy and Inflation," in *The Public Stake in Union Power,* 1958. See also my paper "Theoretical Reflections on the Trade of Socialist Countries" in *International Trade and Central Planning,* ed. A. A. Brown and E. Neuberger, (Berkeley, University of California Press, 1968).

6. Even in this area monopoly power should not be exaggerated. In many cases it has been substantially diluted by technological progress.

NOTES

Electricity competes with gas, and the railroads have been subjected to the powerful competition of road and air transport.

7. Import restriction under the guise of antidumping measures are equally objectionable. The antiinflationary and competition-promoting effects of cheap imports in no way depend on whether these imports are made possible by a natural comparative advantage of foreign producers or by subsidies or tax privileges granted by foreign governments or by price discrimination in favor of the *importing* country on the part of foreign producers. (For details and some minor qualifications, the readers should consult the authoritative and definitive treatment of the problem in Jacob Viner's *Dumping: A Problem in International Trade*, Chicago, 1923).

8. This has been pointed out many times. I commented on it in *Inflation: Its Causes and Cures*, 1966 ed., pp. 14, 65, 116-17.

9. The opposite shift, an increase in the share of GNP going to labor, is also possible. This may happen because of technological change and improvements, despite the fact that historically the capital-labor ratio has gone up more or less continuously. (It should be observed that we speak here of the capital-*labor* ratio, not the capital-*output* ratio. Also, as a consequence of technological change and improvements, the latter—the capital-*output* ratio—historically does *not* display a continuous increase.)

10. On this see R. M. Solow, "The Case Against the Case Against the Guideposts," in *Guidelines: Informal Controls and the Market Place*, ed. G. P. Shultz and R. Z. Aliber (Chicago, 1966), pp. 48-49.
It should be observed that this argument applies to *money* wages only. It assumes that *real* wages are not entirely rigid. If the rate of growth of real wages were set at the level of the rate of growth of labor productivity (for example, by adjusting the money wage growth continuously to the rise in the cost of living), unemployment would result whenever the underlying situation required a decline in the share of national income going to labor.

11. This is certainly true for the United States. In some foreign (non-Communist) countries that have all-embracing labor unions—e.g., in the Netherlands—it has sometimes been possible to negotiate uniform wage changes over a large part of the economy. Thus, incomes policy was thought to have been relatively successful in the Netherlands for several years. But after a while it broke down, partly because many Dutch workers could take jobs at much higher wages across the border in Germany. Holland thus experienced a veritable wage explosion.

12. The guidepost theory was developed in reports of the Council of Economic Advisors, during the Eisenhower administration, and further elaborated by the Kennedy and Johnson councils. See especially the reports of 1958 and 1962. On the evolution of the doctrine see Thomas

257

Moore, *U.S. Incomes Policy: Its Rationale and Development*, American Enterprise Institute, (Washington, D.C., 1971). Reprinted in *Economic Policy and Inflation in the Sixties* with an introduction by William Fellner, Washington, D.C., American Enterprise Institute, 1972.

Incomes policies in other countries have been described and analyzed by Eric Schiff, *Incomes Policies Abroad*, Part I-1971, Part II-1972, American Enterprise Institute; and by Lloyd Ulman and Robert J. Flanagan, *Wage Restraints: A Study of Incomes Policy in Western Europe* (Berkeley, Cal., 1971). Both works come to the conclusion that income policy has not worked well anywhere.

13. Similar formulations can be found already in the 1958 report of the Council of Economic Advisors. The rules—or "guides"—for "noninflationary price behavior and the corresponding modifications" are even more complicated than those for wages. They largely turn on comparative productivity trends in different industries [p. 189].

14. The reports for later years have added nothing to the analysis of the problem. On the contrary, the formulations have become cruder and more dogmatic and the "modifications" have been deemphasized for the simple but unconfessed reason that they are in practice totally unworkable. Even the Kennedy and Johnson Council of Economic Advisors have always rejected general wage and price fixing.

15. Indeed, years before the guideline approach to wage setting was first proposed by the Council of Economic Advisors, some of its problems and dilemmas were clearly foreseen and analyzed by no one less than the late Professor Sir Dennis Robertson in the first report of the *British Council on Prices, Productivity and Incomes*. (The first report of the so-called "Cohen Council," named after its chairman, Lord Cohen, was largely Sir Dennis's handiwork, especially its analytical parts).

Concerning "the suggestion that from time to time a percentage figure should be announced by which average money wages could increase without damage to the national interest," the report has this to say:

> We are conscious of the attractiveness of this proposal offering as it does the hope of establishing a link between the rate of wage increases and the growth in overall productivity. There are, however, serious practical objections to it. There would always be industries in which there were good reasons for the advance in wages to exceed the average; others in which much less good reasons for it to do so could be thought up; very few in which the case for lagging behind the average would be readily conceded. There would thus be a real danger that the prescribed average would always become a minimum, and the process of wage inflation therefore built into the system.

16. The 1965 report of the Council of Economic Advisors said "that during recent years of still excessive unemployment and idle capacity, strong competition for jobs and markets reinforced a growing sense of responsibility on the part of labor and management." The "growing sense of responsibility" is vaguely attributed to the operation of the guidepost policy. This sounds like a witch rainmaker saying, when the rain came, that favorable atmospheric conditions reinforced his efforts!

17. The experience of seeing the guidepost policy falling into disuse and disrepute under its own weight has not prevented the economists, who unsuccessfully tried to make the policy work, from chiding their successors for not using this ineffective instrument.

18. This does not, of course, mean that the labor market, in the absence of unions, would necessarily be perfect and that nothing can be done to remove imperfections.

19. The only major country where industry-wide collective bargaining still is the exception rather than the rule is Japan. Largely for this reason, Japanese wages have retained considerable downward flexibility. This fact surely is responsible for Japan's remarkable ability to cope with inflationary bouts and balance-of-payments difficulties by means of orthodox monetary measures (credit restriction) without creating more than very mild and short recessions.
In 1973, however, the good record of Japanese labor relation seemed in danger of being drowned in a wave of demand inflation. One gets the impression that Japan is rapidly adopting American and European institutions and practices.

20. I refer again to the authoritative study by Roscoe Pound, "Legal Immunities of Labor Unions," in *Labor Unions and Public Policy,* American Enterprise Association (Washington, D.C., 1958). The same volume contains an excellent analysis, "Economic Analysis of Labor Union Power," by E. H. Chamberlin.

21. In Great Britain where union power has been more abused than in the United States, the conservative government of Edward Heath has recently undertaken a major reform of the rules of collective bargaining.

22. Arthur F. Burns, *The Management of Prosperity* (New York, 1966), p. 46. An early analysis of the pernicious effects of minimum wages, especially when applied uniformly to the regions in different stages of economic development, has been given by John V. Van Sickle in *Planning for the South: Enquiry into the Economics of Regionalism* (Nashville, Tenn., Vanderbilt University Press, 1943) and in "Geographical Aspects of a Minimum Wage" *(Harvard Business Review,* spring 1946).

23. It was suspended, but the suspension was later rescinded and replaced by a complicated "largely self-regulating system of wage constraints" and "monitoring" construction prices. Many states have their own "little Davis-Bacon Acts" which contribute to the "skyrocketing" wage and price increases in the construction industry. All these wage-boosting measures are the legacy of the New Deal of the early 1930s. See John P. Gould, *Davis-Bacon Act: The Economics of Prevailing Wage Laws*, American Enterprise Institute (Washington, D.C., 1971).

On the highly damaging effect of minimum wages on young, inexperienced and otherwise disadvantaged workers, see the previously quoted work by Martin Feldstein, "The Economics of the New Unemployment," in *The Public Interest*, no. 33 (Fall 1973), and *Lowering the Permanent Rate of Unemployment*, Study Prepared for the Joint Economic Committee, U.S. Congress, Joint Committee Print (Washington, D.C., Government Printing Office, 1973). Not only are many underprivileged workers deprived of employment for considerable periods, but they are robbed of some of their lifetime income by losing highly important on-the-job training.

24. See John V. Van Sickle, *The Walsh-Healy Public Contracts Act*, American Enterprise Institute (New York, 1952).

25. The reform of collective bargaining proposed by the government of Edward Heath tries to put an end to or at least have a sharp reduction of public financing of strikes.

26. The rise of the consumer price index over its level twelve months earlier reached its highest level, 6.3 percent, in February 1970. The rate of increase fell steadily to 4.4 percent in August 1971 and 4 percent in September 1971. The decline continued to 3.3 percent in September 1972.

27. To give one example of what must be expected, I quote what an administration spokesman, Assistant Secretary of the Treasury Edgar E. Fiedler, said in a speech before the National Economists Club (Washington, D.C., Nov. 15, 1972):

> Although economic distortions do not currently appear to be numerous there is one major sector of the economy where significant distortions are reported: softwood lumber, which is under heavy demand-pull pressure from the extraordinary boom in homebuilding. It is widely reported by industry sources that:
> — Lumber production is being held 5 to 10 percent below levels that would be achieved in the absence of controls, primarily to avoid violation of the Price Commission's profit margin rule.
> — Minor operations are being performed on standard cuts of

lumber to create "new products" that are exempt from price control.

- Railroad cars full of lumber are being shipped around the country from middleman to middleman, accumulating markups (which are individually legal) but not getting the lumber to the final user.
- Phony export and reimport transactions are being recorded—the paperwork is there but no lumber ever leaves the country—to circumvent the Price Commission's regulations.

Another well-known case where price control has caused considerable damage is that of natural gas. By fixing the price at the wellhead too low, exploration and production have been discouraged. This has contributed to the fuel shortage and has encouraged imports which are not subject to control. With the passage of time the number of distortions has rapidly multiplied and the damage done to the economy is mounting from day to day.

28. From a political standpoint the new policy was a masterstroke. Yielding to the tremendous pressures coming from all sides to introduce controls, the new policy left the political opposition and news media without argument in the economic field. And going, as it did, with the trend—which although quite visible was not seen at the time by those who were clamoring for controls—the new policy minimized possible damage.

29. See also Sidney Weintraub, "An Incomes Policy to Stop Inflation" in *Lloyds Bank Review,* London, Jan. 1971.

30. *The Economist* of London ("A Real Incomes Policy," issue of Apr. 24, 1971) proposed that increases in wage incomes exceeding the growth in labor productivity—say, 3 percent—should be taxed 100 percent. That would indeed remove any incentive to ask—or to strike—for larger wage increases. But an "incomes policy" as stiff as that would be equivalent to a wage freeze. In an acute crisis such a measure may become necessary. But it could not be maintained for any length of time without causing the same distortions and wastes.

Upgrading of labor, granting of all sorts of hidden fringe benefits and similar devices would be the inevitable, wasteful, inefficient, discriminatory and distorting methods of evasion—discriminatory and distorting because different types of work and employment lend themselves unequally to the application of these stratagems.

31. Added in the proofs, December 1973. For background and details see *A New Look at Inflation: Economic Policy in the Early 1970s* (Washington, D.C., 1973).

NOTES TO CHAPTER 8

1. Alfred Marshall, *Principles of Economics*. Quoted by Ragnar Nurkse in *Equilibrium and Growth of the World Economy* (Cambridge, Mass., 1961, p. 242).

2. See my paper "Theoretical Reflections on the Trade of Socialist Countries" in *International Trade and Central Planning*, ed. A. A. Brown and E. Neuberger (Berkeley, Calif., 1968), and the literature quoted there.

3. The late Jacob Viner, one of the great economists of our times and the leading American expert on international trade, once said, "The best arguments for protection have been invented by free traders."

4. Agriculture is a different story. The agricultural policy of the EEC (or EC–European Community, as it is now usually called) has been highly protectionist and interventionist. The same experience with respect to the removal of industrial tariffs has been made in the so-called European Free Trade Area (EFTA) or the "outer seven" (Great Britain, the Scandinavian countries, Austria, Switzerland and Portugal).

An experience on a much larger scale that demonstrates the amazing adaptability of a modern industrial free enterprise economy is the smooth transition from a war to a peace economy both after the First and the Second World War. The dire predictions that the cessation of war production would cause prolonged mass unemployment were proved entirely wrong by events. The so-called postwar depression in the United States after the First World War in 1920-1921 had nothing to do with difficulties in shifting productive resources from war to peace production. It was a *financial* and *monetary* aftermath of war. As such, it could have been avoided by antideflationary policies. This was corroborated by the fact that after the Second World War, when financial management was much better than after the First World War, no severe depression occurred, confuting again many dire predictions by well-known experts.

In 1970-1971 winding down the war in Vietnam, cutting expenditures on defense and on outer space explorations (moonshots and the like) have caused widespread unemployment in defense, aerospace and related industries. But unemployment surely would have been much less of a problem if it had not been necessary to restrain aggregate effective demand in order to hold down inflation. If the wage-push could be stopped and the reins on the expansion of aggregate demand loosened, the existing pockets of unemployment would be speedily absorbed.

5. An early but excellent statement can be found in the famous *Report on Manufactures* by Alexander Hamilton, Secretary of the Treasury, 1791. This was a report to Congress in response to a resolution passed in the House in January 1790. The best-known German proponent of infant

industry protection was Friedrich List (1789-1846) who was strongly influenced during his stay in the United States (1825-1832) by American thought. His main work where he propounded his theory of infant industry protection was *The National System of Political Economy*, German ed., 1841. A much better and more precise early statement of the infant industry idea can be found in John Stuart Mill's *Principles*, bk. 5, ch. X, 1, illustrating Viner's *dictum* that the best arguments (or at any rate the best presentation of arguments) for protection come from free trade economists.

6. For a theoretical analysis and demonstration of the close connection between the new concepts and the old infant industry idea, see my paper "An Assessment of the Current Relevance of the Theory of Comparative Advantage to Agricultural Production and Trade," *The International Journal of Agrarian Affairs*, vol. IV, no. 3, May 1964, pp. 130-49, reprinted in J. D. Theberge, ed., *Economics of Trade and Development*, pp. 168-87. This volume contains an excellent selection of the modern literature and an extensive bibliography.

7. It has often been pointed out that protection in the form of a subsidy would be more efficient than in the form of import tariffs, for two reasons. First, the cost of protection to the consumer, even if eventually successful, is more obvious in the case of a subsidy; therefore the chances are better that protection will be discontinued after it has served its purpose, that is to say, after the industry has "grown up." Second, an import duty (or quota) distorts the price structure and reduces consumer satisfaction from the same income. This argument, which has become very popular among modern theorists, does not deny that even if eventually successful, infant industry protection implies a temporary burden; but it makes the point that the burden is less if it is imposed by a direct tax to finance the subsidy than by an indirect tax such as an import duty. It would lead too far to go into further details. In my opinion it is not a matter of great importance, for direct taxes, too, produce distortions and blunt incentives.

8. This is obscured and minimized by the untenable but very popular assumption that there exists large-scale "disguised" unemployment in agriculture in less-developed countries. For a criticism of this notion, see my above-mentioned article and the literature cited there.

9. Henry Rosovsky, *Capital Formation in Japan* (New York, 1961), pp. 100-101. See also the literature mentioned there.

10. See F. W. Taussig, *U.S. Tariff History*, many eds.; and *Some Aspects of the Tariff Question*, 3rd ed. (Cambridge, Mass., 1931).

11. See Taussig's *U.S. Tariff History*.

12. For supporting evidence see especially an earlier volume of the present series—John V. Van Sickle, *Freedom in Jeopardy: The Tyranny of Idealism* (New York: World Publishing Co., 1969), pp. 89-94 and 189; notes 7, 8 and 9 and an earlier paper by the same author, "The Southeast: A Case of Delayed Industrialization," in Papers and Proceedings, *American Economic Review,* vol. 41, May 1951.

13. See Albert Hirschman, "The Political Economy of Import-Substituting Industrialization in Latin America," *Quarterly Journal of Economics,* Feb. 1968. Hirschman speaks of the "Disenchantment with industrialization." He does not, however, try to assess the cost of the policy and leans over backward in trying to prove that the "disenchantment" has gone too far. See also my paper "Protectionism or Freer Trade in the Less Developed Countries," 11 Politico, University of Pavia, 1969, XXXIV, no. 3.

14. The quote comes from Harry G. Johnson, "A Word to the Third World: A Western Economist's Frank Advice," *Encounter,* Oct. 1971 (a slightly different version of the paper was published under the title "Controls vs. Competition in Economic Development" in the *Bulletin of the United Malayan Banking Corporation,* Kuala Lumpur, Malaysia, 1972). Johnson discusses the results of planning in general, not just protection, in historical perspective. Some of his results are: " . . . central planning . . . has been both a failure in terms of results achieved and a shocking waste both of the time of the world's very scarce supply of educated manpower and of the political energies of the peoples of the developing countries. Whatever the theoretical appeal of deliberate economic planning, we have in practice lacked the capacity to execute it properly; and in consequence, we have squandered human and natural resources . . .", and "Much worse, we have developed ways of thinking and of doing things that perpetuate the initial faith in the control approach, and its methods, without in fact being capable of delivering the promised goods." [op. cit., p. 3]

The two comprehensive empirical studies are: (1) I. Little, T. Scitovsky and M. Scott, *Industry and Trade in Some Developing Countries—A Comparative Study* (London, 1970). This volume, sponsored by the Development Center of OECD (Paris) is based on detailed studies, published as separate volumes, covering Brazil, India, Pakistan, Taiwan and the Philippines. (2) Bela Balassa and associates, *The Structure of Protection in Developing Countries* (Baltimore, Md., 1971), sponsored by *The International Bank for Reconstruction and Development.* See also Bela Balassa, "Trade Policies in Developing Countries," *American Economic Review,* May 1972, which is based on the aforementioned volume and cites other material; and Richard N. Cooper, "Third World Tariff Tangle: Pros and Cons of Preferences," *Foreign Policy* (Cambridge, Mass., no. 4, 1971). On the whole question of development policy, see also P. T. Bauer, *Dissent on Development Studies and Debates in Development Economics* (London, 1972). This impressive and exciting work presents a detailed and devas-

NOTES

tating criticism of the prevailing interventionist-protectionist theories and policies of development of less-developed countries.

15. See Jack Baranson, "Integrated Automobiles for Latin America?" in *Finance and Development,* vol. 5, no. 4, Dec. 1968, published by IMF and LBRD, and by the same author *Automotive Industries in Developing Countries,* World Bank Occasional Paper (Washington, D.C., 1969).
L. J. Johnson, "Problems of Import Substitution: The Chilean Automobile Industry," in *Economic Development and Cultural Change,* vol. 15, Jan. 1967, pp. 202-16, and B. Munk, "The Welfare Cost of Content Protection: The Automotive Industry of Latin America," *Journal of Political Economy,* Jan.-Feb., 1969.

16. For facts and figures and other examples, see the papers by Balassa and Cooper cited above (note 14). On Malaysia, see the study by Wolfgang Kasper, *Malaysia: A Case Study in Successful Development,* American Enterprise Institute (Washington, D.C., 1974).

17. This test is important to make sure that under the spur of foreign competition the hitherto protected industries maintain their efficiency and do not lapse into lazy monopoly. But it does *not* follow that if an industry can get along without protection, or even if it has become an exporter itself, we have absolute proof that the policy of protection has benefited the country. It is possible that the industry in question would have grown up anyway or that the resources (human and material) invested in that industry would have yielded higher returns elsewhere.

17a. The choice example is the Bank for International Settlement (B.I.S.) in Basel, Switzerland, which had been solemnly declared dead and ordered to be interred (in an annex by the Bretton Woods charter for the I.M.F.), but is still very much alive.

18. There existed under the gold standard a built-in mechanism which was supposed to counteract tendencies of the price level to decline or to rise. When prices declined the resulting rise in the "real value" (purchasing power) of gold would stimulate gold production by making it profitable to mine poorer ore and to prospect more vigorously for gold deposits.
But this clearly was a slow and haphazard process which could not and did not provide the world with a smoothly growing supply of basic money.

19. It is often thought that, before Keynes, the cycle was conceived entirely in terms of prices and monetary flows and that it was Keynes who directed attention to output and employment. That is not true. For example, A. C. Pigou whom Keynes criticized as an archclassicist, analyzed the business cycle—"industrial fluctuations," he called it—long before Keynes in terms of output and employment. See his *Economics of Welfare,* 1st ed. (London, 1920). The part dealing with business cycles in that

book, entitled "The Variability of the National Dividend," was later expanded into a separate monograph *Industrial Fluctuations*, 1st ed., London, 1927; 2nd rev. ed., 1929.

20. *Communiqué*, March 27, 1973, of "The Committee of 20" of the IMF, charged with making proposals for reform of the international monetary system.

21. Immediately after the First World War, the pound was at a discount vis-à-vis the dollar and gold, and deflationary measures were taken to restore the prewar parity. The return to gold at the prewar parity was accomplished in 1925 under Winston Churchill as Chancellor of the Exchequer. As a consequence the pound was overvalued, and the British economy was depressed throughout the 1920s when other countries enjoyed brisk prosperity. Keynes had correctly predicted this outcome in his famous pamphlet *The Economic Consequences of Mr. Churchill* (London, 1925, reprinted in *Essays in Persuasion*, London, 1931, and in vol. IX of the *Collected Writings of John Maynard Keynes*, London, 1972). Keynes had recommended a voluntary 10 percent cut in money wages to compensate for the overvaluation of the pound.

It should perhaps be added that Keynes' warning about overvaluation of the currency was entirely in the classical tradition. A hundred years earlier, after the Napoleonic Wars, David Ricardo, a leading member of the British classical school, had said that he would never recommend return to the prewar parity if prices had risen substantially. Actually Britain made exactly the same mistake after the Napoleonic Wars with the same deleterious consequences.

The full story of the British return to gold in 1925 has been told only recently after hitherto secret official papers have become available. See D. E. Moggridge, *British Monetary Policy 1924-1931: The Norman Conquest of $4.86* (Cambridge, 1972). The subtitle is an allusion to Montague Norman, the powerful governor of the Bank of England, who was to a large extent responsible for the return to gold at the prewar parity of $4.86. The new material tends to exonerate Churchill. In a remarkable "most secret" memorandum, addressed to his advisors before the decision to return to gold at the old parity was made, Churchill had asked all the relevant questions. But he received wrong or misleading answers. Keynes objected not to restoration of the gold standard as such, but to the time and to the rate of $4.86.

22. The reader may ask what is the difference between the gold exchange standard and dollar standard? The two terms are often used interchangeably. True, it would be more correct to speak of the gold exchange standard so long as the dollar was convertible into gold and of a (pure) dollar standard since the dollar became inconvertible into gold. But in most contexts it does not do any harm if the terms are used interchangeably, inasmuch as the date at which the convertibility of the dollar

into gold came to an end is an ambiguous matter. On August 5, 1971, the dollar was officially declared inconvertible. But even before that it was de facto inconvertible except for small drawings. (For private individuals the dollar had been inconvertible into gold for a long time. The same is true of all other currencies.)

When the dollar was formally declared inconvertible into gold on August 15, 1971, many commentators, academics and others, proclaimed that the dollar standard had broken down and was finished. Actually the opposite is true. A pure dollar standard had formally replaced the gold-exchange standard. The world-wide dollar standard was phased out as more and more currencies floated and may be said to have come to an end in March 1973 when the major European currencies let their currencies float. However, many smaller countries continue to peg their currencies to the dollar. There exists in other words a dollar bloc and the dollar is still the world's foremost official reserve and private transactions currency.

23. To a considerable extent, although perhaps not entirely, other countries could have protected themselves against infection with the depression bacillus from abroad by depreciating their currencies or still better by letting them float down, or by controls. But controls to ward off speculative capital flows are not enough. To protect surplus countries from imported inflation current account (trade) controls would be required. And these are analytically equivalent to disguised, messy, discriminatory and distorting exchange rate changes. They are the prototype of objectionable beggar-my-neighbor policies. These issues are further discussed below.

24. The preceding analysis should be qualified and elaborated in one respect: The statement that countries which peg their currencies to the dollar must participate in the U.S. inflation does not mean that their consumer price indexes must rise by precisely the same percentage as the American index. In fact in some countries, notably in Japan, consumer prices have risen significantly faster than in the United States. Despite this, Japan has had a large trade surplus which was clearly an inflationary factor in the Japanese economy. This is due to the fact that export prices in Japan have risen less relative to Japanese prices generally than American export prices have risen relative to American prices in general. The reader will perhaps ask why attribute world inflation to the U.S. inflation if there were many other countries that spontaneously pursued inflationary policies? Did their inflation not tend to spread to others including the U.S. itself? The answer is first that this is an analytical causal and not a moral attribution and second that while in principle under fixed exchange rates inflation spreads in *all* directions, there actually exists a quantitative if not a qualitative asymmetry between the U.S. and other Western countries. This asymmetry stems from three facts, first that the dollar is the world's most important official reserve and private transactions currency, second that the international trade sector in the American economy is much smaller than in any other Western country and third that U.S. domestic

macro-economic policies which determine the U.S. inflation have become almost entirely independent of the state of the balance of payments. (On these important issues, see Harry G. Johnson "Secular Inflation and the International Monetary System" in *Journal of Money, Credit and Banking,* vol. V, No. 1, Part II, 1973, p. 509-519 and G. Haberler "International Aspects of U.S. Inflation" in *A New Look at Inflation Economic Policy in the Early 1970s,* Washington, D.C., 1973, American Enterprise Institute, pp. 79-106.)

25. Other factors responsible for smooth functioning of the inter-regional adjustment mechanism which are often mentioned are: absence of trade barriers, free mobility of capital and labor and the fact that inside a country the central government's tax revenues and expenditures may act as a partial offset or buffer if any part of the country gets into trouble. Concerning the last-mentioned factor, the underlying idea is that there exist, in fact, regional balance-of-payments difficulties, but that they are masked as regional stagnations or booms. However, if a region is relatively depressed it gets relief from the fact that the central government's tax revenues from the depressed region automatically decline while expenditures for welfare, unemployment benefits and possibly ad hoc grants increase. In addition to the automatic relief to depressed regions the central government is likely to take ad hoc discretionary rescue measures in the form of special subsidies and tax abatements. In the European Economic Community a substantial regional fund has been set up partly for the purpose of reducing the risks of "monetary unification" (rigidly fixed exchange rates).

It would lead too far to pursue these problems further. The factor discussed in the text would seem to be sufficient to explain the relative ease of adjustments between regions and the difficulties of adjustment between sovereign countries.

26. Small and medium-sized countries are in better position to get away with oversized devaluations. The reason is that other countries can more easily absorb the surplus of a small country. France succeeded on several occasions to depreciate the franc so much that she was able later to develop a large surplus and accumulate a large reserve of gold. This happened in 1926, following the postwar inflation, and again in 1958 when General de Gaulle devalued the franc. (It must not be forgotten, however, that in both cases prudent financial and economic policies were necessary conditions of success.) The United States, on the other hand, was not able to devalue the dollar sufficiently in the Smithsonian agreement of December 18, 1971, because other countries were not willing to take the risk of a large American surplus which might have resulted from a larger devaluation of the dollar.

The basic fact is that it is impossible to know what an equilibrium pattern of exchange rates is. There is no presumption that the haggling at an international conference will produce such an ideal pattern of rates.

Nor is the application of elaborate econometric models a guarantee for success. The pattern of exchange rates, including the devaluation of the dollar, that emerged from the Smithsonian conference (December 1971) was based on econometric research carried out in the IMF. In a few months it turned out that the Smithsonian pattern of rates was wholly inappropriate.

27. I say "as a minimum" because many experts add to the required list what they call "common regional policies." What they have in mind is an agreement of the participating countries collectively to finance measures to support and develop regions in any member country that may be damaged by the adoption of a common monetary system (impossibility of changing parities), or in some proposals by less-prosperous (backward) regions in general (see for example Giovanni Magnifico., *European Monetary Unification*, London, 1973).

The European Economic Community has accepted this principle and has set up machinery to implement it.

Whether this additional requirement is economically really justified will not be further discussed here. So much is certain, if this postulate is accepted (which is politically probably unavoidable), it will tremendously complicate monetary unification.

28. In March 1973 when the Germans proposed a common float of the European Common Market currencies against the dollar, the British proposed exactly that scheme as a condition for hitching sterling to the mark and other continental currencies in a common float against the dollar. Naturally the proposal was not accepted by the continentals.

Later in 1973 several currencies in the common float were upvalued, the German mark in June, the Dutch guilder in September and the Norwegian crown in November. As was to be expected under semi-fixed rates (adjustable peg) each change caused a mini-crisis in the form of heavy speculative capital flows into the currency that was suspected to go up, i.e., the German mark.

29. The bank also lost on the dollar reserves that it had on hand when the 1969 speculation started. But these losses could be shrugged off as unavoidable.

30. It is true, however, that toward the end of the first period of float, in 1961-1962, the government started to manipulate the rate. This did not work well at all and Canada was then pressured by the United States and the IMF to restabilize. It is, however, quite incorrect to say that the system of the freely floating rate broke down because of malfunctioning. The fact is that the government did not allow it to function any more. On the Canadian experience, see Paul Wonnacott, *The Floating Canadian Dollar: Exchange Flexibility and Monetary Independence* (Washington, D.C., American Enterprise Institute, 1972). For a detailed analysis of the

Canadian experience, see Richard E. Caves and Grant L. Ranber, *Capital Transfers and Economic Policy, Canada 1951-1962* (Cambridge, Mass., Harvard University Press, 1971).

31. On the Brazilian system and its lessons see *Brazil's Trotting Peg: A New Approach to Greater Exchange Rate Flexibility in Less Developed Countries,* by Juergen B. Donges, revised and translated by the author with the aid of Eric Schiff and a foreword by Gottfried Haberler, (Washington, D.C., American Enterprise Institute, 1971).

The unfortunate fact that inflation rates in Europe and Japan have recently reached Brazilian levels, has greatly enhanced the relevance of the Brazilian example for the industrial countries.

32. In 1962 the "clean" (unmanaged) float was replaced by a "dirty" (poorly managed) float with disastrous consequences which led to the abandonment of the float until June 1970.

33. Another gimmick is to "twist interest rates" (operation twist). A deficit country which suffers from recession would try to keep long-term interest rates relatively low and short-term rates relatively high on the theory that low long-term rates have a favorable effect on internal equilibrium (alleviate the recession) while high short-term rates improve the balance of payments by attracting capital from abroad or by inducing domestic capital to stay at home.

Actually the twisting interest rates as tried in the United States in the 1960s is even less effective than changing the mix of monetary and fiscal policies. Obviously there is little room for a divergent movement of long- and short-term rates, and it is very doubtful whether short- and long-term rates can have a pronounced differential impact on internal and external equilibrium. Even if the policy succeeded, the effect would be similar to running down international reserves, the only difference being that under some definition of deficit, private capital attracted by high short-term interest rates would go "above the line" in the international accounts.

The theory of these policies has been developed by Robert Mundell and later elaborated by Harry G. Johnson in "Some Aspects of the Theory of Economic Policy in a World of Capital Mobility." (Originally published in *Essays in Honour of Marco Fanno,* Padova, Italy, 1966. Reprinted in H. G. Johnson, *Further Essays in Monetary Economics,* Cambridge, Mass., 1973. This paper contains useful references to the literature.) Johnson has, however, become skeptical about the usefulness of the devices. In the introduction to the 1973 book, he says that he now thinks that these "extensions of Keynesian international policy models . . . are both far too easy for the mathematically competent theorist and not very illuminating for the policy maker." [op. cit., p. 12]

33a. It should perhaps be pointed out because it is often misunderstood that in the 1930s the controls were not the consequence of floating but on the contrary the result of excessively rigid parities. Each time a major country devalued its currency—Great Britain in 1931, the United States in 1933/34—others were prevented by gold standard mentality to follow suit; instead they protected their parities by controls (import restrictions). The vicious process became known and remembered as "competitive depreciation." Depreciating one's currency to snatch a trade advantage and thereby to stimulate the economy is a beggar-my-neighbor policy and the very opposite of floating.

34. A halfway house between exchange rate changes and controls is a general import surcharge. The United States imposed an import surcharge of 10 percent in August 1971 to force other countries to realign their exchange rates. When this was accomplished in the so-called Smithsonian agreement of December 18, 1971, the surcharge was abolished. But during the currency crisis early in 1973 the possibility of a surcharge, even a discriminatory one directed against the imports from certain countries, was frequently mentioned, sometimes as a measure of "last resort." This is most unfortunate, for although a surcharge "across the board" is better than import restrictions on selected commodities, especially quantitative ones (quotas), it is obvious that a devaluation of say 10 percent is always better and more effective than an import surcharge of 10 percent. The reason is that devaluation, although it restricts imports, also stimulates exports, while a surcharge only restricts imports. A surcharge is a protectionist method and destructive of trade while a devaluation is neither.

35. It should be mentioned that if a deficit country levies a surcharge of X percent on all imports and at the same time grants a subsidy of X percent on all exports, it would achieve, as far as commodity trade is concerned, exactly the same effect as a devaluation of X percent. (Similarly, an import subsidy plus an export tax of X percent is equivalent to an appreciation of X percent.) The tax-subsidy method was, in fact, proposed as a substitute for exchange rate changes, e.g., by Keynes before Great Britain devalued sterling in 1931. In the postwar period the method has been occasionally applied although never in a "clean" form of a *uniform* tax and subsidy. This is precisely the difficulty, that it is likely to be used in a selective and discriminatory manner and technically cannot be applied to service transactions (tourism, for example). For further discussion see G. Haberler, "Import Border Taxes and Export-Tax Refunds Versus Exchange Rate Changes" in *Approaches to Greater Flexibility of Exchange Rate Changes: The Bürgenstock Papers* ed. Fred Bergsten et al. (Princeton, N.J., 1970).

36. It would be most desirable if they used "negative controls" in the sense of eliminating existing import restrictions (tariffs, quotas) and export subsidies. Unfortunately not much use has been made of this method.

37. A sophisticated argument against the efficacy of exchange rate changes which on closer analysis turns out to be based on the existence of an internal policy dilemma can be found in the modern monetarist

271

literature. It has become popular to argue that at least in a wide-open economy a depreciation would not work because prices will quickly adjust, workers will ask for higher wages and any initial balance-of-payments improvement will disappear. It requires money illusion, it is said, to achieve a lasting effect and those who advocate exchange rate changes are criticized for unrealistically "relying on the presence of international money illusion but absence of domestic money illusion" (Michael Parkin, "An Overwhelming Case for European Monetary Union" in *The Banker*, London, Sept. 1972, p. 114d). An earlier, more cautious version can be found in Ronald McKinnon's well-known paper "Optimum Currency Areas" *(American Economic Review*, vol. 33, 1963, pp. 717-24). Speaking of a "highly open economy," McKinnon says: "Changes in the exchange rate will necessarily be completely offset by internal price-level repercussions with no improvement in the trade balance." (see p. 719. McKinnon refers to Robert Mundell's famous article on Optimum Currency Areas AER, 1961, which expressed similar views.)

This theory has far-reaching implications of which the authors do not seem to be fully aware. Under full employment, elimination of a deficit which is financed by drawing on reserves or running into debt requires some belt-tightening (cut in "absorption"), for exports must go up and/or imports go down thus reducing what is available for domestic consumption and investment. (On this point see my pamphlet *Money in the International Economy*, 1st ed., Cambridge, Mass., 1965, p. 30; 2nd ed., 1969, p. 45.) Keeping in mind that in these models for simplicity "labor" stands for all factors and "wages" for all incomes, the criticized theory, in effect, assumes that nobody is willing to accept a cut in his real income. If this is the case, if real incomes cannot be reduced, equilibrium in the balance of payments can be restored neither by floating nor by depreciation nor by internal credit contraction, except through the creation of unemployment. (This has been clearly recognized by W. M. Corden, *Monetary Integration: Essays in International Finance No. 93*, Princeton, N.J., 1972, p. 9.)

The crucial domestic implication of this theory is that Keynesian policies would be ineffective in reducing unemployment. If the money illusion is really gone, if unions bargain in real terms, and insist on wage increases exceeding productivity growth, unemployment is unavoidable. Harry Johnson's treatment of the problem is unsatisfactory (See his essay, "The Monetary Approach to Balance-of-Payments Theory" in *International Trade and Money* ed. M. Connolly and A. Swoboda, London 1973, p. 236.) Discussing the criticism of what he calls the "standard model" on the ground that it assumes "that workers can be cheated out of their real marginal product by devaluation," he says:

> The charge . . . is incorrect: if rectification of a balance-of-payments deficit requires that the domestic marginal product of labour in terms of foreign goods falls, because the price of domestic goods relative to foreign goods must be reduced in the foreign and home

markets to induce substitution between these goods favourable to the balance of payments, it requires no money illusion but only economic realism for the workers to accept this fact.

The criticism is, however, correct, he continues:

> ... if the elasticities of substitution between domestic and foreign goods are in fact high (approximately infinite), and it is nevertheless assumed that wages will remain unchanged in terms of domestic currency. For in this case it is being expected that workers will be content to accept wages below the international value of their marginal product.

If a country lives beyond its national product by depleting reserves or running into debt and if then an attempt is made through a devaluation and a rise in the price level to reduce absorption to the level of the national product—can that be described as "cheating workers out of their real marginal product?" I don't think so. Wages are reduced to the real marginal product. As in the first case it "requires only economic realism" to understand that a country cannot live forever beyond its means. Three more remarks seem to be in order. *First,* the whole problem can arise only if there are powerful monopolistic labor unions. In a moderately competitive labor market real wages would not be rigid. *Second,* I doubt very much that we have really reached the stage where unions bargain in real terms. Money illusion has been weakened, but is not yet dead. *Third,* it should be kept in mind that in many cases the purpose of a devaluation is not to eliminate a deficit but to restore convertibility. In these cases the deficit has already been suppressed by controls. Hence devaluation or floating does not require any further belt-tightening. On the contrary, belts can be loosened a little bit because the elimination of controls will make the economy more efficient. (For the last point, see my *Money in the International Economy,* 1st ed., p. 30; 2nd ed., p. 45.) A thorough discussion of these problems can be found in the paper "Controlled Floating and Confused Issue of Money Illusion," by William Fellner in Banca Nazionale de Lavoro, Quarterly Review, September 1973.

38. There have been lengthy discussions and disagreements among experts (especially in the German literature) whether inflationary (or deflationary) influences from abroad cannot be transmitted directly, rather than via the balance of payments. Consider a small country with a large foreign trade sector. If inflation goes on abroad, export and import prices will be immediately affected and through them the price level may quickly be jacked up, without any prior surplus in the balance of payments (increase in international reserves) having developed.

It is a question of the speed with which a country adjusts to inflation (or deflation) abroad. Whether slow or fast, with a lengthy or a short or in the limiting case no intermediate phase of a balance-of-payments surplus (deficit), *under fixed exchanges* prices must eventually adjust *and* so must the monetary circulations, either automatically via conversion of the increased international reserves or by internal credit expansion.

What is said in the text about the possibility of avoiding imported inflation (or deflation) is, in principle, independent of the speed of adjustment.

39. The reason why deflation and depressions cause more profound real dislocations than inflation is (as has been pointed out earlier) that wages and prices are rigid downward; they adjust much more easily in an upward direction during an inflation than downward during a deflation.

40. See especially C. P. Kindleberger, "The Benefits of International Money," *Journal of International Economics,* vol. 2, no. 4, Sept. 1972.

41. Advocates of fixed exchange rates sometimes try to support their case by asserting that the logic of floating requires that existing unified currency areas should be broken up. If flexibility of exchange rates is a good thing for the United States and Canada, why not also for the U.S. South or West vis-à-vis the East? Where should the line be drawn? The answer is that the line should be drawn where the basic conditions for monetary unions, sufficient unification of basic economic policies, are fulfilled; and that is usually, although not always, in the existing sovereign states. The advocate of flexibility is not forced by the logic of his theory to recommend that the United States should be broken up into several currency areas because inside the United States the conditions for monetary unification and sufficient unification of economic policies are fulfilled.

These problems have been more obscured than clarified by the so-called theories of the "optimum currency" areas, i.e., speculations about the economic criteria that determine whether any two or more countries qualify for monetary unification. The criteria usually mentioned are factor mobility (Mundell) and degree of "openness" of the economies concerned (McKinnon). (See R. A. Mundell, "A Theory of Optimum Currency Areas," *American Economic Review* vol. 51, 1961; and R. I. McKinnon, "Optimum Currency Areas," *American Economic Review* vol. 53, 1963.) Surely the overriding condition for monetary union is political: Countries must be able to agree and stay agreed on common basic economic theories.

42. Most advocates of floating believe that some interventions in the market by monetary authorities (central banks) can be justified. I speak of "managed" or "controlled" floating (not of "dirty" floating), if interventions merely consist of buying and selling of foreign exchange in the market to prevent short run fluctuations or to moderate excessive swings. Practically all floats, including the Canadian, have been of the managed

kind. Experience seems to show that so long as the authorities avoid rigid pegging of a particular rate, managed floating remains quite effective, in the sense that it discourages destabilizing speculation. I call it "dirty" floating if the interventions go beyond the mere buying and selling of foreign exchange in the market. Floating of this type involves such things as "split markets" and dual or multiple exchange rates for different types of transactions, a flexible unpegged (or mildly pegged) rate for "financial" or "capital" transactions and a pegged rate for "commercial" or "current" transactions. Dirty floating has been practiced in recent years by a number of European countries, notably France and Belgium. It requires more or less arbitrary distinctions between what is a "commercial" and "financial" transaction and detailed supervision of substantially *all* transactions to keep the two markets apart. Since it is easy to camouflage current transactions as capital transactions and *vice versa* dirty floating requires a large beurocratic apparatus and gives rise to legal or illegal, wasteful, corrupting and distorting evasions or avoidances.

NOTES TO APPENDIX B

1. See the pioneering article by George J. Stigler "Information in the Labor Market," *Journal of Political Economy Supplement,* Oct. 1962, and *Microeconomic Foundations of Employment and Inflation Theory,* a collection of essays ed. Edmund S. Phelps (New York, 1970), especially Armen A. Alchian's essay "Information Costs, Pricing, and Resource Unemployment." This essay has references to the earlier literature, especially J. R. Hicks' *The Theory of Wages* (London, 1943) and W. H. Hutt *The Theory of Idle Resources* (London, 1939). An excellent more elementary exposition can be found in Arman A. Alchian and William R. Allen, *University Economics,* 2nd ed. (Belmont, Cal., 1967). See also James Tobin's presidential address, "Inflation and Unemployment," *American Economic Review,* March 1972.

2. This is the so-called "Keynes effect." B. P. Pesek and T. R. Saving in *Money, Wealth and Economic Theory* (New York, 1967) assert that he also recognized the "Pigou effect." But we need not go into that here.

3. A. C. Pigou, *Lapses from Full Employment* (London, 1945, p. V). True, this was a post-Keynesian book. But Pigou had taken the same position in his earlier *Industrial Fluctuations* (London, 1927).

NOTES TO APPENDIX C

1. *Economica,* vol. 25, Nov. 1958, pp. 283-99. There have, of course, been many earlier attempts to connect inflation with the level of unemployment. But Phillips' work was couched in econometric terms. This fact probably accounts for its strong appeal to contemporary economists.

2. There exist several good reviews with lengthy bibliographies of the literature that took its starting point from Phillips' work. Monographs are: R. G. Bodkin, *The Wage-Price Productivity Nexus* (Philadelphia, 1966) and G. L. Perry, *Aggregate Wage Determination and the Problems of Inflation* (Cambridge, Mass., 1966). Elaborate discussions and fairly complete bibliographies can be found in the articles by Edwin Kuh, "A Productivity Theory of Wage Levels—An Alternative to the Phillips Curve" (*The Review of Economic Studies,* vol. XXXIV (4), Oct. 1967, pp. 333-60) and Edmund S. Phelps, "Money Wage Dynamics and Labor-Market Equilibrium" (*Journal of Political Economy,* vol. 76, July-August 1968, pp. 678-711).

3. In a progressive economy, where output per man-hour (labor productivity) increases steadily, price stability is compatible with rising money wages and, of course, with rising real wages as well. Hence it takes less unemployment to keep prices stable than it would take to keep money wages stable.

4. Phillips, op. cit., p. 283.

5. If there exists an irresistible wage-push which imposes a minimum wage increase of, say, 2 percent, the curve would become horizontal at that rate. This stiuation would still be compatible with *price* stability if the annual wage increase imposed by the wage-push is lower than the annual rise in labor productivity.

6. If money wages, more precisely the wage *level*, remained stable, prices would fall roughly in proportion to the increase in labor productivity so that *real* wages would rise just as much as with rising money wages.

7. Phillips' assumption of a stable trade-off over this long period thus reflects an extreme version of the demand-pull theory of inflation because it implies that market power of labor has no influence on wages and unemployment. This goes far beyond the position of the modern critics of the wage-push theory of inflation which we discussed earlier. These critics do not deny that the large increase in market or monopoly power of labor unions that has taken place during the period studied by Phillips has had a

profound influence on the level of unemployment and presumably also on the *short-run* trade-off between inflation and unemployment.

8. See especially his masterful presidential address, "The Role of Monetary Policy," *American Economic Review*, vol. 58, Mar. 1968, pp. 8-11, and his contribution to *Guidelines, Informal Controls and the Market Place*, ed. G. P. Shultz and R. Z. Aliber (Chicago, 1966), pp. 55-61. The "Trade-off" and "Equilibrium" views have been well analyzed and compared by R. W. Spencer in "The Relation Between Prices and Employment: Two Views," in *Review* (Federal Reserve Bank of St. Louis, vol. 51, no. 3, Mar. 1969). This article contains numerous references to the literature.

9. As explained earlier, this does not mean that inflation must inexorably accelerate. Restrictive monetary policy can always prevent acceleration, in principle, at least, notwithstanding certain technical difficulties to keep it exactly at a particular level. But what monetary policy cannot prevent is adjustment of nominal wages and interest rates to the (constant) rate of inflation. When these adjustments are made, unemployment will rise again; in other words, the Phillips curve will shift upward and not stay put. With the same rate of inflation more and more unemployment will be associated.

10. This, of course, does not mean that government policy cannot reduce the equilibrium level of employment and unemployment. Improvements in the structure of the labor market, better information of workers about job opportunities, training and retraining programs, elimination of minimum wages and similar regulations, restraints on the monopoly power of labor unions through the withdrawal of the far-reaching legal and de facto privileges which they presently enjoy—these and similar measures would serve to reduce the equilibrium level of unemployment and bring about a lasting increased output and employment.

11. Friedman, in his presidential address, offers some cautious observations and guesses about the time these various reactions may take; op. cit., p. 11.

12. Henry Wallich, in his remarkable paper "The American Council of Economic Advisers and the German Sachverstaendigenrat: A Study in the Economics of Advice," *Quarterly Journal of Economics*, Aug. 1968, has some interesting observations: "The Phillips curve retains its familiar shape only so long as there is money illusion. Without money illusion, i.e., if inflation is fully and instantaneously discounted, the Phillips curve becomes a vertical line over the point of 'equilibrium unemployment.' This is the rate of unemployment where wage increases equal productivity gains plus changes in income shares. The unemployment-price stability trade-off is gone." [pp. 356-57].

The Phillips curve becomes a vertical straight line, because if inflation were fully foreseen and instantaneously anticipated the equilibrium rate of unemployment would persist whatever the price rise. Needless to add that perfect foresight and full anticipation are extreme assumptions describing an "ideal type" which may be approached but will never be fully realized in the actual world.

Author Index

Subject Index